DISCLOSURE OF THE ULTIMATE:
Fundamental Theology Reconsidered

Richard W. Rousseau, S.J.

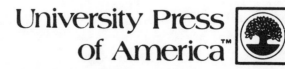

University Press
of America™

Library of Congress Catalog Card Number: 80-8259

FOREWORD

I would like to express my thanks
to the Weston School of Theology's
Board of Directors whose grant of
a year's sabbatical leave greatly
facilitated the preparation of this
book as well as to the members of
the Georgetown University Jesuit
Community and the Staff of the
Woodstock Library for their help
and encouragement during that time.

CHAPTERS

CHAPTER ONE

WHAT IS

FUNDAMENTAL THEOLOGY?

Fundamental theology is the serious reflection of the christians of each age upon the how and why of their living faith. Fundamental theology is also called philosophical theology and both are distinguished from apologetics and natural theology. Apologetics was intended to convert unbelievers to christianity by the presentation of such "evidences" as prophets and miracles. In fact, it was usually more effective in confirming christians in their faith. Natural theology tried to supply a rational basis for theology by starting from generally accepted premises and arguing to a number of basic truths which were then used as foundational by systematic and symbolic theology.

Though apologetics and natural theology played an important role in their day, in recent times they have been heavily criticized on both theological and philosophical grounds and have become largely ineffective. It has been easier to criticize than to replace, however, and, in both Catholic and Protestant circles a number of efforts to reestablish the foundations of theology have been undertaken with varying measures of success.

DISCLOSURE OF THE ULTIMATE

This book, as the first sentence indicates, takes a stand on the nature and scope of modern fundamental theology which it will attempt to justify in the course of its development. Despite the brevity of the definition, it harbors a number of important positions. These will be developed in what hopefully will be an ecuminical enterprise. At the same time, since the Roman Catholic community is in special need of intensive discussion in this area due to the sudden collapse of a previous "apologetic" consensus as recently as the 1960's,/1/ special attention will be paid from time to time to points of concern to Catholics.

Contrast Between the Old Apologetics

and Modern Fundamental Theology

As a start, the old apologetics and the new fundamental theology will be compared to see how they differ. Recent discussions of this area will be synthesized into ten basic contrasts. /2/

The first contrast between the older apologetics and the new fundamental theology is between the old view that the sources of fundamental theology should be confined to theology and revelation and the view that these sources should include philosophy, science, psychology, history, and other aspects of human culture.

This contrast is in part a consequence of historical growth. At one time, fundamental theology was scarcely distinguishable from systematic theology and consequently the sources proper to systematic were indiscriminately applied to fundamental. With the more careful distinctions of later years, and with the greater autonomy of the secular disciplines themselves, it has become easier to see that the sources of fundamental theology are different from those of systematic.

WHAT IS FUNDAMENTAL THEOLOGY?

Second Contrast

The second contrast is between the older view of fundamental theology as a description of the sources involved and the new view of it as a critical examination of theological method itself. In concluding his History of Apologetics, Avery Dulles says,"The 20th century has seen more clearly than previous periods that apologetics stands or falls with the question of method. In the past few decades, apologetical science has merged to an increasing degree with the epistemology of religious knowledge. It is in this difficult area that the most important work remains to be done." /3/

Third Contrast

The third contrast is between the old view that fundamental theology is primarily directed against error and the new view that its primary purpose is to give an account of one's own belief.

For centuries arguments were addressed to unbelievers such as Roman pagans and medieval Muslims, and the newly discovered peoples of the age of exploration. A good deal of apologetic energy on both sides also went into the debates among christians at the time of the Reformation and after. In the nineteenth and twentieth centuries, the focus was frequently on atheists, agnostics, and secularists.

There is an acknowledgement today, however, that doubt and unbelief are not confined to the world outside the church. There is greater recognition that christians must struggle with their own doubts and not pretend that they do not have any. In addressing the doubts of the believers, then, fundamental theology both gives witness to christian life, and reaffirms christians in their commitment. As Johannes Baptist Metz puts it,

Hence the clear and responsible

account of the possibility of faith
is not just a secondary development,
a sort of theoretical superstructure
for the educated faithful or an arse-
nal of agreements in ideological
controversy with non-believers. It
is becoming more and more an intrinsic
element of the individual believer's
situation and a condition of possibility for his own belief. /4/

Fourth Contrast

The fourth contrast is between the old view
that apologetics must passively accept the terms
of the debate from someone else and try to respond
to the objections raised, and the new view that
fundamental theology is a testifying to personal
belief and an active search for common ground in
solving common problems.

One of the difficulties with a counterattack
is that it must conform to what is already there.
Others set the parameters of the discussion and
sometimes even set the theme of the debate. Too
often this involves an unconscious acceptance of
certain of the challenger's assumptions, even
though this unacknowledged acceptance means that
the argument has been lost even before it begins.
Insofar as such an attitude of attack assumes that
an opponent is ignorant or suffers from ill will,
it is narrow and self-defeating.

Fifth Contrast

The fifth contrast is between the old view
that the arguments of apologetics were based on
observable fact and the new view that fundamental
theology deals with the religious dimension of
human life and the experience of faith.

Since this is one of the main areas of discussion in this book, suffice it to say for the

moment that the new view rules out an automatic
acceptance of the influential objective-subjective
model of human and religious knowledge.

Sixth Contrast

The sixth contrast is between the old view
that the most important thing about revelation is
its factuality and the new view that the most important thing about it is its message.

This implies a distinction between the fact
that God reveals and what he reveals. Though an
emphasis upon the factuality of revelation may
have had merit in the past, many people today have
more difficulty with the content of revelation. To
someone who is having trouble with the Incarnation,
for example, it does not really settle the question
in his mind to tell him that after all it is revealed.

Seventh Contrast

The seventh contrast is between the old view
that the truth of one's position demands that it
be fixed and unchangeable and the new view that
firmness of personal conviction is compatible with
change and development, and, sometimes, even with
learning from one's opponents.

The old view presupposed that truth was to be
understood as a kind of fortress under siege and
that in order to defend it, it was necessary to
prevent even the slightest breach in the walls.
Since we are dealing with the great questions that
affect the nature and destiny of man, such a physical, mechanical understanding of them is inappropriate. It it is a law of life that we must grow
and change as individuals, why should it seem
strange that we must grow and change as christians?

DISCLOSURE OF THE ULTIMATE

Eighth Contrast

The eighth contrast is between the old view that apologetics should bring about conversion through clarity of argument and the new view that understanding is as important as conversion and that growth in understanding comes from many sources besides propositional clarity.

Under the influence of the Enlightenment and the continued rise of science in the world, great importance was attributed to deductive reason with its clear and distinct ideas. But this has been seen as not enough. Man has within himself and in the context of life as a whole, further complex powers which must also be taken into consideration.

Ninth Contrast

The ninth contrast is between the old view that these fundamental questions must be viewed through the optic of Western culture and even of one Christian denomination, and the new view that questions basic to human nature and God's dealing with man must take into account the experiences of other Churches and other world religions.

Tenth Contrast

The tenth contrast is between the old view that apologetics is very much concerned with the historical achievements of the church and the personal accomplishments of christians, and the new view that fundamental theology must go beyond the institutional, no matter how great, and beyond the ethical, no matter how noble, to the basic religious and revelational experiences of man.

This is in no way to deride those works which examine in detail the historical continuity of the christian church, its moderating and civilizing influence on society. its impact on literature and the arts, its universality, its unity amid diversity./5/ Nor is it to deny the wonderful lives and accomplishments of christian saints and heroes. It merely says that these discussions are more appropriate for a christianized society and that, as far as the more secularized modern world is concerned, they do not go deep enough.

Directions for Fundamental Theology

The following directions for fundamental theology emerge from this series of contrasts between the older apologetics and the newer approach:

1. Fundamental theology should include philosophy, science, history, psychology, and other areas of human culture among its sources and not confine itself to theology and revelation.

2. It should be a critical examination of theological method itself rather than a mere description of theology's sources.

3. It should be more concerned with giving an account of belief than reacting against error.

4. It should testify to personal belief and an active search for common ground in solving common human and religious problems rather than passively accepting the terms of the debate from someone else.

5. It should deal with the religious dimension of human life and the experience of faith rather than confine itself to the forum of observable fact.

6. It should consider its revelational message as more important than the factuality of revelation itself.

7. It should combine firmness of conviction

with openness to change rather than consider truth
as something fixed once and for all.

8. It should consider the self understanding
of faith and its growth from many sources to be as
important as conversion of others through clarity
of argument.

9. In dealing with issues so basic it should
take into account the experience of all the christian churches and that of other world religions
rather than relying on a narrow optic.

10. It should go beyond the institutional and
ethical, no matter how great, to the basic religious and revealed experience of man, rather than
concern itself primarily with the historical
achievements of the christian church and the accomplishments of individual christians.

European Catholicism

This comparison between old and new approaches
in theology, looking backward as it does, helps
only so much. What is needed besides is the development of a formally worked out system. Two
German speaking Catholic theologians, Hans Kung
and Karl Rahner, have published works which, along
with a number of other concerns, attempt to work
out a new approach to fundamental theology.

Hans Kung

Hans Kung's On *Being a Christian* was a best
seller in Germany and has also been widely read
in the United States./6/ It has also stimulated
a considerable amount of serious theological
discussion. In the book Kung attempts to answer
such questions as: can the christian faith continue to meet the challenges of the modern world;
is the message of christianity really responsive
to the needs of twentieth century men and women?

8

WHAT IS FUNDAMENTAL THEOLOGY?

He bases his affirmative answers to these questions
on the uniqueness of christianity and its "roots"
in the historical Christ. He also examines the
role of christianity in the world of politics and
economics as well as the interrelationships between christians and Jews, and between christians
and other world religions. The christian community
is analyzed in considerable depth. It ia a monumental world which has received much attention.

Can On Being a Christian, however, be considered as the new model for contemporary fundamental
theology? Whatever its other values, it is doubt-
ful that it will be considered as such by the
Anglo-American christian community. Quite apart
from the perfectly normal presuppositions, categories and emphases drawn from and directed towards
Germanic christians, the book passes over quickly
a number of issues basic to fundamental theology:
epistemology, the phenomenology of the religious
dimension of experience and the debates of linguistic analysis concerning the meaninglessness of
religious language.

Kung's emphasis is Christological, as the
statistics of the book indicate. The first three
chapters on humanism, transcendence and world
religions take up 116 pages, while the concluding
sections on ecclesiology and ethics take up 139
pages more for a total of 255 pages. The remaining
465 pages are devoted to Christological questions.
While Christology can be taken up in a context of
fundamental theology, a number of prior questions
need to be settled first and it is these prior
questions that Kung's book deals with less
thoroughly.

What about Karl Rahner's long awaited book
Foundations of Christian Faith? /7/ Can this
serve as a model of modern fundamental theology?
It comes closer than Kung because it does include
both Rahner's epistemology and metaphysics. Rahner
deals with the theology of God's self communication

9

to man in Christ, sin and forgiveness, the church,
christian life and eschatology and, at the end, he
appends three creedal statements in which he attempts to express in more understandable form the
basics of christian faith.

There are two methodological considerations
that have to be taken into account in any judgement with regard to this work as a model of modern
fundamental theology. The first is its very
massiveness. It includes a broad sweep of christian life and thought and has been called by one
commentator the closest thing we are going to have
to a Summa from this master of the theological
essay. /8/ Second, though it does include a more
explicit epistemology and metaphysics, these are
based on Rahner's well known version of transcendental thomism. This constitutes an important
contribution to twentieth century theology and the
issues of fundamental theology in Foundations are
obviously derived from it. It is therefore no
derogation of Rahner's system or monumental
achievements to suggest, in the spirit of the
theological pluralism that he himself encourages,
an alternative approach to fundamental theology
which would be more limited in scope and which
would be based on premises which are more empirical, more experiental and more American.

In contrast to Kung, then, this work will be
more explicitly epistemological; in contrast to
Rahner, more empirical, and in contrast to both,
more restricted to the introductory areas of
theology.

American Catholicism

In Blessed Rage for Order: The New Pluralism
in Theology, by David Tracy, an American Catholic
understanding of fundamental theology is proposed
with great skill and erudition. /9/ In order to
present Tracy's stimulating system very briefly

and also to clarify the positions being developed in this book, each of Tracy's five theses for a revisionist model of theology /10/ will be examined and evaluated briefly. Since such a process may be unfair to both Tracy and to the theory of fundamental theology proposed here, it is suggested that the difficulty may be alleviated by referring to Tracy's full text and to the later chapters of this book.

The First Thesis

Tracy's first thesis for a revisionist model of theology is, "The two principal sources for theology are christian texts and common human experience and language." /11/ The following is suggested as an alternative: the two principal sources of theology are human experience and language in general and christian experience and language in particular.

Tracy calls this common human experience fides or the conviction, supported by various psychological and biological drives for survival and value, that existence is worthwhile. But the question can legitimately be asked whether or not this leaves out a considerable spectrum of human experience, dealing with the absurd and the discouraging? "I suspect that on as profound a level of common human experience there is that further characteristic which one might term 'desperation,' the mood and question (and even threat) that indeed existence is cruel and absurd and not worthwhile after all."/12/ "Human experience and language" in the alternative phrasing is therefore more inclusive, encompassing both optimistic and pessimistic outlooks on life and drawing upon contemporary experience and the accumulated historical experiences of mankind.

Also does not seeing common human experience as fides involve secularism or the "fundamental attitude which affirms the ultimate significance and the worth of our lives, our thoughts and actions

11

here and now, in nature and history."? /13/ Avery
Dulles finds it so,

> Personally, I have no difficulty
> in accepting the worthwhileness of
> existence--even if existence be under-
> stood as confined to the present world.
> The christian warrants tell us that
> creation is good, even if secular exper-
> ience sometimes leaves this point
> ambiguous. I fail to understand, how-
> ever, what Tracy means by asserting
> that our lives and actions, here and
> now, within history, have ultimate
> significance and final worth....For a
> believer, only God has ultimate meaning
> and value. /14/

These comments on common human experience can
be applied in the same fashion to language.

None of this should be taken as opposition to
Tracy's emphasis upon the phenomenological analysis
of human experience. The difference lies in the
way it is applied, more broadly or less broadly, as
will be noted below.

The Second Thesis

Tracy's second thesis is "The theological
task will involve a critical correlation of the
results of the investigation of the two sources
of theology." /15/ The alternative suggested is,
The theological task will involve a critical questioning and reflection upon these two principal
sources.

Simple sounding as these two statements are,
they involve some strong methodological variations.
Correlation as described by Tracy means that
christian texts provide "an existentially appropriate symbolic representation of the fundamental
faith of secularity." /16/ As Dulles describes it,
this "seems to be a one-way process in which the

christian positions are shown to be consistent
with the secular vision of life. I doubt whether
anyone is likely to become a christian simply in
order to have his secular faith elucidated or
expressed by better symbols." /17/

This correlative method is a logical one, however, if one is searching for a neutral justification of christian answers. "Tracy takes the stand
that beliefs are data for inquiry and believing is
not a constitutive part of the subject-theologian"s
stance toward the data." He is not required to be
"a member of the christian community or classified
as a believer." /18/ Apart from the fact that
such a procedure would offer a number of philosophers a share in the task of fundamental theology
that would be denied to most christian theologians
trying to work in this area, such a position is
based on a systematic doubt which is understood
to be scientific and modern. For Tracy, "beliefs
become not merely a subject matter for exploration,
clarification and even justification, they become
questionable, i.e. in such a state that I must
authentically and systematically wonder and doubt
whether they are true." /19/ Thus those who do not
wonder and doubt in this fashion cannot be fundamental theologians.

This methodological lack of commitment to
christianity could conceivably lead the fundamental
theologian to reject christianity on the basis of
the evidence examined.

> The prime loyalty of the theologian
> according to Tracy, is not to church or
> tradition, but to the community of scien-
> tific inquiry....I wonder what concept
> of science is at work here?....In
> safequarding the autonomy of the scientific
> community, is he prepared to forfeit the
> autonomy of the community of faith?....
> Tracy is quite prepared to challenge the
> reigning models of theology, but he seems

less prepared to call into question
certain popular conceptions of science. /20/

And here we have finally come to one of the
core issues.Though Tracy's avowed purpose is to go
the theological roots, he seems in fact to have
taken secondary root systems for primary. He presupposes a theory of knowledge strongly influenced
by the classic empiricist tradition, where only
sensible, factual knowledge is real and where all
value judgements are considered subjective.

The theory of fundamental theology presented
in this book, however, does not accept any such
unquestionable assumption that only factual knowledge is real knowledge; it does not accept the
assumption that in order to really know it is necessary or even possible for a human being to be
cognitively neutral; it does not accept the assumption that the value laden dimensions of human life
such as the ethical, the artistic and the religious
are fully subjective and without genuine cognitivity.
This work will not stop at negative disagreements,
however. It will present a positive alternative: a
consciously developed theory of knowledge which will
be called intersective realism. This will attempt
to show that all thought, including scientific,
involves a personalistic, heuristic element, which
in no way invalidates its genuine cognivity.
Methodologically then, instead of striving for an
unattainable neutrality, a fundamental theologian
would strive to question and to understand his belief.
Insofar as Tracy lacks a developed epistemology. and
insofar as he presupposes certain theories of knowledge over-influenced by an out-of-date scientism,
his approach to later questions is weakened.

The Third Thesis

Tracy's third thesis is, "The principal method
of investigation of the source 'common human experience and language' can be described as a phenomenology of the 'religious dimension' present in everyday and scientific experience and language." /21/

14

WHAT IS FUNDAMENTAL THEOLOGY?

The suggested alternative is, <u>The principal method of investigation of general human experience and language can be described as a phenomenology of the "religious dimension" of that experience and language</u>.

This brings us back to the discussion of common human experience and language. Though it would perhaps be going too far to suggest that Tracy is simply identifying common and secular, it does seem to be true that by common he means ordinary. But, as Dulles says, "I do not understand why there could not be certain uncommon experiences from which one could perceive more about the ultimate nature of reality than is given in ordinary experience." /22/ Thus, he seems to understand Tracy to be saying that while the religious aspect of common human experience is the affirmation that the final reality in our lives is trustworthy, the self-enclosed nature of that affirmation keeps it from opening out to a new order of reality, thus blurring the widely acknowledged distinction between the sacred and the profane.

Though this book will examine the religious dimension in secular experiences of limit, it will also examine other more extraordinary experiences of limit and the holy. It will also attempt to show the relationship between the religious dimension of human experience and revelation.

The Fourth Thesis

Tracy's fourth thesis is, "<u>The principal method of investigation of the source 'the christian tradition' can be described as an historical and hermeneutical investigation of classical christian texts</u>." /23/ The suggested alternative is, <u>The principal methods of investigation of christian experience are the hermeneutical examination of biblical texts and their interpretation in the christian community and a theological analysis of revealed dimension of christian experience</u>.

15

The emphasis by Tracy on the words christian
facts and _texts_ and the bracketing of "christian
tradition" is "intended to be as neutral as possible
and to avoid suggesting as 'Scripture', 'Tradition'
and 'Gospel' might do, any normative status." /24/
Here Tracy is being consistent with his so called
scientifically neutral stance. It is an equally
legitimate view, however, that without passionate
concern with christian tradition on the part of the
theologian, and without the faith commitment to a
more authentic life that this implies, "the object
on which the theologian reflects begins to disappear
and we are left with nothing except, precisely,
texts." /25/

Furthermore, Tracy, in adapting Ricoeur's
hermeneutical method, seems to be implying that
the meaning of christian texts is imbedded there
quite independently of the intention of the authors
and of the understanding of the christian community
inwhich, over the centuries, these texts have been
developed, read, interpreted and lived. In which
case, the primary meaning to be discovered would
be existential, a "mode-of-being-in-the-world" thus
pushing even further away cognitive claims on the
part of the Bible or of religion.

> Many Protestants, not to say
> Catholics and Orthodox, have recognized
> that the Bible is not truly a theolo-
> gical source when read by itself alone,
> apart from the whole history of interpre-
> tation which it has engendered. It does
> not yield its deeper significance except
> to those who participate existentially
> in the community of faith. /26/

The fact that Tracy's premises have led him to
this theory of an existential interpretation of a
text-in-a-vacuum, will lead later to a postpone-
ment of the christological question on the grounds
that fundamental theology in the form conceived
is able to see Jesus only "as a Christ-myth that

tells us something about God," /27/ and that anything further must wait until a more directly dogmatic evaluation. But there does not seem to be any reason why fundamental theology, if it is already theology, cannot at least begin to give us an authentic insight into Jesus.

The Fifth Thesis

Tracy's fifth thesis is "To determine the truth-status of the results of one's investigations into the meaning of both common human experience and christian texts the theologian should employ an explicitly transcendental or metaphysical mode of reflection." /28/ The suggested alternative is, To determine the truth-status of one's investigation into general human experience and language and into christian experience and language, the theologian should employ an appropriately realistic theory of knowledge out of which will then flow further metaphysical reflections.

The new point at issue here is the use of constructive or systematic metaphysics not only before the proper epistemological foundations have been laid, but as a substitute for them. This is not to quarrel with an emphasis upon metaphysics. On the contrary, when it is absent, we all suffer from a lack of conceptual clarity and precision, to say nothing of depth and perception. But what justification is there for not providing a developed epistemology as the foundation of a metaphysical superstructure?

Implied in Tracy's fifth thesis is the position that a believer initially does not really know. He does not know because in order to know he must systematically doubt and this radical doubt can be solved only by lengthy metaphysical analysis and construction. But this does not correspond to life as it is really lived. "Christians know that God exists and knowwhat he means, and know that he has entered their lives imparting knowledge of him surer than any other. And they 'know' these things usually long before they wonder (if they ever do!) about the transcendental conditions of their experience." /29/

A couple of distinctions might be helpful here. Radical doubt is one thing, critical questioning is another. The first rules out belief, the second does not. Also, doubt in everyday life, leading either to conversion or to despair, is not quite the same thing as theoretical, systematic doubt.

> The theologian, then, may try to understand what has happened to the community and how it has happened rather than <u>necessarily</u> wonder whether it should have happened or whether it has been truly expressed. I am quite willing to admit here that this can with good reason be called a dogmatic rather than a critical task if some find this terminology helpful. But is the dogmatic stance illegitimate?....Is this a fidelist position? This is the question that Tracy so ably forces upon me. Not a fundamental fidelism, I think. I accept the value of philosophical theology. I think that God's existence is known in believing and philosophical theology is necessary to clarify how we arrive at and how we can defend that knowledge. But I do not think he is known aside from grace and without surrender. The experience of christians confirms this. And I accept the "circle" implied. /30/

Though it would be unfair to demand it is what are basically only review articles, neither Shea and Dulles, in the papers quoted in the course of this discussion of the five theses of Tracy, attempt to develop the positive theory of knowledge that underlies their own criticisms of Tracy's. This book will try to develop an explicit theory of

WHAT IS FUNDAMENTAL THEOLOGY?

knowledge as an integral and necessary part of fundamental theology. Theories of knowledge have always been controversial, of course, and no doubt this one, called intersective realism will be as well. But is seems far more appropriate for such controversies to take place where they belong, namely in the premises, rather than in the working conclusions drawn from them.

Protestant Foundational Theology

Since Protestant theologians have been wrestling with the basic challenges posed to christianity by modern science and culture since at least the time of Schleirmacher, they have a considerably larger body of achievement and a higher level of sophistication in dealing with problems of fundamental theology than Roman Catholics. At the same time, the demise of natural theology in Protestant circles has signalled a drop in interest in these foundational areas. So both Catholic and Protestant theologians have something to gain by close and continued dialogue on fundamental theology.

There are two main, all-inclusive schools of Protestant foundational thought, the Neo-Orthodox and the liberal. Neo-orthodoxy, in its classical, Barthian form, focuses primarily on the authority of revelation. Insofar as apologetics attempts to substitute human efforts for the work of the Holy Spirit, they are considered unworthy. Scripture and biblical theology are the genuine sources of enlightenment in a life where we see through a glass darkly. In its more recent forms, neo-orthodoxy turned away from the questions of origins to those of influence or the way revelation sheds light on the situation of modern secular man. Thus in the writing of Reinhold Niebuhr and Emil Brunner there are many reflections upon economic, political and even military matters.

DISCLOSURE OF THE ULTIMATE

The other school, unlike the neo-orthodox, does not have any leading figure of Barthian magnitude, but its influence is widespread. In contrast to the neo-orthodox, the liberals hold that faith may be mediated by such secular things as psychology, sociology, history, science and so on. Some are metaphysically inclined, like such process theologians as John Cobb, Jr. Others are more empirically inclined, seeing existence and experience as the proper starting point for philosophical and foundational theology.

Peter Berger and Theological Reductionism

Rather than develop this historical description of liberal Protestant approaches to foundational theology, it might be more helpful to examine in some detail an article by the sociologist Peter Berger /31/ in which he comments on four books by three important American liberal theologians, two Protestant and one Catholic: Schubert Ogden, Langdon Gilkey and David Tracy, whom we have already examined at some length. /32/

Berger sees these works as "impeccably academic in content, sedate in tone and on an indisputably high level of intellectual sophistication.... these are good books; which, precisely, is the reason why they are interesting for the purpose at hand." /33/

What Berger sees as common to all these books is what he calls their theological reductionism. By this he means that the translation of the contents of religious tradition fully into language that will not clash with the presupposition and language of the secular milieu of the modern world is reductionistic because it reduces religion to the secular and throws the baby out with bath. He does not mean that the reductionism which he finds in these books is simplistic or popular. Popular reductionism which identifies itself with such things as emancipatory political movements is frequently hortatory and intellectually vulgar in

20

tone. The sophisticated reductionims of these books,in Berger's opinion, is quite another thing, and consists mainly in a common attitude of opposition to "supernaturalism."

In examining Schubert Ogden's <u>The Reality of God</u>, Berger finds support for this understanding in such quotes as, "there is an irreconcilable oppostion between the premises of supernaturalistic theism and the whole direction of our experience and reflection as secular men." /34/ Also, that in his opposition to a monopolar God (and advocacy of a process dipolar one) Ogden says, "sooner or later, the conclusion must be faced that the God conceived by this form of theism cannot be the God of secular man." /35/

Berger understands Langdon Gilkey's <u>Naming the Whirlwind: The Renewal of God Language</u>, to be an attempt to reconstruct theology on the foundations of secularity. Thus he sees Gilkey as saying that secularity is not merely the starting point but the criterion of theology, "A creative theology cannot point our minds and spirits to another realm or use language intelligible only if we enter special religious situations and special religious places." /36/ Berger comments on the above, "It is <u>this</u> life, it is <u>this</u> world, which are disclosed in this ultimate ground as one approaches the limits of human experience. Whatever transcendence may mean, it does <u>not</u> mean an'other realm' of experience." /37/

Berger sees these same themes repeated in Gilkey's other book, <u>Catholicism Confronts Modernity</u>. There he finds that the word transcendence is used in constant contrast to supernaturalism, "The goal of christian life, then is not to transcend this life into another, into a supernatural level characterized by a sharing in the divine life that abrogates or absorbs natural life, for the perfection of nature is the sole value." /38/

DISCLOSURE OF THE ULTIMATE

As for Tracy, Berger summarizes his method as follows, "The centerpiece of the book is an analysis of the religious dimension of common human experience. The key concept here is that of limit ...(For Tracy) the religious significance of human life is revealed (more precisely, disclosed) as the latter is pushed to certain boundaries. The limit experiences are not in themselves religious; rather they open up a religious horizon." /39/

Tracy is quoted as saying that "Religious language does not present a new, a supernatural world wherein we may escape the only world we know or wish to know." Thus confirming the fact, as Berger claims, that throughout the book, "the notion of supernaturalism is used synonymously with 'fundamentalism.'" /40/

Points of Agreement and Disagreement in Berger

It is quite clear that Berger is in serious disagreement with these three theologians. He feels that it is not enough to speak of religious symbols as disclosing the limits of this world; they should also be understood as disclosing the impingement of another world upon it. For Berger religious experience is not exclusively this world; the world itself must be seen as a symbol of the reality that lies behind it. "A secular theology understands religious language as signs of the human condition; quite another theology is possible, which seeks for the 'signals of transcendence' within the human condition--indeed within the common experience as well." /41/

Despite this strong criticism, Berger does admit that, on a number of points, he is in agreement with these three authors. First of all, he agrees that their description of the current cultural situation as a pervasively secularistic one is correct.

Second, he agrees that when external authority is generally weakened as it is today, it is natural and even necessary to turn inward towards experience. He says that "faith based on some sort of individual decision may be deemed superior to faith supported solely by culturally taken-for-granted authority." /42/

Third, he agrees that since the nature of the experience dealt with is of great importance it is necessary to go beyond many of the social and cultural circumstances historically embedded in religious language.

Fourth, Berger agrees that disclosure as a method is a good one, highly appropriate to both theology and christianity. By disclosure he means that the symbols of christianity (or those of other religions, for that matter), "disclose some hitherto hidden aspects of the human condition." /43/ Limit language can thus be understood as a language of disclosure.

Some Conclusions from This Debate

In the light of the theory of fundamental theology developed in this book, Berger's critique of Ogden, Gilkey and Tracy, while helpful in clarifying what are some of the main points at issue, and pointing in some interesting directions, nevertheless ultimately fails. /44/

The first reason for this failure is the fact that it is quite possible that a great deal of his disagreement is based on a misunderstanding of the word "transcendence." Though disputes about word-meanings are usually not very productive and though they tend to get tangled in semantical charges and countercharges, it may nevertheless be helpful to point out that those whom Berger calls the "reductionists" tend to interpret transcendence spatially, whereas Berger himself tends to interpret it as a combination of temporal and spatial dimensions. Ogden, Gilkey and Tracy have difficulty with an overly spatial dimension of transcendence because

of its overconcrete descriptiveness and its assoc-
iation with various kinds of church authoritarianism. It would seem to be going too far, however,
to see this rejection of a historically conditioned
understanding of transcendence as a refusal to
accept any kind of transcendent dimension at all
and as a reduction of religion to nothing more than
secularity.

Second, the above is confirmed by the impression that their intentions do not seem to be
reductionistic in this sense. When Berger divides
all theology, like Gaul, into three parts: the
deductive, the reductive and the inductive, and
classifies Ogden, Gilkey and Tracy in the reductive, he is overstating his case. /45/ It is
unconvincing to argue that these practicing
christians and active theologians would seek to
describe their faith through the denial involved
in complete secularistic reductionism.

Third, after his lengthy and detailed criticism of these three theologians, Berger does not
offer a great deal in the way of positive theological alternatives. After accepting a great deal
of their program, including the central concept
of disclosure, he adds merely that the task at
hand is to determine the shape of supernaturalistic
experience through "a return to a phenomenology of
religion, in the line of Rudolf Otto, Gerhardus
van der Leeuw and Mircea Eliade. Additional
conceptual tools could be borrowed from Alfred
Schutz' work." And, in a footnote, he mentions
Louis Dupre. /46/ It is not clear what relationship his own Rumor of Angels bears to this
description. /47/ Ultimately, then, he raises
more questions than he answers, though some of
these questions contain hints that point in constructive directions.

Further Definition of Fundamental Theology

This book isin thorough agreement with the empirical, experiential approach to foundational theology seen in Tracy, Gilkey, Ogden and others because it overcomes many of the disadvantages of other approaches and has many advantages of its own, as will be developed later. But if Tracy's definition of fundamental theology is to be taken as emblematic it is possible to argue, as shall be argued in this book, that this particular version of the experiential approach goes too far in some respects and not far enough in others.

Foundational theology is described by Tracy as "a phenomenological-transcendental philosophy of religion upon the christian fact," and, "a philosophical reflection upon common human experience and the christian fact." /48/ These definitions imply two methodological issues for fundamental theology.

The first methodological issue is the scope of the experiential method. If experiential is understood to mean that only factual knowledge is real knowledge and that religious knowledge is necessarily subjective and non-cognitive, as it does seem to mean in Tracy, then it may be argued that the method has been pushed too far; that the christian theologian should not be forced to set aside his own faith experience in order to approach these questions.

The second methodological issue involves the restriction of the experiential-phenomenological method to common human experience and christian facts and texts. If this is so, as Tracy seems to indicate, then it is possible to argue that the method does not go far enough. By its own principles it needs as wide a range of phenomena as possible for examination. It is unconvincing to say that fundamental theology, on methodological

25

grounds, needs to set aside the full sweep of man's
religious experience from the sublimely mystical
to the steadfastness of day-to-day conviction.

At the beginning of this chapter, the following
definition was proposed,"Fundamental theology is
the serious reflection of the christians of each
age upon the how and why of their living faith."
Support for this view is found in a recent review
of Rahner's Foundations of Christian Faith by
Gerald McCool:

> A philosophical-theological
> reflection that provides explicit
> intellectual justification for the
> reasonableness of the christian's
> concrete faith commitment is what
> Rahner means by fundamental theology.
> It is a new and distinct discipline.
> Unlike the old apologetics, faith
> through "pure reason". Neither does
> it prescind from the content of faith
> to focus its attention on the assent
> alone. On the contrary, the content
> of faith enters into the arguments
> that it presents to the believing
> christian to justify the reasonable-
> ness of his lived commitment. /49/

There are some nuances of difference of course,
Rahner emphasizes the explicit intellectuality of
the process of reflection and sounds what might be
called an apologetic note in his emphasis upon
justification. Reflection is taken here, however,
as a broader term which includes phenomenological
description, metaphorical allusion, theoretical
modularity and metaphysical elaboration. Also,
Rahner's justificational language does not clearly
include both self-clarification and the ability to
explain belief to others, whereas our own descrip-
tionimplies both. These nuances, however, do not
affect a substantial agreement between the two with
their joint focus upon the christian believer in

search of understanding. Bernard Lonergan's definition of theology as "reflection on religion in
a culture," while more restricted and austere
points in the same general direction. /50/

Finally, the following is the full definition
of fundamental theology operational in this book,
one which now contains the methodological insights
developed in the course of this chapter:

Fundamental theology is the serious reflection
of the christian of each age upon the how and why
of their living faith. This reflection uses an
appropriately realistic theory of knowledge to
support a phenomenological study of the disclosure
of the ultimate in the religious dimension of
experience and language and the revealed dimension
of christian experience and language.

The following chapter will take up this
religious dimension of experience and the following
two will develop a foundational theory of
knowledge.

NOTES

[1] Andrew Greely, _The New Agenda_ (Garden City, N.Y.: Doubleday, 1975), pp. 33-68.

[2] Johannes B. Metz, ed. _The Development of Fundamental Theology._ Concilium Series, n. 46 (N.Y.: Paulist Press, 1969). This book contains a series of articles that can be taken as typical of recent discussions in this area, many of whose ideas are synthesized in the ten point contrast developed. Among the authors included are Claude Geffré, Réné Latourelle, Heinrigh Fries, Jan Walgrané and Karl Rahner. The points made in the contrasts, however, should not be directly attributed to them.

[3] Avery Dulles, _A History of Apologetics_ (N.Y.:Corpus, 1971), p. 246.

[4] Metz, "Apologetics," in _Sacramentum Mundi._

[5] In Europe an example of such work is Juan Donoso Cortes' _Ensavo sobre el catolicismo, el liberalismo y el secularismo_ (Barcelona, 1851). In the United States a number of the essays of Bishop John England, first Bishop of Charleston, North Carolina (1821-1842), were along the same line. Cf. _The Works of the Rt. Rev. John England First Bishop of Charleston._ Ed. Messmer, 7 vols. (Cleveland: Clark, 1908).

[6] Hans Kung, _On Being a Christian._ Transl. by E. Quinn (Garden City, N.Y.: Doubleday, 1976)

[7] Karl Rahner, _Foundations of Christian Faith_ (N.Y.: Seabury Press, 1978)

[8]Gerald A. McCool, S.J., "Karl Rahner on Christian Faith," _America_ (February 25, 1978) 138.

[9]David Tracy, _Blessed Rage for Order: The New Pluralism in Theology_ (N.Y.:Seabury Press, 1975)

[10]Ibid., Chapter 3, pp. 43-63. Also, an earlier version of this chapter which appeared as "The Task of Fundamental Theology," in _The Journal of Religion_ 54 (1974) 13-34, which shows that Tracy introduced a few small changes in the wording of his revisionist theses when they appeared in book form, among which was the insertion of the word "language" here and there.

[11]Tracy, _Blessed Rage_, p. 43.

[12]William M. Shea, "The Stance and Task of the Foundational Theologian: Critical or Dogmatic?" _The Heythrop Journal_ XVII (1976) 286

[13]Tracy, op. cit., p. 13.

[14]Avery Dulles, "Method in Fundamental Theology: Reflections on David Tracy's _Blessed Rage for Order_," _Theological Studies_ 37 (1976) 307.

[15]Tracy, op. cit., p. 45.

[16]Ibid., p. 9.

[17]Dulles, op. cit., p. 310.

[18]Shea, op. cit., pp. 282-283.

[19]Ibid., p. 285.

[20]Dulles, op. cit., p. 306.

[21]Tracy, op. cit., p. 47.

[22]Dulles, op. cit., p. 307.

[23]Tracy, op. cit., p. 49.

[24]Dulles, op. cit., p. 309.

[25]Ibid., pp. 309-310.

[26]Ibid., p. 311.

[27]Ibid., p. 314

[28]Tracy, op. cit., p. 52.

[29]Shea, op. cit., p. 288.

[30]Ibid., pp. 289-290.

[31]Peter C. Berger, "Secular Theology and the Supernatural: Reflections on Present Trends," *Theological Studies* 38 (March, 1977) 39-56.

[32]Schubert Ogden, *The Reality of God* (N.Y.: Harper and Row, 1966);
Langdon Gilkey, *Naming the Whirlwind: The Renewal of God Language* (Indianapolis: Bobbs-Merrill, 1969);
_____, *Catholicism Confronts Modernity* (N.Y.:Seabury Press, 1975)
David Tracy, *Blessed Rage for Order*

[33]Berger. op. cit., p. 40.

[34]Ogden, op. cit., p. 17; quoted Berger, p. 42.

[35]Ogden, op. cit., p. 51 and foll.; quoted Berger, p. 43.

[36]Gilkey, Naming the Whirlwind, pp. 250 and foll.; quoted Berger, pp. 45-46.

[37]Berger, op. cit., p. 46.

[38]Gilkey, Catholicism Confronts Modernity, p. 66.

[39]Berger, op. cit., p. 49.

[40]Tracy, Blessed Rage, p. 135; quoted Berger, p. 50.

[41]Berger, op. cit., p. 53.

[42]Ibid., p. 51.

[43]Ibid., p. 53.

[44]For the individual replies of these three theologians to Berger's Critique, see Theological Studies for September 1978, pp. 486-507.

[45]Ibid., p. 55.

[46]Ibid., p. 54.

[47]Peter Berger, Rumor of Angels: Modern Secularity and the Rediscovery of the Supernatural (Garden City, N.Y.: Doubleday, 1969)

[48]David Tracy, "Foundational Theology as

Contemporary Possibility," _Dunwoodie Review_ 12 (1974) 3; _Blessed Rage_, p. 43.

[49] Gerald McCool, op. cit., p. 138.

[50] Bernard Lonergan, _Method in Theology_ (N.Y.: Herder & Herder, 1972), Chapter XI, pp. 170, 267, 332 and 355.

CHAPTER TWO

RELIGIOUS SYMBOLISM

Alfred North Whitehead's now classic definition of religion is an appropriate way to begin,

> Religion is the vision of
> something which stands behind, and
> within; the passing flux of immediate
> things; something which is real, and
> yet waiting to be realized; something
> which is a remote possibility and yet
> the greatest of present facts; some-
> thing that gives meaning to all that
> passes, and yet eludes apprehension;
> something whose possession is the
> final good, and yet is beyond all
> reach; something which is the ultimate
> ideal and the hopeless quest. The
> immediate reaction of human nature to
> the religious vision is worship....
> That religion is strong which in its
> ritual and its modes of thought evokes
> an apprehension of the commanding
> vision. The worship of God is not a
> rule of safety--it is an adventure of

the Spirit, a flight after the
unattainable. The death of religion
comes with the repression of the high
hope of adventure. /1/

Religious Symbolism and Religious Experience

In the light of that definition it is important to distinguish between relisious symbolism
and religious experience. They differ much in the
same way that a sign differs from a symbol. A
sign stands for something else while having no
internal connection with it. A flashing yellow
light at an intersection, for example, has no
internal connection with its meaning of caution.
That is something assigned to it arbitrarily by
city ordinances. A symbol, on the other hand,
does have an internal connection with what it
represents. Easter eggs, for example, stand for
new life and contain new life. Such a distinction
is important because when a symbol juxtaposes two
differing frames of reference and creates a new
insight, this can be understood as a cognitive
process.

Religious experience is a late nineteenth
century term introduced as an explanation of the
empirical side of religion. William James in his
Varieties of Religious Experience /2/ investigated
a number of phenomena such as mystical experience,
conversion and prayer. He saw their functions as
helping people to cope with their problems, large
and small, long range and short range, and their
source as the inner energy of the subconscious in
man.

The paralellism between religious experience
so understood and signs lies in the fact that the
cultural framework within which religious experience was and is examined imposes the same kind
of cognitive limits that are endemic to signs.
Thus there was a deliberate attempt made to equate

34

such religious experience with the facts and data
needed for the pursuit of the scientific method.
There was also a presupposition at work that experience is a set of hard data, singular in nature
and present to the mind of the individual self,
with solipsistic implications.

In an analysis of this difficulty, John Smith
says that this approach leads to a dilemma with
two choices, neither of which is completely satisfactory: "an absolute distinction between immediacy and mediation, or between immediate experience and inference." /3/ The difficulty with
the inferential part of this distinction is that
religion is so intimate, so personal, so important
an affair in the commitments it evokes, that a
God who is argued to by inference and not genuinely
experienced in some way is too weak to support
such vitality and dedication. The difficulty
with the experiential part is that though in
mystical experience the reality of God is disclosed
in a way that is as close and pure as can be, it
is nevertheless mediated in some way. For however
one interprets the role of <u>analogy</u> in dealing with
God, it does express the fundamental human conviction that the greatness and unfathomability of
God requires some means of interpretation if the
limited human mind is going to be able to deal with
it at all.

For these reasons Smith suggests a way out of
the two-pronged dilemma by raising a third possibility, namely, "interpreted experience." /4/
Since the medium always comes between the person
experiencing and God, and since inference means
that what is being experienced is not God, but
something else which is considered to necessarily
point to God, then one way out is to try to weave
interpretation and experience together in some way.
This brings together the need for a medium and an
acknowledgement that that medium is genuinely
related to the reality with which it is involved.

DISCLOSURE OF THE ULTIMATE

These are some of the reasons why those religious apologists who attempted to build a defense of religion and to explain the existence of God upon the "facts" of religious experience ultimately failed. They had unconsciously accepted certain methodological and epistemological presuppositions that doomed their efforts from the start.

The "religious dimension of experience" is a term which deliberately attempts to avoid the factual narrowness of "religious experience." Although it continues to be thoroughly experiential, it also includes a interpretative element. It implies not merely a quest for meaning and value but a confidence that these are discoverable and influential. Beacuse we are dealing with the mysterious depths of the human psyche and of the universe, all this is difficult to express and needs a medium. That is where religious symbolism comes in. It is a medium of expression of this religious dimension of experience. As such it is doubly interpretative: it shares in the intrinsicity and cognivity of symbols in general and it shares in the interpretative understanding active in the religious dimension of experience.

As indicated in the last chapter, theories of knowledge are the ultimate foundation stones of fundamental theology. And we will take this up explicitly in the following two chapters. For the moment, and introductory to that, we will examine briefly the rich complexities of religious symbolism in three areas: psychology, comparative religion, and phenomenology. At the end. we will see how and why some early social scientists dealt with religious symbolism and religion.

Ernst Cassirer and the Psychological Sources
of Religious Symbolism

Cassirer has an explanation of the psychological nature and origin of religious symbolism that differs from James' by going deeper and from Freud's

36

by challenging his interpretation of their source.
In a commemorative article on the occasion of the
death of Dr. Cassirer, Suzanne K. Langer compares
him with Freud and says, "Each in his own way came
upon their common fundamental insight--the realization that all human life is pervaded with symbolic
values and all thinking mediated by symbolization,
much of which goes on below the level of consciousness." /5/

Cassirer was interested in the what of this
process of unconscious mental activity as in the
how. He saw them as developing in the same way
that metaphors do. The first stage of this metaphorical insight involves a sense of significance,
a sense of the "holy," which always includes a
feeling of awe and an awareness of mysterious
power. This, for Cassirer, was the beginning of
myth, magic, ritual and religion.

Most importantly, for Cassirer such unconscious symbol formation does not arise out of an
unhealthy suppressed core of evil, as Freud
suggested, but out of a normal, though immature
stage of symbolization. The helter-skelter,
tumbling-over-one-another production of images and
symbols is characteristic of an early stage of
human culture where new concepts are as yet undif-
ferentiated. As Langer says,

> This proto-symbolism, according
> to this view, probably appeared first
> in emotionally engendered ritual, which
> was mystical and magical, but--unlike
> a neurotic's compulsive ritualized
> practices--not subjective, personal
> and private, but objective and public,
> and with the rise of tribal organization,
> morally sanctioned. It lives on through
> the epoch of language--making and
> provides the story material of communi-
> cation in social intercourse, the
> fabric of myth and religion. It is the

37

beginning of intellectual life. /6/

One of the essential aspects of Cassirer's
thought is his view that every symbolic form should
stand in its own right. He felt it inappropriate
to look upon form as merely the "primitive" stage
of a form that develops later on in growth of
civilization. As John Smith says in a companion
piece to Langer's,

> The point is nicely illustrated
> in his refusal to accept any theory
> of myth which asserts that the mythical
> imagination is merely a primitive
> attempt to achieve scientific under-
> standing of theoretical knowledge. On
> the contrary, for him myth lives and
> moves in its own immediate human world
> of feelings and concerns and does not
> at all develop against a background
> of a "nature" defined in terms of
> physical objects determined in their
> behavior by general laws. /7/

It was this view that led Cassirer to empha-
size the sympathetic relation of man to nature,
that man and the whole world are bound together
in indissoluble ties. (Religio: to bind) This
confident assertion of the ultimate meaningfulness
of life can be found in man's history all the way
back into the fog of proto-history. It is quite
the opposite of a childish fear of the world and
even death. Fear, then, as an explanation of the
origins of religion, seems at best only partial.
Magic as the manipulation of the world was an
undoubted factor in the life of primitive man,
but there is no evidence to indicate that it constituted a prior, self-contained period that was
superseded by a new and higher period called the
religious. Their foci were quite distinct and they
could very well have coexisted as moral options,
as, in some sense, they do today. Smith adds one
insight concerning Cassirer that is helpful in the

matter of the pursuit of the nature and meaning
of religious symbols,

> Cassirer was able to steer clear
> of the two most common pitfalls which
> threaten the success of every philo-
> sophical analysis of religion. On the
> one hand, we are offered a dialectical
> development on concepts or personal
> opinions with no special relation to
> the facts of the religious conscious-
> ness, or, on the other hand, we are
> presented with vast quantities of
> historical information about religious
> traditions which are devoid of philoso-
> phical interpretation or examined
> assumptions about the "essence" of
> religion. /8/

Mircea Eliade and Religious Symbolism

in Comparative Religion

Mircea Eliade's studies in comparative religion do combine in many ways the two important
elements suggested above by Smith. He presents
some fairly sharp basic philosophical views on the
nature of religious symbolism, but these are
derived from and supported by vastly complex
studies of actual religious symbols in various
religions and at various periods in history.

Eliade says that "the world 'speaks' or
'reveals' itself through symbols; not however, in
a utilitarian and objective language. The symbol
is not a mere reflection of objective reality. It
reveals more profound and basic." /9/

This basic position is developed at some
length in six points. First, that religious
symbols are involved in the very structures of
life itself and indicate a level more mysterious
and deep than that which is reached in everyday

experience.

Second, that since for the primitive the sacred and the real and equivalent, then symbols which point to the real are always sacred.

Third, that religious symbolism is multivalent or has the power to express at the same time a number of meanings which are not to be so united by ordinary experience.

Fourth, and flowing from the third, that there is thepossibility of constructing integrated systems from diverse elements, thus creating a unified view of the world and of man's role in it.

Fifth, that religious symbolism has the power to express paradoxes which are otherwise inexpressible, by somehow bringing together contradictory aspects as an expression of the existential polarity of man and the world.

Sixth and finally, that religious symbolism has "existential" value because "a symbol always aims at a reality or a situation in which human existence is engaged." /10/ Symbols remain in contact with life in a way that concepts do not. Or, as Paul Ricoeur puts it, "the symbol gives rise to the thought." /11/ Religiously speaking, they express the religious as something lived and not merely thought. They do not merely unveil a structure of reality, they give a meaning to life. Man now feels part of the world, which opens out to embrace him. The externality of the symbol allows man to escape his subjectivity and to see that what for him is personal is also universal and real.

A number of other thinkers point in the same direction. For admittedly different reasons, they urge us to heed the power of the symbols in our lives, especially religious symbols, because they spring from the good and creative center of man's psyche. These include Jung's archetypes of the

collective unconscious, Ira Progoff's dynatypes
and cognitypes, Joseph Campbell's creative myths,
and Paul Ricoeur's thought inducing symbols.

All of which indicates that according to Eliade
and others, the religious dimension of experience
and the symbols and myths which express it need to
be taken seriously. They cannot be brushed aside
as magical substitutes, as primitive and outmoded,
as crude scientific imaginings, or as validations
of some specific social order. This is not to say
that such characterizations are totally false;
there is a limited historical and psychological
validity to them. But whether taken individually
or collectively, they do not add up to a disquali-
fication or a denigration of this area of human
life. They persist, despite all, and their power
endures. They go beyond emotion considered as a
subjective, personal, self-enclosed kind of experience, to a relationship with a reality which is
none the less central and meaningful for being
hidden and mysterious.

The Phenomenology of Religious Symbols

What then are some of the actual symbols of
the religious dimension of experience, or, to put
it another way, how does humanity go about symbol-
izing the disclosure of the ultimate? This is a
vast subject, one which fills many books and
shelves. For our limited purposes, however, we
will take three types of symbols as examples;
nature symbols, as seen in Eliade himself, transcendence symbols of various kinds and limit
symbols. One important caveat before beginning
is that such symbol synthesizing is not intended
to reduce them to a rationalistic common denomina-
tor as if that were the cake and the symbols
themselves only the frosting. As Eliade says,

> One cannot insist strongly enough
> that the search for symbolic structures
> is not a work of reduction but of

integration. We compare or contrast
two expressions of a symbol not in
order to reduce them to a single,
pre-existent expression...but in
order to discover the process whereby
a structure is likely to assume
enriched meanings. /12/

Some Religious Symbols from Nature

Among Eliade's many works, one which carries
out such a program most ambitiously and most
meticulously is his Pattern in Comparative Religion, /13/ where he studies in great detail how
a number of elements in a manifestation of nature
are taken by man as religious symbols. Some of
these will be examined briefly as examples.

The Moon: The moon can be said to hold a mirror
up to man, showing him his true condition. There
is sadness there as well as consolation. The moon
is seen as affecting both fertility and death.
The moon is always changing, yet at the same time,
is always returning. There is a rhythm to it that
men find congenial and disturbing. Life is fragile.
It can disappear at any moment. Yet, like the moon
it can reappear again. This law of life, at once
harsh and merciful, can, however, be transcended
by reaching an absolute level of existence. Sometimes (Tantric) attempts are made to somehow
unite the sun and the moon and go beyond this dualistic opposition between life and death to emerge
into some kind of original, undeviating unity.
This myth of reintegration is well nigh universal
in religions and includes all kinds of variations.
It is born of the desire to do away with dualism,
returnings and fragmentations. It is found in
the earliest stages of man's existence, showing
that man has always tried to get beyond his human
situation as symbolized by the moon.

The Waters: The world is seen as born from water,

and men too are understood to be born from water.
Whole continents are said to have fallen into the
death of water: witness the continuing vitality
of the Atlantis myth. This phenomenon is something
that needs to be repeated periodically. In human
terms this is done through a second death in
burial libations and the initiatory rites of baptism (death). But this immersion in water does
not mean a final disappearance; it is simply a
temporary return to the formless. From it a new
creation will emerge, a new life or a new man,
depending on whether the reintegration is cosmic,
biological, or redemptive. The deluge is comparable to baptism. Water disintegrates and abolishes forms, it washes, it purifies, and gives
new life. Separated from water, everything begins
to decay, everything needs periodic regeneration.
Ritual lustrations are performed to remind us of
and bring into the present that time long ago
when creation took place in water.

The Earth Mother: Though sometimes seen as bisexual,
the earth mother from primitive times was considered to be the source of all things living, the
source of food, the keeper of children, the womb
where the dead were laid to rest and from which
they would eventually be reborn, thanks to the
holiness of mother earth.

Plant Life: The forces of plant life show the
realities of the whole universe. Man is part
and parcel with nature, and he tries to use the
life he finds there for his own purposes. That
is why he takes "signs" of vegetation (Maypoles,
blossoming branches, etc.) and venerates them
(sacred trees). But there has never been an
exclusively vegetative cult. It is usually
associated with other elements such as the cult of
the sun or of water. They are usually considered
to be seasonal celebrations of the more complex
dramas that take place in the universe. It is the
ritual celebration which confers its significance
to the coming of spring, showing the full nature

of the renewal of vegetation and the start of a new "life".

The Sky: The sky has a number of hierophanies of transcendence: height, being on high, infinite space. The meteorological life of the sky is also a sign of life and power: thunder and lightning, eclipses. The supreme beings of the primitive races and the high gods of the early great civilizations are all connected in some way with the sky and what happens in it.

These sky gods gradually begin to disappear from worship. They are replaced by worship of the gods and spirits of nature, of ancestors, fertility, great goddesses, etc. The movement is always in the direction of a more concrete. more active, more fertile divinity. What wins out is what represents life.

Sometimes with the appearance of agriculture, the sky god becomes reborn as the storm god who inseminates nature. His power of omnipotence is thus limited. It was against this orgiastic god that the Yahwistic revolution toward "heavenly" values took place, quality against quantity. A few sky gods retained their position by becoming sovereign gods as well: Jupiter, Zeus, T'ien, and those who were the subject of monotheistic revolutions: Yahweh, Ahura Mazda.

But even when religious life was no longer supported by worship of sky gods, the heavens, the starry regions, ascension myths, and so on, all continued to be important, sacrally speaking. Thus what is "on high" still reveals the transcendent. The sacred idea of the sky remains a living idea everywhere and in all circumstances. This sky symbolism remained the foundation of a number of other rites: initiation, coronation, myths of the cosmic mountain, the cosmic tree, the chain of arrows, etc. The myth of the Centre, so important in all the great religions is made up

of sky elements. That of the centre or axis of
the world depends on it.

The Sun: Sun worship is limited historically to
Egypt, Asia, Peru, and Mexico. It seems to go
with the development of a certain level of political organization. Where history is on the
march as it were, thanks to kings, heroes and
empires, there is sun worship. Sky gods tend to
turn into sun gods in the sense described above
where sky divinities become fecundators or fertility gods. This happened frequently in Africa.
Sun worship was strongest in ancient Egypt. Ra
becomes supreme. Sun hierophanies tend to become
the privilege of a closed circle, a minority of
the elect. The result is a hastening of the process of rationalization.

Agriculture: The most important contribution of
agriculture to the development of humanity was
not the increase it brought in food production and
the consequent greater assurance of survival. More
important was the perception of man in the agricul-
tural process and what he learned from it with
regard to his own life. He found there fundamental
processes of organic life and the interrelation of
all things. From this he drew simpler analogies
between women and fields, between sex and sowing,
and further deeper syntheses: life as rhythmic,
death as a return. Redemption is one of the
greatest human discoveries in agriculture, for like
seed hidden in the earth which eventually stirs,
breaks the ground and reaches towards the sun, so
man when he is dead can hope to return to life in
a new but similar form. At the same time, all is
not cheery, for life itself is also like the
flowers of the field, here today and gone tomorrow.

Because primitive and early men saw the holy
in nature and later generations more clearly distinguished between God and nature, it does not

follow that early men were somehow less human and
their religious integrity less worthy than modern
man's. There was simply less cultural development
and differentiation. Furthermore, despite his
sophistication, modern man is not beyond being
moved, frightened, awed, or influenced by the mysterious powers he continues to perceive at the
heart of nature, particularly at its most catacly-
smic moments.

The Multi-Dimensional Symbolism

of the Transcendent

One of the clarifications that developed in
the course of time was an understanding of the
transcendent, and this is the second major area of
religious symbolism or our phenomenological study.
This can of course mean many things--self-transcen-
dence to the transcendent object, depending upon
the general frame of reference within which it is
used. But if used in its most generic sense of
going beyond oneself, then it can be studied for
a number of helpful insights.

If we pursue the "going beyond" image in order to
develop an analysis of its directionality, then
it is worthwhile to examine these various directions in which it can move or towards which man
can be attracted. Norman Geisler has developed
this dimensionality in considerable detail in one
of his books, which we will now examine. /14/
Maybe there is a certain artificiality in such an
analysis, and though there is some overlapping
among the directions, such a method does have the
distinct advantage of clearing up a lot of the
ambiguities and confusions that so often surround
any such discussion, especially when the controversy revolves around not the acceptance or denial
of a transcendent dimension, but around that
directionality which is most appropriately qualified as transcendent.

Since transcending is a going beyond oneself,
it can be understood as directional or dimensional
in character. And, if so, then it is legitimate
to talk about and examine the various directions
involved. None of these directions should be
understood as absolute or totally self-contained,
for there are overlappings among them.

Toward the Beginning: In archaic times, man
turned backward to reach the transcendent. Mircea
Eliade has studied this is great detail. The
transcendent in his view is called the "Sacred,"
and this world is called the "Profane." When the
Sacred somehow shows itself in the midst of the
Profane, this is called a hierophany.

The real world is the original world, what
happened "ab inito", or "in Illo tempore." This
is what the gods did at the beginning. Mythical
time of the past can be recovered and made present
by ritual, for time is continuous or circular.
The time of origin thus becomes a kind of eternal
present. Man is able to transcend personal situations and gain access to the world of the spirit
by returning to the divine origins of the world
through ritual which abolishes the barriers of
time. They find there the paradigmatic solutions
to their problems, as opposed to profane man
who has nothing to fall back on but his limited
personal experience.

The "Beginning" in Greek philosophy. Though
the Greek philosophers disassociated themselves
from these cosmogonic myths of their ancestors and
fellow Greeks, they went essentially in the same
direction, namely backwards, to try to identify
the source of being, the arche. The "going back"
was accomplished no longer by ritual but by a
process of thought. Thus it can be said that both
mythos and logos find their common origin in a
religious source, namely the desire to know the
answer to the problem of source, beginning, or
origin.

47

DISCLOSURE OF THE ULTIMATE

<u>Toward the Highest</u>: This is the tendency to leave this world of hard matter and suffering, of shadows and fear, by going up towards a world of pure form. Begun in Plato, it reaches its full development in Plotinus.

Plotinus believed that all things come from the One and all things return to it. The first great movement in his thought is from unity to multiplicity, continuing all the way to matter which has the greatest multiplicity. The further things are from unity, the less reality they have. At the bottom is the evil of almost total multiplicity. Man is stained by his contact with matter and must purify himself by ascending toward a higher unity.

The first step in this ascent is from the sensible to the intellectual. The inner unity of the mind of man is greater than the outwards multiplicity that assails his senses.

The second step is the ascent from the intellectual to the intuitional. In the intellectual realm called <u>nous</u> the intellect arrives at a higher unity where the knower and the known become identified. But since the duality of knower and known remains, and there is a multiplicity of Forms or Ideas by which things are known, there remains one final step.

The third stage in this vertical transcendence is where one finds oneself alone with the Alone. This unity cannot be known intellectually. It comes to us by a presence which is neither scientific or intellectual. To know the one, a person must merge with it and become one, thus reaching the top of the ladder. Greek rationalism went beyond itself and returned to its religious roots. Mysticism fulfilled rationalism. It is not a question of origins as for primitive man, but of unity, not backwards but upwards; natural, not supernatural.

RELIGIOUS SYMBOLISM

Toward the Beyond or Outwards: Here the
transcendent is found at the outermost limits of
human experience. Some of the mystics speak of
the transcendent as a great encompassing circle
that surrounds us and that can be reached by
thrusting outwards as far as we can go in any direction. (This can include a direction inwards
to the core of the center as well.) It could
also be described as neither up nor down but only
out and away.

It is this implied which lies behind the
conception of the universe as structured into
three stories or levels: heaven, earth and hell.

Modern man has in many ways rejected this
multileveled universe and has demythologized it.
Just as Greek rationalization made obsolete the
mythological going backwards towards the transcendent, so the demythologization of vertical
transcendence has developed interest in a forward
moving or eschatological transcendence. This is
a further development of the Christian understanding
of time as linear instead of circular.

Toward the End: With the development in the
19th century of the evolutionary emphasis and the
growing faith in theinevitability of progress, a
movement developed in modern thought that emphasized
the Transcendent as the end of the whole process
of the universe and the development of man. It saw
God as the terminal point towards which all else is
moving. Thus instead of the movement backwards of
primitive man, modern man has tended to move forward towards the transcendent, which is always out
there ahead beckoning him on. Teilhard de Chardin
has developed this directional in considerable
detail. Christ as the omega point of the universe
has become that distant star toward which all is
moving. There are some elements of this directionality to be found also in Whitman and De Tocqueville.

Toward the Center: With the emphasis on the

"death of God" as a reality "out there" or "up there," the emphasis has shifted towards eschato-logical transcendence and perhaps even more strongly towards immanence in the human. All theology is transformed into anthropology. God cannot be found out there but only in others and one must become a "man for others." Thus religion can be secularized by being humanized. But the strange thing is that the human impulse towards the transcendent begins to operate even within these apparently restrictive limits of the human, and men begin looking for the Transcendent by turning deep within themselves for something that is greater than themselves.

This looking towards the center of human life and experience, however, is not something totally new in human history and that of religious exper-ience. Primitive man seeks to situate himself at the "center" of the cosmos, and the many sacred poles, tents, and temples established as "centers" of the universe attest to this. Mystics too have spoken as merging with God by finding their center in the center. Teilhard de Chardin talked of a transcendent Center called the "Divine Milieu," the Ultimate Point toward which all realities converge. He urged union with the center while remaining oneself and remaining close to the Jesus of the Gospel. Some of this same tendency is to be found in Emerson.

Toward the Depth: In rejecting the Transcen-dent "back there" or "up there" or even "up ahead," many moderns have sought it by plunging into the depths of man. The supposition is that in man there lie depths that we know not of and that cannot be encompassed by scientific or purely limited means. Thus man can see the unlimited in the limited relationships of life and then respond to it in an unlimited way through personal commit-ment. Tillich spoke of this depth as the "ground" of being.

It is only another step to a consideration
of the subconscious as either identified with or
closely related to the Transcendent. The subconscious is seen as a mysterious realm which has
great power and over which men seem to have no
conscious control. Some hold that with the demise
of a communal mythology such as the ancients had,
or, in a modified form, Christians had, the subconscious provides a kind of personal mythology that
is saving for it puts man in contact with the
source of life or the Transcendent within. Some
qualify this by saying that this does not deny the
idea of God, but says only that there is one he
can only touch as through the subconscious region.
It there is a transformation power there, it is
legitimate to ask whether it can then be simply
identified with the human, whether subconscious
or conscious, collective or personal.

Transcending Around in a Circle: This could
be described as the Transcendence of atheists.
Nietzsche, for example, never conceded the possibility of any kind of theism or even pantheism.
"God is dead," he said formally. But he complained
of the emptiness and loneliness of his life, and
found solace in what he called the need for
"eternal recurrence." Man must want the same
things to happen over and over again, otherwise
nothing makes any sense. Life is something real
because it is eternally reappearing. The eternal
cycle becomes important rather than the center.
Linear time is replaced by the old cyclical time.

According to some existentialists, life is
meaningless, but man must continue to live and
continue to resist the meaninglessness of life.
This is a self-initiated and self-created form
of transcendence that seeks to overcome the otherwise nihilistic demands of an absurd universe.

DISCLOSURE OF THE ULTIMATE

Conclusion

What is especially interesting about this
analysis of transcendental directionality is the
insight it gives into historical disagreements
about transcendence. How often the charge that
transcendence is being denied really means that
one directional transcendence is being preferred
over another. Perhaps it has been a mistake to
too quickly call the rejection of a transcendent
"out there" or "up there" as atheistic, when what
was being affirmed implicitly or even explicitly,
was a transcendent "out ahead" or "deep within."

The Religious Symbolism of Limit Experiences

Such discussions of transcendence remain
unsatisfactory, however, for many more secularly
inclined persons. There is little question that,
historically speaking, religious experiences in
the past expressed themselves in terms of a
culturally conditioned duality of worlds, one
below and one above, one natural and one supernatural. The first was obviously our own world,
the stage on which we live and move and have our
being, and which includes ourselves as players.
The second was a mysterious "other" world with
controlling powers over the first, imposing upon
is a variety of limits, especially that of death.

Since modern man has strongly experienced a
sense of limit, to him a limit means precisely
that: a limit, and any claims to go beyond it, to
have some real knowledge, even if only partial,
of that other world, have generally been dismissed
in our modern secularized world as superstitious
wish-fulfillment.

Thus the two positions are deadlocked, both
aware of the limitations of human experience, one
understood to claim an at least obscure knowledge
of what lies beyond the limits, the other denying
any such possibility, with the matter resting in

frozen opposition.

There is a third alternative, however, which
deserves examination. This alternative is to
examine more carefully and in phenomenological
depth the experiential basis from which
the awareness of limit is derived, and this is
the third major area of phenomenological study.
Though modest, such an enterprise at least opens
up the possibility of dialogue between two adam-
antly opposed and uncomprehending positions.

Such a method substitutes a new duality for
the old. Instead of a duality between two worlds,
natural and supernatural, a new duality is explored, one between experience and its limits.

Langdon Gilkey and the Experience of Limit

This is the enterprise to which Langdon
Gilkey sets himself in his previously mentioned
Naming the Whirlwind. He says there that he
intends "to show that within an ordinary secular
experience, that deeper range, which we have
called that of ultimacy, and which religious
language seeks to conceptualize, does appear." /15/

His methodological principles are carefully
defined and important to recall. He says that
this will be an ontic rather than a$\ ontological
search, in the sense that it deals with the
concrete experience of being in the world. In
the course of this concrete search, the dimension
of ultimacy will appear covertly, rather than
overtly, as an implication of human feelings and
behavior. This appearance will also take a form
more often negative than positive. No important
area of human life will be without the influence
and presence of such a dimension. And, finally,
if asked to put the dimensions of ultimacy in
tangible, verbal form, they could be phrased in
terms of questions as: Who am I? What is it all

about? Where am I going and why? How can I become whole again?

What then are some of the characteristics of this dimension of ultimacy, according to Gilkey? He says that it appears in our experience, first of all, as the source or origin of what we are. This gradually emerges as we become aware of our fundamental and lasting limits, not merely our superficial and passing ones. It also shows itself to be the source of our values, values without which we feel that we have and are nothing. And finally, because of the paradoxical affirmation-negation nature of this dimension of ultimacy and its unveiling, it has an element of mysteriousness about it, both in the way we experience it and in the way we speak about it.

Gilkey then develops in great detail a phenomenological analysis of limit in human life: joy in living is limited by the terror of mystery; the dynamism of life is limited by the possibility of meaninglessness; the freedom of life is limited by forces beyond one's control; the wholeness and peace of life are limited by the lack of genuine possibilities of forgiveness and reconciliation. The richness and depth of this complex analysis must be savored at first hand. /16/

Religious Limit Experiences in Literature

While methodologically difficult, the pursuit of interdisciplinary connections between religion and literature can be extremely rich. This is especially true in this area of basic religious symbolism where the imaginative and the metaphorical play such a large role. The following then are some random suggestions concerning religious symbolism in literature that could be taken as seminal for further investigation.

Ernest Hemingway in his For Whom the Bell

Tolls shows alienation as a consequence of evil
when Pablo, just back from his desertion of the
small band of republicans operating behind enemy
lines, speaks of a loneliness that had become
unbearable.

Herman Melville in the Pequod refers to the
Islanders as "Isolatoes" because they each seem
to be living on separate continents. William
Faulkner, in Light in August, describes Joe Christ-
mas as rootless, with no town or street or space
to call his own. Jean Paul Sartre devotes a whole
play. No Exit, to the hellishness of being unable
to escape from a situation of physical closeness
but psychological alienation. In his play, The
Cocktail Party T. S. Eliot has Celia Coplestone
express a strong sense of guilt. In searching for
an escape from alienation and guilt, she tries to
become at-one with the world. In his frightening
and disturbing novels, The Trial and The Castle,
Franz Kafka pursues the same theme of alienation.
But it is Albert Camus who deals with this question
in what is probably the fullest and most satisfying
way.

Camus' works need to be divided into two
major groups, the first containing The Stranger and
The Myth of Sisyphus, and the second containing
The Plague and The Rebel. The first group is more
nihilistic, the second more humanistic, but all
involve the problem of alienation and meaninglessness. Camus moves from a posing of suicide as the
only valid solution to the problem of life to an
affirmation of encounter that is as moving as it
is ambiguous.

An Analysis of Limit Experiences

Gordon Kaufman, in a careful analysis,
suggests that for all the illuminating insights
to be gained from the existentialists, their
understanding of ultimate limit leaves something

to be desired /17/ He says that it is inadequate
to suggest that the experience of ultimate limit
is a particular, immediate kind of experience to
be contrasted with the experience of limits less
than ultimate--in other words, that the difference
is merely quantitative when, in fact, it is qualitative.

He suggests, rather, that we experience
directly only such things as suffering, death of
others, peace, happiness and so on. It is only
through reflection upon these that an awareness
of our limitations gradually emerges. It is this
reflective awareness that is the source of anxiety,
alienation, revolt, fear, and despair. It is this
complexus of direct experience, indirect reflection, and emotional reverberations that is called
the experience of limit.

Limit is of course an abstract word; wall is
a concrete one. Generally speaking, they both
mean the same thing. But there is a difference.
A wall can be measured, felt, tested, and in some
cases, even walked around, looked at on the other
side, and even sat upon. A limit, is something
that cannot be measured, and certainly cannot be
gone beyond. What is at issue is not a limit to
objects, but a limit to the self. The human mind
however, is restless, and when it realizes that it
cannot penetrate beyond such an ultimate limit, it
raises questions about just what this is that
hems in the self. To put it another way, the mind
asks how it is possible to think about something
beyond which it cannot go?

Kaufman suggests four fundamental types of
limiting experiences which can be taken as models
of how to conceive or think about this ultimate
limit. In one sense there is no necessity of
moving this far and there may be arbitrariness
involved in the conceptions proposed, yet the
human mind surges restlessly at this barrier, and
the attempt must be made. This last development

is another way of putting the question of God.

Four basic analogies are proposed: first, the organic analogy, with its limit to life; second, the normative analogy, with its limit to meaning; third, the physical analogy, with its limit to time; finally, the personal analogy, with this limits to freedom. Each of these analogies can be pursued in considerable detail, as was seen above in Gilkey's work.

Other Kinds of Religious Symbolism

The following are suggested areas for further exploration of the symbolism of the religious dimension of experience. First there is the positive side of the analogies of limit just examined. Any balanced analysis must take the joyful aspects of life to account along with the tragic. One of the most significant contributions of Peter Berger's Rumor of Angels, is his stress on the positive or ecstatic aspects of religious experiences of limit.

According to William Johson, five contemporary thinkers who would not consider themselves to be religious nevertheless find and express transcendence in their own way. According to him then, Charles Reich finds transcendence in personal liberation; Herbert Marcuse in the possibility of historical alternative; R. D. Laing in creatio-ex-nihilo; Ernst Bloch in the future and Karl Jung in self-realization. /18/

A related recent development is transpersonal psychology,

Transpersonal psychology is the title given to an emerging force in the psychology field by a group of psychologists and professional men and women from other fields who are

57

DISCLOSURE OF THE ULTIMATE

The major criticism of religion by the early social sciences was that it was not scientific enough and could not be tested by verifiable hypotheses. Its symbolism could therefore not be genuinely cognitive, and its object, as Freud pointed out, was an illusion, beneficial perhaps, but illusory nonetheless. But if this is so, how explain the fact of its presence and its power over the minds and hearts of people through the countless millenia of man's recorded history as well as its continued validity in today's scientific world? The basic answer of the early social sciences was to explain religion in terms of its functional consequences.

One of the first attempts to explain the functional consequences of religion was the one which saw it as the support of various historical tyrannies and political despotisms brought about by an alliance of self-interest between priests and the ruling political figures. This "reduced" religion to a form of politics, and not a very noble one at that. This kind of explanation has been called "consequential reductionism." /21/

Not all functional explanations were so crude, however. Others admitted an authentic side to religion and conceded some objectivity to religious symbolism, but claimed that this authenticity had been misinterpreted and misunderstood. What was needed were newer and better explanations. This approach has been called "symbolic reductionism."

One of the earliest examples of such symbolically reductive explanations was the one which considered religion as a phase of the history of science. Since primitive man could not really understand the mysteries of the stars, the fertility of crops and the rotation of the seasons, he supposedly developed these fantastic theories to try to explain them. As science gradually developed, however, its factual, sensible explanations took the place of the imaginary ones.

Durkeim and others saw religion as a stage in the development of ethics or morality. In mankind's early period, such ethics as there were emerged out of community pressures and the collective spirit. As man matured, however, a sense of personal ethical responsibility developed and replaced the symbol systems which had been necessary to sustain a tribally oriented system of morality.

Many social scientists today find such explanations exaggerated. They say that even though some aspects of primitive religion can be understood as attempts at crude scientific explanation, these were generally not at the core of the religious system. Also, further research has found that primitive man was not so primitive after all. His science, especially in such fields as astronomy, was amazingly accurate and developed, and his understanding of symbolism was considerably more sophisticated and complex than had been thought.

All this obviously oversimplifies the work of the great social scientists and their important contribution to modern culture. But their helpful explanations of the milieu of religion and of certain historically conditioned aspects of religion should not be expected by them and by others to give a satisfactory explanation of the nature of religion and of religious symbolism because it goes beyond their professional expertise. But if that is true, why did they attempt to do so? And why were their analyses generally so negative? Robert Bellah offers the following as an explanation,

> It is my contention that implicit
> in the work of the great symbolic
> reductionists was another position
> with entirely different implication
> for the place of religion in our
> culture, a position which I will
> call 'symbolic realism'...Not only

the great social scientistsbut many
philosophical, literary, linguistic
and religious thinkers have contributed
to this position which has been gestating for a long time and has become
increasingly explicit in the last
twenty years. Both consequential
reductionism and symbolic reductionism
are expressions of an objective cognitive bias which has dominated Western
thought ever since the discovery of
scientific method in the seventeenth
century. This position has held that
the only valid knowledge is in the form
of falsifiable scientific hypotheses. /22/

Down through the centuries men have existed
as though there really were answers to their
problems and their basic needs. They were sensible
enough, of course, to realize that because a need
is not fulfilled in the concrete, this does not
mean that it is unfulfillable. They knew that
because a man doesn't have a home, this didn't
mean that houses are impossible. No matter how
much religious fulfillment might elude the grasp
of some individuals or groups, few men believed
that basic human needs were there to be basically
unfulfillable. These expectations and these needs
for a transcendent object were expressed in religious symbolism. Historically and psychologically,
this dimension of human experience and these hopes
have been so strong and the accumulated weight of
religious symbolism has been so massive, that it
would seem more reasonable to expect the burden of
any proof to fall on the side of those who claim
that it is all illusion or, at least, sublimation.

For these reasons, then, it is imperative
that in the following chapter, the cognivity of
religious symbols be examined in depth and a theory
of knowledge developed that will deal directly
rather than indirectly with these basic epistemological questions.

NOTES

[1]Alfred North Whitehead, Science and the Modern
World (N. Y.: Macmillan, 1935), pp. 275-276.

[2]William James, Varieties of Religious Experience (N. Y.: Lomgans-Green, 1912).

[3]John E. Smith, Experience and God (N. Y.:
Oxford University Press, 1968), p. 52.

[4]Ibid., p. 52.

[5]Suzanne K. Langer, "De Profundis," Revue
Internationale de Philosophie 110 (1974), 449-50.

[6]Ibid., p. 454.

[7]John E. Smith, "Some Comments on Cassirer's
Interpretation of Religion," Revue Internationale
de Philosophie 110 (1974), 480-481.

[8]Ibid., p. 483.

[9]Mircea Eliade, "Methodological Remarks on the
Study of Religious Symbolism," in Eliade and
Kitagawa, eds., The History of Religion: Essays
in Methodology (Chicago: University of Chicago
Press, 1959), pp. 97-98.

[10]Ibid., p. 102.

[11]Paul Ricoeur, The Symbolism of Evil (Boston:
Beacon Press, 1967/69)

[12]Eliade, op. cit., p. 97.

[13]Mircea Eliade, Patterns in Comparative Religion (N. Y.: New American Library, 1958).

[14]Norman Geisler, Philosophy of Religion (Grand Rapids: Zondervan, 1974).

[15]Langdon Gilkey, Naming the Whirlwind: The Renewal of God Language (Indianapolis: Bobbs-Merrill, 1969), p. 306.

[16]David Tracy in Chapter five of his Blessed Rage for Order (N. Y.: Seabury, 1975), develops the same analysis of limit. He says, "My contention will be that all significantly explicit religious language and experience (the 'religious') and all significant implisitly religious characteristics of our common experience (the 'religious dimension') will bear at least the family resemblance of articulating or implying a limit experience, a limit language or a limit dimension." p. 93. Cf. also p. 98 where Tracy finds agreement with the transcendental analysis in Louis Dupré's Hegelian phenomenology, Alfred North Whitehead's process philosophy and for scientific ideals. Cf. also pp. 102 and 105.

[17]Gordon D. Kaufman, "On the Naming of 'God': "Transcendence Without Mythology," in Herbert W. Richardson and Donald R. Cutler, eds., Transcendence (Boston: Beacon Press, 1969), pp. 114-142.

[18]William A. Johnson, The Search for Transcendence: A Theological Analysis of Non-theological Attempts to Define Transcendence (N. Y.: Harper and Row, 1974)

[19]Anthony Sutich in the _Journal of Transpersonal Psychology_ (Spring, 1969), as quoted by Charles T. Tart in _Transpersonal Psychologies_ (N. Y.: Harper and Row, 1974), frontispiece.

[20]Raymond A. Moody, Jr., _Life after Life_ (Atlanta: Mockingbird Books, 1975).

[21]Robert Bellah, "Christianity and Symbolic Realism," _The Journal for the Scientific Study of Religion_. 9 (Summer, 1970) 89.

[22]Ibid., p. 92.

DISCLOSURE OF THE ULTIMATE

CHAPTER THREE

WAYS OF KNOWING

One of the difficulties with many theological works that deal with such basic issues as religious experience, faith, revelation and religious language, is that they do not take the time to make explicit their epistemological foundations. They accept the premises of current epistemologies even when trying to respond to the charges against religion based on these theories. Even in their more straightforward discussions and expositions, they rely on the methodologies and principles of epistemologies whose implications and background they have not examined. Within these parameters, many problems prove to be extremely intractable and in some cases, insoluble. It is imperative, then, that these theories and premises be examined in an explicit and formal way. What is a problem within one set of premises, may prove much more within another. At the very least, fundamental theology, as a frontier area of theology, needs to deal with the basic elements of human knowledge as one of its major tasks. Though this involves a journey into philosophy, with attendant complexities and uncertainties, these are lesser problems than those that result from relying on an unexamined system.

What this chapter and the next intend to do, then, is to undertake such an epistemological study. It will try to explore and develop a basic working theory of human knowledge. Postponed for the moment will be a direct discussion of the implications of all this for religious knowledge.

In this chapter two important epistemological systems will be studied. It will be contended that they are closely related despite some secondary differences. As a conclusion this work's guiding epistemological principles will be specified. In the following chapter, a number of other contemporary thinkers will be examined briefly and in apart to indicate that a number of their ideas bear a remarkable resemblance to and convergence with the major principles of the theory of knowledge developed. Whatever its weaknesses such an attempt to develop an explicit theory of knowledge is preferable to an unexamined and unconscious use of someone else's premises.

Brief History of the Question

It will be helpful to start with a look at a few highpoints in the historical development of theories of knowledge. These theories divide up roughly into rationalistic and empirical systems. The rationalistic philosophies claim to have discovered certain truths in the human mind. Plato in his <u>Dialogues</u> /1/ holds that certain knowledge, knowledge in the strictest sense, can be obtained through universals. These universals, sometimes called "Platonic Ideas," are grasped through what Plato calls the recollection of their Forms. Strenuous training, usually mathematical, is required to do this. But when one eventually becomes aware of these innate ideas, certainty is achieved.

Many centuries later, Réné Descartes in his
Discourse on Method /2/ arrived at similar conclusions from different premises. Growing up as he
did in a world of rapid change: religious, scientific, commercial, even philosophical, Descartes
came to suspect all traditional systems especially
those based on the authority of antiquity. In
constructing his own system, he began with systematic doubt, not out of complete skepticism, but
in order to discover a more satisfactory and viable
basis for knowledge and certainty. Looking around
for a firm foundation with which to begin, he
discovered certainty only in himself, in his own
existence. He felt that though he could doubt
the existence of the world, and though his cons-
iousness of the so-called external world was
possibly the result of deception, he could not
possibly deceive himself about his own ideas and
his own existence. Thus his famous maxim, "Cogito,
ergo sum--I think, therefore I am. /3/

Descartes concluded that "I am, I Exist," is
true every time that it is thought and uttered.
Certainty comes from the clarity and the distinct-
ness of the idea of one's own existence. Though
these two words, "clear and distinct," have slightly
different meanings in Descartes' system, they both
indicate the source of the certainty he claimed:
the lucid operations of the human mind.

Having worked out one fundamental, clear idea,
Descartes turned to another, the idea of God as
the perfect being. Since this too is a clear and
distinct idea we can be sure of it as well. And
since a perfect being could not be deceptive, it
follows that faith can be placed in the knowledge
that comes to us from him. Descartes theory of
knowledge, then, though it begins in doubt, ends
in a double certainty: the clear and distinct ideas
of one's own existence and that of God, the perfect
being who cannot deceive us.

In the years following Descartes, rationalistic

theories of knowledge began to lose their influence. This was due in part to conflicting claims
among rationalistic philosophers as to what the
foundational certainties were. It is difficult
to accept the claim that a whole intellectual
superstructure can be raised on such a principle,
when another philosopher denies it and makes the
same claim for an opposite principle. Multiply
this a bit and these philosophical systems, whatever their worth, begin to lose their influence.
Also involved were the great cultural and historical changes taking place in the emerging modern
world. Solutions which might have seemed plausible
in a simpler society, now seemed inadequate to
cope with the flood of new information and even
new problems that these developments were bringing
in their wake. The very sum of knowledge itself
began to increase geometrically, further compli-
cating things. Though the more rationalistically
inclined responded to these critiques and developments by saying that their ideas and principles
were based primarily on what is timeless and
unchanging in the human mind, and therefore above
these culturally and historically conditioned
changes, there were a number of contra-indications.
Even within mathematics, for example, some theorems
once thought to be self-evident and intellectually
clear, had to be discarded because of later
developments, such as non-Euclidian geometry,
where different theorems could be true in alternative systems.

All of this led to the development of empirical theories of knowledge. One of the concerns
of empiricism is to try to be more consistent with
the ways ordinary human beings live and think.
Another is to find where in fact our information
comes from and what is its reliability. Thus
empirical systems turned away from ideas, innate
or otherwise, towards sense experience. It is no
accident that these ideas have developed especially
in countries with strong practical bent: England
and the United States. Though such an approach

for whatever reason, found less favor among the philosophers of other countries, it nevertheless represents a very important stream of contemporary thought that needs to be dealt with in developing any current theory of knowledge.

Two great empirical philosophers were John Locke (1632-1704) and David Hume (1711-1776).

In his main work, The Essay Concerning Human Understanding /4/, Locke's approach to knowledge is a commonsensical reflection on ordinary experience. He rejects innate ideas saying that ideas are derived from sensation. Upon reflection, the mind can become aware of its internal operations of willing, thinking, wanting, and so on. He divides ideas into two classes: simple and complex. Simple ideas arise from external objects, internal processes or combinations of these, and complex ideas are combinations of simple.

Whether ideas are simple or complex, the mind understands ideas. Knowledge, therefore, is apprehending how ideas agree or disagree.

It there are no innate ideas, something must be the cause of simple ideas. Things that affect man must therefore exist. But since man knows the effect on him, the thing itself must remain unknown. Substance is a name given to a collection of secondary sense qualities such as color, taste, odor, touch and sound.

The difficulty with Locke's theory of knowledge is its initial assumption, namely that what is known is only an affection of the knowing subject. It begins and ends in the mind. This leads to severe subjectivism. Locke recognized the difficulty and tried to deal with it, but without complete success.

David Hume in his A Treatise on Human Nature /5/ and Enquiry Concerning Human Understanding /6/

pursued these questions to their ultimate conclusion. Beginning with sense experience, he came to
the conclusion that it is impossible to know anything about the world. What we do have is a series
of disconnected sense impressions. From these we
get our ideas. We then put these ideas together in
our minds, not because there is any unifying basis
in the impressions themselves, but simply because
that is the way our minds work. These impressions
belong to nobody and are contained in no-self.
Thus the only basis we have for ordering our experiences is our mental habits. But what about men
with different sets of mental habits? In that
case, which beliefs correspond to the true world?
Hume says that there is no answer to that question,
since there is no justification for believing one
thing rather than another. All we have is a strong
feeling that this is so. No matter how irrational
we discover our beliefs to be, we find we cannot
help believing. We are compelled by human nature
to live and speak on the basis of belief in certain
things.

In this Hume also displayed some inconsistency.
On the onehand, he doubted everything, and on the
other, he believed a number of things because he
felt he had to.

Starting with sense experience then, did not
lead the empiricists to the kind of certainty
calimed by the rationalists. On the contrary, it
led to a kind of skepticism. Perhaps because of
this the empiricist position could not be called
fanciful in the way the rationalistic one could.
It reflected more the actual features of everyday
experience. What was suggested could be examined
and tested by everybody. As a matter of fact, one
of the results of the empiricist tradition has
been to question the premise that in order for
human beings to live we need to have absolutely
clear certainty about things. On the contrary,
it is possible to conclude that normal lives are
possible with only probable knowledge. The

certainty found in day-to-day lives of most people comes closer to the probable than to the certain. Somehow human beings are able to transcend this limitation.

Radical American Empiricism

The "gentle scepticism" exemplified by Hime is not the only conclusion that can be drawn from a philosophical theory of knowledge based on experience. Building upon more than a century of further scientific and cultural development, a group of American philosophers drew considerably different conclusions, all the while remaining as thoroughly empirical as their predecessors. Continuing to avoid the rationalistic certainty of innate ideas, they tried to avoid as well the dead-end skepticism inherent in earlier theories of experience.

The three main empirical American philosophers are Charles S. Pierce (1839-1914), William James (1842-1910), and John Dewey (1859-1952). Each of them approached the question of experience differently. Each of them had his own individualistic understanding of it. It would be inappropriate to the present task to go into those details here. Despite these differences, however, there are enough similarities to justify speaking of a broad pattern or consensus among them. This American empirical theory was developed in conscious opposition to the classical British theory. It accepted the basic premise of classical empiricism: experience as opposed to innate ideas, but then went on to develop another and different theory of experience. It was broader and more comprehensive than the previous narrow focus upon strict sensation.

A distinguished contemporary philosopher, John E. Smith, has, in his various works, presented a study and synthesis of this American empirical school, to which he gives the name radical empiricism. /7/

DISCLOSURE OF THE ULTIMATE

The following section of this chapter is a presentation of Smith's synthesis of these American radical empiricists or pragmatists.

No appeal to experience is naive. It always involves a presupposed theory. So the most honest and straightforward thing to do is to state one's own theory of knowledge clearly and unambiguously from the outset. Smith does this in at least two places; first in <u>Religion and Empiricism</u>, he says, "Experience is understood as the record and result of complex interactions and transactions between the human organism or language-using animal and the environment in which that organism lives and moves." /8/ And in <u>Experience and God</u> he says, "Experience is the many-sided product of complex encounters between what there is and a being capable of undergoing, enduring, taking note of responding to and expressing it." /9/

Smith makes clear from the very beginning that he considers the epistemological position that experience is a primarily mental, subjective affair to be just a theory like other theories. He says that there is no need for us to agonize endlessly over how to break out of the prison of subjectivity --an ideological circle if ever there was one-- for the simple reason that we have never been and are not in that prison.

He suggests that for too long the burden of proof has been placed on those with a more realistic theory of knowledge, despite the fact that this seems to correspond more closely to how people understand their own ways of daily knowing and living. It would seem more reasonable to suggest that the burden of proof should be the other way around. Or at least should not subjectivistic theories of knowledge stop requiring other theories of knowledge to prove their case to their satisfaction. For the claim that we can be certain of our perception because what is immediately present to the mind must be beyond doubt is itself a theoret-

ical/assumption, proved neither empirically nor
intuitively. It has dominated the field largely
because it has been sheltered itself in the great
shadow and prestige of natural science. Fairness
demands they should have to fully argue their case
like anyone else.

Smith deals at considerable length and in
various places with the three claims of classical
empiricism and its later day forms of positivism
and some types of linguistic analysis. These claims
are: that experience is co-extensive with what can
be sensed;that it is a body of data present to the
mind of a theoretical knower; and that it is primarily a private, mental content standing as well
before the world.

Of the three, the third is the most important
and will be taken up firth.

In opposing it, Smith claims that "experience
is an objective disclosure of what is there to be
encountered, whatever it may prove to be." /10/,
ot that it is "a valid medium of disclosure through
which we come to know what there is." /11/

This view is of course opposed to the view
that experience is some kind of veil or wall
standing between the person who experiences and
the so-called external world. It is opposed to the
claim that human certainty begins as a private
affair which then has to deal with a world out
there through an inferential process. It is opposed
to the understanding of experience as primarily
something mental immediately present to the apprehending subject. It is opposed, in other words, to
any understanding of experience, as purely self-
reflexive, leaving out whatever realities present
themselves for encounter.

Underlying this classical theory, he sees two
basic assumptions usually unquestioned, but which
very much need examination. The first assumption

is "that whereas we may by mistaken about the
existence and the nature of the object before us,
we cannot be mistaken about our perception at least
of the nature of the object, because what is immediately present to the mind, i.e., our perception,
is beyond all doubt." /12/ And the second is that
since perceptions are seen to vary, as, for example,
a pencil appears to the eye to be broken when
placed in a glass of water, then this experiencing
of the pencil is unreliable and the only reliability
there is resides in experiencings or personal
feelings about it. The net results of these assumptions, erected into a theory of perception, is that
"experience, instead of disclosing what there is,
actually encloses itself within a circle of priv-
acy." /13/

Reconstructed or radical empiricism rejects
as uncritical the assumption that experience is
merely a mental record, a passive receiving of
something totally within the mind or feelings of
a person. It claims, instead, and many modern
psychological studies of perception tend to support
it, /14/ that it is rather "a product of the intersection of something encountered and a being capable of having an encounter." /15/ Since it is
a product or process, it takes time and has a
temporal structure. It is true that at times an
experience will seem to be pressed into an
instantaneous flash of apprehension, something
above or beyond time, yet this phenomenon, trus as
it may be, makes sense only it seen as embedded
in and the result of an ongoing temporal flow of
experience. Someone who suddenly sees the solution
of a dogged problem on arising in the morning, has
usually been chewing on it, studying it, reading
about it and even sleeping on it for some time.

Smith adds that there is a lack of balance,
an asymmetry between these cooperative factors.
The human person who encounters has "to reflect
what is there to be encountered in a way that does
full justice to the nature and being of the

encountered material." /16/ What is experienced
on the other hand, is just there; it need reflect'
nothing.

In a number of ancient philosophical systems,
and assumed as well by more modern theories of
perception, is the understanding of the human mind
as a kind of _tabula rasa_ or blank blackboard, upon
which the world somehow writes. According to this
view, learning is essentially a passive experience.
Other theories see man as having a structure of his
own that enters actively into the experiencing
process. Nor is this merely a question of combining a few subjective elements with an objective
reality. "The one who experiences refracts as well
as reflects and it is through such refraction that
the material of encounter comes to be 'taken' or
interpreted in different contexts of meaning." /17/

Each of the two elements that intersect in
experience, the person and what is being experienced, have grounds pointing to their natures.
Neither one totally produces or absolutely influences the other. Each has its own integrity which
needs to be recognized and respected.

Second Element

This leads to the second of Smith's three
major points, namely that experience is "the
funded and meaningful result of a multidimensional
encounter between a concrete person and whatever
is there to be encountered." /18/ By this he
denies that experience and sense are co-extensive,
or that such sensory things as taste, color, sound
and so on are of exclusive importance in experience.
This opposes the position that if such sense data
cannot be produced, as it cannot be for many
genuine dimensions of human life, then these are
ruled to be inexperiencable and purely subjective.

DISCLOSURE OF THE ULTIMATE

Without denying that all our encounters with
the world involve our senses, it is possible to
hold that the identification of sense with experience flies in the face of much that we do and
know. Smith offers the example of two persons
speaking to each other. The point of the conversation is mutual communication. Although all that
can be seen is a face, a body, hands, all moving
and gesturing in one way or another, yet it is
assumed "that these words and gestures are intel-
lible and can be interpreted because they are the
expression of a center of attention or purposive
unity which constitutes that person as the self."
/19/ Yet according to classical empiricism, that
purposive, central unity cannot be "experienced"
because it is not an ingredient of sensory activity.

We encounter meaningful unities not merely in
dealing with other selves but also within ourselves
in a variet of dimensions. A house can be experienced as high, deep, dark and silent, but that is
only the beginning. It can also be considered by
a family as a home, perhaps an ancestral one; by
an engineer as an obstacle in the way of a highway
which needs to be removed; by a house painter as a
possible source of income; by a photographer or
an artist as a beautiful object, particularly at
certain seasons of the year; by a tax collector as
a source of revenue, and so on. Yet all are seeing
the same house, and their senses are responding to
it in the same basic way. The difference is in
the meaning they attach to the experience. But if
it be true that experience is only sensory, then
this meaning has to be something added by the subjective psyche of these various individuals. To
say this, however, is to deprive the world of "the
full depth of meaning which it reveals--moral,
esthetic, religious--and it is supposed instead
that man simply 'adds' this meaning through his own
mind and feeling to an otherwise 'neutral material.'" /20/

Men are not cameras or tape recorders; there
is always interaction between content and meaning.
Another way of putting this is to say, with Dewey,
that in experience thought is present from the
beginning. Something catches our attention and we
begin a process of critical inquiry which enables
us to reach what is there. "The point is that the
recovery of the given is never a matter of reaching
bare, sensible data." /21/

Third Element

This brings us to the third element of Smith's
position, namely that experience embraces a number
of dimensions, "moral, esthetic, scientific and
religious, which give point and purpose to the life
of an individual person." /22/

This view stands over against the one that
sees the experiencer as merely a theoretical observer whose primary, even sole intent is the knowing
of data. The difficulty with this view is that it
takes one element of man's life, albeit an important one, and elevates it to a unique and supreme
position, forcing all other elements either to
conform to it or to give it some form of obeisance.
It claims that other forms of knowledge partake
less of reality the further away they get from the
quality of active knowledge. This makes "the
world, including other selves ... appear as nothing
more than a body of phenomena to be explained in
scientific terms." /23/

The only value that things and even persons
have, according to this view, is to be known by a
scientific observer. Important as science is, and
wonderful as are the things it has brought to modern
man, the fact remains that it is a distorted view
of human nature to have to reduce all knowing to a
scientifically modelled theoretical level in order
to be able to consider it genuine.

77

DISCLOSURE OF THE ULTIMATE

As human beings, we are much more than knowers.
We are complex experiencers. There are many situations where we are not interested in explanation as
much as we are in realization, in involvement and
in the acting out of concern. One of the great
contributions made by the modern existentialist
movement has been its protest against this "object-
ification" of man. They have insisted that genuine
commitment is as valid, perhaps more so, than
theoretical knowledge.

Error

One final major point centers around the question of error, or, to put it the other way round,
the question of certainty. For the "subjectivist
supposition is itself part of a theory for explaining error." /24/

Starting with an analysis of the nature of
the human self, classical empiricism assumes that
it is complete from the start. Though the self
may receive impressions from the outside, like the
blackboard to which it is compared, it remains
basically unchanged by these impressions. An analysis of actual experience, however, indicates that
it is a shock for an individual self to realize
that it is distinct from the world. In order to
see itself as distinct, the self has to begin to
excercise its powers of discrimination, choise and
judgement. For "at the moment when we discover
that we have a selective interest in things, we
become aware that we are individual, active beings
and not merely 'passive' recorders of given facts."
/25/ Without this kind of awareness and interest
there would be only a river of consciousness, unen-
ding, unbroken and unstoppable. Self-awareness
and selfhood would not be possible.

With this emergence of self-awareness the
problem of error also emerges. One question of
error is involved in the possibility of distin-

guishing between the self and what is "really
there." To presuppose that the child begins "by
knowing that all of its experience is private, personal and confined wholly to its own consciousness,
and that it must then find a way of surmounting
that subjectivity in order to reach the 'external
world,'" /26/ is a theory and no more.

If this theory of certainty is rejected, how
is error dealt with? It is helpful to recognize,
first, that there are different kinds of error:
error of due recognition and error due to failure
to notice that something is present. In order to
avoid these it is not necessary to retreat into a
world of private experience over against the
"external world." It makes more sense to start by
accepting that what we encounter is there to be
encountered, objectively and publicly, not merely
privately. It is at best only a theory and at
worst only an illusion to make the self a container-
enclosure for errors allowing the continuance
outside the self of the error-free world of scientific objectivity.

A factor that needs to be introduced at this
point is intersubjectivity. For "experience is
repeated encounter with what there is; it requires
continuity and identity both in what is experienced
and in the one who experiences." /27/ Meaning
presupposes the possibility of critical comparison
and correlation, for in our world, no object or
person is ever fully revealed in the flesh of an
instant or in an absolutely isolated encounter.
Time is required for meaning to grow and develop
as it emerges out of an interconnection of disclosures within a variety of experiences. One encounter helps to evaluate and criticize the other. This
is really nothing new. It is done all the time in
the sciences, where the experiments of one person
are compared with and checked by those of other
persons.

This is not to imply that such comparisons
take place only between separate selves. They also

79

take place within the individual self. When a
person is spoken of as "experienced," this means
that he has learned from a number of concrete
experiences just what something means or how something is done. Such appeals to experience "always
make reference to a cululative product or to a
deposit of insight or skill that has taken years
to acquire." /28/

Context and Tendency

Finally, Smith uses two words that help to
bring analysis to a conclusion. He says that all
experiences must have context and tendency. With
regard to context he says, "experience is not
merely the disclosure of the world's content, but
it also reflects the many ways on which reality
can be approached." /29/ By this he refers to the
many domains of human life such as the scientific,
the economic, the ethical, the esthetic, the religious and other ways that men live and act in the
world. This implies that experience is not merely
a question meeting what is there in isolation, but
of seeing it in many different contexts of meaning.

By tendency is meant that experience encounters far more than the merely sensible qualities
of a passing moment. Though these are of course
acknowledged, "we are also aware of their flowing
into each other, of clustering together or of
succeeding each other in various purposeful
patterns." /30/

Personal Knowledge

This section will take up the epistemology
of Michael Polanyi. In his major work Personal
Knowledge /31/, he developed a theory of knowledge which can be taken as a useful complement
to the positions developed so far. This does not
imply any direct or necessary connection with the

radical empiricismof the American pragmatists.
Polanyi began as a scientist and developed his
ideas in the context of the philosophy and history
of science. His system constitutes an explicit and
orderly rejection of what he considered to be the
false scientific ideal of wholly explicit and wholly
impersonal knowledge. His own experience as a
scientist and his own meditations as a philosopher
led him to an alternative approach which he called
personal knowledge.

The Quest for Discovery

Plato's question posed in the _Meno_ is a very
basic and fruitful one. Socrates says, "But if he
always possessed this knowledge he would always
have known; or if he has acquired the knowledge he
could not have acquired it in this life unless he
had been taught geometry; for he may be made to do
the same with all geometry and every other branch
of knowledge. Now has any one ever taught him all
this...?" To which Meno replies, "I am certain
that no one ever did teach him." /32/ What he is
referring to is the way that the boy is led through
a series of questions to develop a geometrical
theorem though he apparently knew nothing about it
beforehand. Thus the problem: how can you look for
something you don't know about, and how can you
recognize it when you find it? Plato himself
solved the problem by postulating what he called
the recollection of ideas from a previous existence;
the rationalists sought the answer in clear and
distinct ideas and the classical expiricists in the
certainty of sense data. The radical expiricists
insisted on expanding the foundations of knowledge
to go beyond the explicity formulated mental and
the concretely limited physical, to a broader, more
comprehensive human experience. And it is this
broader aspect of human knowing and experiencing
that Polanyi has pursued in depth.

DISCLOSURE OF THE ULTIMATE

Polanyi's basic thrust is similar to Plato's: a quest for discovery. As long as knowledge is treated as something wholly articulated and explicit, then there is no answer to the problem posed in the _Meno_. Why look for something totally unknown? How would we be able to test the results if we did? Polanyi, however, suggests a solution to this dilemma by claiming that our knowledge contains many hidden things. Thus ut us possible for us to have a mysterious foreknowledge of what is as yet not explicitly discovered without recourse to recollection or similar solutions. He sees all knowledge as directed towards discovery because of man's stubborn and undeniable thirst for truth. Here is how he phrases it. "The pursuit of discovery is conducted from the start in these terms: all the time we are guided by sensing the presence of a hidden reality toward which our clues are pointing; and the discovery which terminates and satisfies the pursuit is still sustained by the same _vision_. It claims to have made contact with reality: a reality which, being real, may yet reveal itself to future eyes in an indefinite range of unexpected manifestations." /33/

Before getting into a more systematic discussion of Polanyi's ideas, however, a word of caution my be useful. Polanyi's writings are difficult and various commentators fasten upon differing poles or aspects, so that they are not at all easy to synthesize. Also since he is challenging one of the basic ideals of the contemporary world, namely the total objectivity of science, reading him can generate a certain uneasiness. As the two editors of a collection of essays on Polanyi say in their introduction,

> _Personal Knowledge_ is an exasperating
> book. It is the very antithesis of
> prepossessing. To some readers, it is
> a book against the overall thrust and
> vision of which it requires no great
> acuity to defend oneself. To others,

it seems too good to be true, too
obvious to be important, or too simplistic
to square with what even the simple
minded know to be the case. To still
others, it presents a comprehensive
review of things towards which even the
most patient and sympathetic reader
must struggle as toward some fugitive
and one seeks more fully to articulate
for oneself its central theses, the
whole enterprise, which seems to betray
a fundamental instability, falls apart. /34/

Of course these authors do not agree with that negative assessment, else they would not be editing a
collection of essays in honor of the author, but it
does give us due warning that the material is
difficult, though ultimately rewarding.

The Tacit Dimension

Tacit and Explicit

The first important and basic distinction
made by Polanyi with regard to knowledge is between
explicit knowledge and tacit knowledge. Explicit
knowledge is of course fully articulated and
conscious knowledge. And we tend to value it more
highly than implicit or tacit knowledge. We also
make it the standard both for knowledge in its
final form and for the process of acquiring knowledge. Polanyi objects to this and suggests a
quite different view:

And yet this exalted valuation
of strictly formalized thought is
self-contradictory. It is true that
the traveller, equipped with a detailed
map of a region across which he plans his
itinerary, enjoys a striking intellectual superiority over the explorer

who first enters a new region--yet the
explorer's fumbling progress is a much
finer achievement than the well briefed
traveller's journey. Even if we
admitted that an exact knowledge of
the universe is our supreme mental
possession, it would still follow that
man's most distinguished act of thought
consists in producing such knowledge; the
human mind is at its greatest when it
brings hitherto uncharted domains under
its control. Such operations renew
the existing articulate framework.
Hence they cannot be performed within
the framework, but have to rely (to
this extent) on the kind of plunging
reorientation which we share with the
animals. /35/

This position can be understood as another
instance of the classical distinction between
lower and higher forms of mind. Thus Aristotle
spoke of demonstrative knowledge (episteme) and
rational intuition (nous), Plato gave us the image
of the divided line, and Descartes spoke of the
deductive and intuitive capacities of man. But
in none of these historical instances do the
philosophers focus upon the body-rooted character
of whatever the higher power is called. The
emphasis is rather in the opposite direction,
namely that this higher power fulfills itself by
detaching itself from the particularities of
person and place.

Polanyi, on the other hand, stresses the
bodily roots of man's intuitive capacity. This
has the great advantage of avoiding the image of
man as a disembodied intelligence, which haunts
so much scientifically influenced modern thought.
At the same time, Polanyi must deal with the problem of the impersonal side of human nature,
philosophically called universals, which these
other systems do deal with. He does so by what

84

he calls the universal intent of personal knowledge, a sense of responsibility or commitment beyond the personal, as will be seen below.

Polanyi has adapted the traditional epistemological axiom according to which all knowledge comes through the senses by saying that all thought has a bodily basis. All explicitations, all articulations depend on inarticulate powers in man. We know more than we can tell.

The accreditation of our utterances as true necessarily involves the inarticulate or tacit area. It involves a reliance upon criteria which cannot be fully defined. The ideal of impersonal, objective knowledge and truth, therefore, needs to be revised. By relying on these various inarticulate powers, we can experience reality more comprehensively and more fully.

Polanyi holds that problem solving is the paradigm example of knowing. Solving a problem involves the whole person. It is something we do rather than something we have. Knowledge is man's chief and proper skill and like all man's skills, it takes time to practice and develop. In every act of knowledge, then, including those related to the natural sciences, the knower is personally involved.

Focal and Subsidiary Awareness

This is formalized in a second distinction between subsidiary and focal awareness, where subsidiary is understood to be the equivalent of tacit.

The distinction emerges from the fact that we can be aware of something in two quite different ways. For example, while travelling on a plane, we notice someone up ahead who catches our eye as we look around the cabin. For a moment, we're not

sure ehy and we pause to consider what the reason
might be. It is a momentary puzzle. Could it be
the hair, graying at the temples, the glasses
perhaps, horn-rimmed, or the tweed jacket? We
focus our attention a bit more, examine the face
a bit more closely despite the distance, try to
think back and suddenly it all falls into place.
It is Professor Jones who gave a paper at a convention a couple of years ago and whom we met at
a reception afterwards. There are several steps
involved: it begins with a problem: should I know
him? goes through questioning and examination and
suddenly coalesces into recognition and even a
name. Another example would be the kind of puzzle
popularized by Gestalt research sometimes seen in
popular journals and papers. A page has a certain
number of lines on it that look like meaningless
squiggles. Is there anything more here? We turn
the page around, upside down, sideways. Suddenly
something catches our eyes, we turn back, look more
closely, and suddenly, of course, a rabbit munching
grass under a bush! How could we have not seen it
before? Other examples are those where the squiggles
are ambiguous. What looks like a face can be facing
right or left. Personal Knowledge contains a
number of such examples, many of them influenced by
Gestalt. /36/

As Polanyi explains it, the details of the
person's face, the squiggly lines on the page,are
particulars, vectors or subsidiary elements of
perception. We go from them to something else. We
go from the awareness of subsidiary detail to focal
awareness of the whole. "All thought contains
components of which we are subsidiarily aware in
the focal content of our thinking, and all thought
dwells in its subsidiaries, as if they were parts
of our body. Hence thinking is not only necessarily
intentional, as Brentano has taught, it is also
necessarily fraught with the roots that it embodies.
It has a from-to structure." /37/

Three Kinds of Wholes

Robert Innis suggests that there are three kinds of such wholes or patterns of consciousness. The first kind he calls perceptual-imagined wholes. These see the world as a set of organized forms, images and events in which we dwell. "Indeed aesthetically man produces forms for perception. In so doing he gives objective shape tp his perceptional possibilities and externalizes permanent patterns of perceptual organization by the generation of an image field with which he interacts ." /38/ He quotes Friedrich Heer to the effect that "it is only through images that man is fashioned in his own true image." /39/

The second kind of whole he calls linguistic-conceptual. These build upon the perceptual-imaginal ones, with intellection and language following upon perception and imaging. Language can embed perceptual experience and, as language is systematically developed, experience is clarified. "When we learn to speak either of ourselves or of the world, we perform an interpretative integration and in so doing we assimilate ourselves into a world."/40/

The third kind of whole suggested is affective. An affective whole is a state of being produced in ourselves. "just as there are subsidiary components in the perceptual-imaginal and linguistic-conceptual domains, so there are subsidiary components in the affective domain which demand integration, so that we can succeed or fail in a form of sensibility." /41/

In his book on The Possibility of Religious Knowledge, Jerry Gill spends considerable amount of time analyzing Polanyi's Personal Knowledge and using it to deal with the problem of religious knowledge. He offers a treatment of these distinctions which, even if in its precision seems to go somewhat beyond Polanyi's himself, is nevertheless conceptually clarifying.

Now to bring these distinctions together for the main point. The first distinction was between focal and subsidiary awareness and the second was between conceptual and bodily activity. When these two sets of distinctions are related to one another the result is . third distinction between explicit and tacit knowledge. The relationship can be visualized by imagining the 'awareness continuum' and the 'activity continuum' as dimensions which intersect each other. When the poles of focal awareness and conceptual activity are related, the result is 'explicit knowledge.' When the poles of subsidiary awareness and bodily activity are related, the result is 'tacit knowledge. As every awareness and activity is a mixture of its respective poles, so every form of knowledge is a mixture of both explicit and tacit elements. In other words, relating the two continua in this way produces yet a third continuum--the knowledge con-continuum--between the explicit and tacit poles. /42/

This can be put into graphic form as follows:

Awareness Continuum	Subsidiary Awareness	Focal Awareness
Knowledge Continuum	Tacit Knowledge	Explicit Knowledge
Activity Continuum	Non-Verbal Activity	Verbal Activity

If these subsidiary awarenesses are so important, it is legitimate to ask why we do not seem
to be more conscious of them. One reason that it
is difficult if not impossible to be aware of them
is that they happen in an automatic kind of way
that the knower cannot really control. Another
reason is that some of these subsidiaries are bodily
processes which remain in the realm of the unconscious. The most important reason, however, why
it is difficult to speak about them is that in order
to do this it would be necessary to turn one's
attention to them formally and explicitly. But just
as the modification of the environment of an experiment can effect the experiment itself, so attending
to these subsidiary functions would have the effect
of transforming them into something else thus making
it impossible for them to function.

Kinds of Tacit Knowing

William T. Scott gives a number of examples
of tacit knowing. /43/ The first is the rooting
of speech in subsidiary and focal awareness. The
second is the tacit foundation of logical argument.
When trying to determine the meaning of a proposition it is necessary to use subsidiary awareness
to read the words that express them. Thus we are
able to judge the logical correctness of something
said by a continuing check to see if the symbols
or words continue to stand for the same entities.
Also in order to appreciate the wholeness of an
argument, it is necessary to have a subsidiary
awareness of the value and merit of its parts.
Organizing principles are perhaps more fully involved in tacit recognition than strictly logical
arguments, because the structural principles involved, such as those of a cell, cannot be translated
into rules. They must be recognized by their
features. Biology, for example, is taught as much
with microscopes as with textbooks. Cells are
recognized rather than merely defined.

89

A third area of tacit knowing is universals. This involves the recognition, for example, that an animal belongs to a particular species. "according to Polanyi, a universal appears as the coherence that unites a number of things into a class. In relying on some members of a class for attending to their common meaning, tacit knowledge of this common meaning is gradually acquired. As more members of the class are seen, this knowledge is verified and extended--or destroyed if the coherence proves finally to be spurious." /44/

A fourth area of tacit knowing is the recognition of an achievement. Subsidiary aspects of the action become part of what is necessary for recognizing that doing something has been done successfully. A football player catching a pass and crossing the line for a touchdown, a man mowing his lawn, an airplane taking off and disappearing into the sky, looking through a windshield of a car to see the directions on the road signs and adjusting lanes in order to be in the right place; these are all examples of achievements that can be recognized by observing them. We know when something has been done correctly, when something is working or when a goal has been achieved. We can recognize successful performance.

This implies of course that we are able also to recognize a performance that does not do what it is supposed to, a non-performance. To do this we have to recognize norms for driving a car, playing football, flying a plane or cutting the grass. Even though we may not see these norms clearly or even explicate them in any way, we are perfectly well aware when they are not observed or fulfilled. This means that there is value-recognition involved here as well as factual recognition. "The recognition of value and the recognition of fact thus occur in similar ways in Polanyi's theory of knowledge, countering the old view that facts are purely objective and values purely subjective, a view which has helped in the past to maintain a sharp distinction between science and religion." /45/

In dealing with values it is just as necessary to pull a group of subsidiary particulars into a focus of wholeness or meaning. While integrating the particulars of physical objects is not in itself a simple task, it is simpler than the process for understanding the concept of values.

A fifth arena of tacit knowing goes beyond the recognition of achievement to the consideration of the achievement itself. In so doing something physical like riding a bicycle or throwing a ball, there already exists in the imagination at the moment of implementation at least, a focal awareness of what is intended. Carrying it out then involves coordinating a whole series of subsidiary activities, muscular and coordinative, or which we are scarcely aware of at all. We aim for the achievement and the parts somehow to arrange themselves to reach it. Achievement in this sense includes extension of our bodies such as instruments and tools.

An interesting conlcusion to the above discussion is its relevance to what actually happens in a scientific procedure for there are definite similarities to procedures in science. To conduct an experiment, the scientist, stirred by a problem, must pull together a number of particulars, guided by his imagination, and by the possibility of arriving at a solution. Later, his critical faculties judge as to whether things really worked themselves out the way he intended them to. Finally, other people are able and need to judge the results if it to be admitted as a contribution to the advancement of the particular field of science involved. The point is that that scientific discovery involves more than abstract methodology. All along the route, responsible judgement is exercised both by the experimenter and by his

91

colleagues in the field.

Tacit knowledge then joins our awareness of particulars into a joint awareness of a comprehensive whole. This focal awareness of a whole is sometimes called a distal term and the subsidiary awareness of the particulars a proximal term. We are subsidiary aware not merely of external things, but, as has been said, also of our own bodies and our own mental operations. In this sense, the body is the basic instrumentality of all our knowing. Tools or instruments, even intellectual ones, such as symbols and language, serve as extensions of our bodies.

Tacit knowing is a combination of action and thought, of doing and knowing, since it combines both body and mental operations as we attempt to understand reality. As Polanyi says, "When we make a thing function as the proximal term of tacit knowing, we incorporate it in our body or extend our body to include it--so that we come to dwell in it." /46/

Indwelling

We indwell by interiorization. Instead of looking at thing in order to understand them, we try to get inside them and dwell in them. Such a process is not directed merely at physical objects around us, houses, trees, mountains, buildings, machines and so on. It also includes other human beings and the whole range of human culture and its products. Indwelling of this type can be called existential. This participation in the thing known by the knower extends to all things known and is at the basis of all knowledge. It can be called a dialectic movement, a to-from and from-to relationship. For the knower, in order to know, must surrender to the object to be known. Once contact has been made or indwelling schieved, a reverse movement occurs, with the object disclosing

itself in return.   This certainly is a more
reassuring approach than the one which understands
the human knower as perpetually locked within a
subjective self-enclosure which cuts him off from
the world.   Indwelling also calls up such words as
empathy and sympathy, emphasizing that knowing is
not a mere theoretical operation, but one which
participates in the emotional and imaginative sides
of man.

   Indwelling can be pursued even further.   It is
appropriate to speak of indwelling in language.   The
act of understanding is constantly trying to articulate itself, and articulation   implies language.
Language is something obviously special to man.
Man uses language not merely to form a link between
persons, but also as the major way of articulating
and understanding experience.   Once the initial
indwelling is specified in language in some form,
it is possible for the human mind to conceptualize
and clarify the experience further, extending man's
powers of comprehension and understanding.   That is
why there has been so much interest in linguistic
studies among contemporary philosophers.

   It is helpful to recall, however, that the
educated human mind living or indwelling in a linguistic framework, is still involved with the tacit
personal particulars that underlie all knowing and
all language.   To put is another way, it is the
understanding that precedes and justifies the
eventual conceptualization.   Language itself is
something of which we are only subsidiarily aware
and it therefore partakes of the same obscure potentialities as other subsidiary particulars.   We are
confident about our indwelling in and use of language because we are supported by our tacit operations.   Knowing and speaking are performances based
on tacit performances.   Articulateness, paradoxically
enough, springs from inarticulateness.   This articulateness can be called explicit knowledge.   Yet it
is a mistake to over-emphasize the explicitness of

explicit language. It is part of a false scientific ideal to demand that all language is and must
totally explicit so that it exhausts that which it
mirrors. Not all tacit knowledge can be articulated.
There is always the area of subsidiary particulars
that remain partially obscure by being what they
are. In an earlier maxim, "we know more than we
can tell," tell means to express in words or to
reduce experience to language

Commitment

According to Polanyi, there is an element
of commitment or belief in every act of human
knowing. In order to start upon the journey of
knowledge, it is necessary to begin by believing
that it is possible to make contact with reality:

> We can account for this capacity
> of ours to know more than we can tell
> if we believe in the presence of an
> external reality with which we can
> establish contact. This I do. I
> declare myself committed to the belief
> in an external reality gradually
> accessible to knowing, and I regard
> all true understanding as an intima-
> tion of such a reality, which, being
> real, may yet reveal itself to our
> deepened understanding in an infinite
> range of manifestations. I accept
> the obligation to search for the
> truth through my own intimations of
> reality, knowing that there is, and
> can be, no strict rule by which my
> conclusions can be justified. My
> reference to reality legitimates my
> acts of unspecifiable knowing, even
> while it duly keeps the exercise of
> such acts within the bounds of a
> rational objectivity. For a claim to
> have made contact with reality

94

necissarily legislates both for
myself and others with a universal
intent. /47/

According to Polanyi, this is not as difficult a claim as it might seem at first, for even
scientists operate from a framework of belief.
"The actual foundations of our scientific beliefs
cannot be asserted at all." /48/ Scientists, in
going about their tasks, work from a set of uniden-
tified presuppositions which become the framework
of experiment and interpretation. The scientific
task, from the setting of a problem to its testing
and eventual conclusion, takes place within the
parameters of these presuppositions. Yet like all
presuppositions, these are not fully conscious nor
always fully admitted, "Science is likewise
founded on faith--faith that is is possible to
find a continuing series of answers to the steadily
unfolding array of puzzles and problems that appear
in man's effort to comprehend the world in which
he lives. Scientific discovery is an interaction
between man and nature, in which the former strives
creatively to discover what the latter has to
reveal." /49/

This situation can be described as a double
belief which intersects in the way the horizontal
and vertical lines intersect on the artificial
horizon on the instrument board of an airplane.
The horizontal line is man's fundamental belief,
expressed so many times over the centuries, and
expressed still today, that it is possible to make
contact with reality. This confidence in a knowable reality is something that either exists or
it does not. It cannot be "proven".

The second element, the vertical one, is the
confidence that man has in his power to know.
Even at the most primitive levels, man can be seen
as driven by a passion to know and to understand.
Urged on by this need, confident in its basic
ability to succeed, man embarks on a path of

exploration, discovery and knowledge. A typical example in the unparalleled excitement the characters in a science fiction novel are made to feel as they step onto a new and yet unexplored planet.

These two confidences combine into a basic outlook or knowledge that stabilizes man and transcends the disjunction between the objective and subjective. To say that knowledge is personal, therefore, is by no means to admit that it is merely subjective. The claim to contact what is really there is a claim to universality. For a contact with reality is not something merely "factual." It includes the dimension of unspecified particulars which reach in many directions both within the world and within the human person, thus providing a universal dimension. Though not all or even most knowledge need be or is conscious of this dimension of universality, this in no way affects its presence.

It is in this context that Polanyi prefers to speak more of validation than verification. Verification is both legitimate and necessary within the context of science itself, with its specific and limited tasks. But it is unnecessary and harmful to extend such a principle into areas where it is inappropriate. Our human powers of knowing simply do not work that way in their broader activities. What may be fine for one kind of activity, is not necessarily suited for all other kinds of activity. And that is why Polanyi says that the kind of commitment involved in human knowing should be called validation rather than verification.

To believe in reality, to be committed to it, to have confidence in man's powers to know and validate, all these involve some risk. But risk is a part of human life. It cannot be avoided by trying to invoke physical criteria for human questions.

Metaphysics and the Principle

of Marginal Control

All this leads into a final metaphysical or
ontological level which will be discussed only
briefly. Polanyi says that the structures of
comprehension reappear in the structures of what
is comprehended. There is reduplication between
the structures of tacit knowing and those principles
of all real and comprehensive entities with which
it deals. He is claiming that just as there are
levels in knowing, so there are levels in things.
"The operations of a higher level cannot be accoun-
ted for by the laws governing its particulars
forming the lower level." /50/

Polanyi gives three major examples of what he
calls the principle of marginal control: First
machines: How can a machine which is obviously
determined by the laws of physics and chemistry
fail to be finally determined by these laws? His
answer is that this is done by shaping or imposing
patterns which, even if artificial, do not impinge
upon the laws of nature. With regard to a machine,
its principles of operation are embodied by artificial shaping called engineering. These principles
as he say "govern the boundary conditions of an
inanimate system." /51/ The operations of the
upper level are embodied artificially in the boun-
daires of the lower level.

A second example is a human one, speechmaking.
Voice production, the lowest level of speech, leaves
open the level of words. Words are themselves
controlled by a vocabulary. Vocabulary is controlled by sentences which are controlled by grammar.
Finally the speech itself is controlled by the
setting, the audience, etc.

A third example is biological. Our bodies are
sustained at rest by our vegetative systems. These

97

are included in physical or muscular movements,
and these are incorporated into patterns of behavior
themselves capable of being further shaped by
intelligence.

"These illustrations of the principles of
marginality," he says, "make it clear that it is
present alike in artifacts, like machines; in
human performances, like speech, and in living
functions at all levels. It underlies the functions
of all comprehensive entities have a fixed structure." /52/

At the beginning of this study of Polanyi's
system of Personal Knowledge, Langford and Poteat
were quoted concerning the difficulties inherent
in Polanyi's major work with that title. It seems
fitting to conclude with another selection from the
same essay, where they render a judgement on the
worthwhileness then, one must begin by attending
from the many independent 'arguments' relying upon
the various rhetorical strategies, in order to
attend to the large coherence they jointly mean;
a comprehensive view of things at once more plainly
at right angles to what we do expect, yet more
consonant with what we should expect than anyone
would realize who dwelt only in its rhetorical
particulars." /53/

Conclusion

The radical empiricism presented by Smith and
the system of personal knowledge developed by Polanyi
can be perceived as complementary opposites.
Smith's presentation is largely negative in the same
that he examines the major positions of the classical
empiricists for their weaknesses then proposes the
more satisfactory solutions of a reconstructed
empiricism. Those solutions, however, are not
developed in depth. Polanyi, on the other hand,
though he refers often unfavorably to various
scientifically influenced theories of knowledge,

spends most of his time developing his own positive theory of personal knowledge.

These two presentations are complementary not merely because they represent negative and positive plans in a state of tension, but because the inner dynamics of both are genuinely close to each other. This is not to say that Polanyi considered himself to be a pragmatist or radical empiricist, or even, at least at the beginning, as a philosopher in the classic sense of the term, or that the American pragmatists would see themselves as all that close to Polanyi. Nevertheless, a close examination of both systems shows the presence of essential lines of agreement arrived at from different perspectives. If there is any major differences between them it lies in the fact that Smith stresses more the end result while Polanyi stresses more the process.

The following is an attempt to integrate them in summary fashion, not merely as a convenient summary of the extended discussions of this chapter but also to help develop a personal working definition of knowledge or experience that will serve as the instrument for further theological discussion in the course of this book.

The radical empiricists deny, according to Smith, that experience (or knowledge) is a veil standing between the person who experiences and the so-called external world; that experience and sensation are co-extensive; and that the experiencer is primarily a theoretical knower of data. They claim instead that experience is an objective disclosure of what is there to be encountered, whatever it may prove to be; that experience is a meaningful result of a multidimensional encounter between a concrete person and whatever there is to be encountered; and that experience embraces a number of dimensions of human life such as the moral, esthetic, scientific, and religious, which give point and purpose to the individual human being.

DISCLOSURE OF THE ULTIMATE

The basic operational presupposition of classical empiricism was that though we can be mistaken
about the nature, shape, or existence of the object
before us, we cannot be mistaken about our perception of that object because what is immediately
present to the mind cannot be mistaken. This is
challenged on the grounds that though its proponents
claim it to be intuitively self-evident, it is not
so at all. It is one theory of experience among
others and is only as valid as its supporting
arguments, many of which are vulnerable when separated out from an atmosphere of unchallenged
domination. Since most persons ordinarily consider
themselves to be in genuine contact with reality,
it would seem that any theory of knowledge that
denied this must bear a heavy burden of proof.
Yet the fact is, due to what might be called scientific imperialism, this subjectivistic theory of
knowledge has sheltered its weaknesses in and
siphoned its strength from the prestige of the
natural sciences. The natural sciences, within
their own parameter, quite naturally insist on
principles of verification. Scientistic omper-
ialism, however, going far beyond this, insists the
methods of the natural sciences are the only truly
legitimate methods of human inquiry and knowledge
and that all other human domains and ways of knowing
must conform to them under the threat of being
declared meaningless and subjective. The present
proposals reject that extravagant claim, harmful
even to true science, and say that the radical
empiricist theory of knowledge, on the basis of
the careful and extensive arguments put forward in
its behalf, is, as a theory of knowledge, more valid
and more acceptable.

In conclusion, here once again is Smith's
definition of experience, "Experience is the many
sided product of complex encounters between what
there is and a being capable of undergoing, enduring,taking note of, responding to and expressing
it." /54/

This is an extremely dense definition and needs to be unpacked. Polanyi's system of personal knowledge can be understood as one way of unpacking ot analyzing it and providing it with a number of conceptual tools.

Polanyi speaks first of a quest for discovery in man arising out of his sense of a hidden reality towards which certain clues are pointing. He then breaks knowledge into its various aspects or complexities, distinguishing first between explicit, fully articulated knowledge and tacit knowledge.

Tacit is clearly related to subsidiary in the further distinction made between subsidiary and focal awareness. Subsidiary awareness is awareness of background particularities, while focal awareness is awareness of the emergent whole. Polanyi sums it up in the formula: "we know more than we can tell." Knowledge is seen as a fusion of doing and knowing, of mind and body. We do not merely look at things and persons, we try to dwell existentially within them. This involves a dialectical movement of surrender to the object known and a return from it. Polanyi calls it a "from-to" movement. Indwelling occurs also in language, whereby the human mind, drawing upon these deeper than conscious riches, progressively conceptualizes and clarifies experience.

Commitment or belief is involved in every act of human knowing. It is necessary, first of all, to believe that it is possible to make contact with reality. Even scientists operate within similar unconscious and unprovable assumptions, for example, that there is sense to be made out of the natural world. It is necessary to believe, correlatively, that man has the power to know. Personal knowledge, therefore, transcends the disjunction between subjective and objective. Its claim to contact reality is a claim to universality since reality includes the dimensions of unspecified particulars which reach out in many directions within the world and within the knower. Certainty and error are dealt with by validation rather than by verification.

Finally, Polanyi makes certain ontological claims, though only briefly and tengentially. He says that there is correspondence btween the structures of knowing and the structures of comprehensive entities. According to the principle involved, the principle of marginal control, the laws governing a comprehensive entity cannot be encompassed by the laws of its parts. The ontological principle that the whole is greater than the sum of its parts balances the epistemological dictum that we know more than we can tell.

By Personal Knowledge then, Polanyi means that all knowledge has bodily base and follows the model of problem solving. Thus all man's articulations depend upon his unarticulated powers.

Because of the complexity of his theory, it might be fairer to let Polanyi himself summarize what he means by personal knowledge, as he does in the Preface to the book of that name:

> I regard knowing as an active compre-
> hension of the things known, an action
> that requires skill. Skillful knowing
> and doing is performed by subordinating a
> set of particulars, as clues or tools,
> to the shaping of a skillful achievement
> whether practical or theoretical. We may
> then be said to become 'subsidiarily
> aware' of those particulars within the
> 'focal awareness' of the coherent entity
> that we achieve. ...

> Such is the personal participation
> of the knower in all acts of understanding.
> But this does not make our understanding
> subjective. Comprehension is neither arbitrary

102

act nor a passive experience, but a responsible act claiming universal validity. Such knowing is indeed objective in the sense of establishing contact with a hidden reality; a contact that is defined as the condition for determining as indeterminate range of yet unknown (and perhaps inconceivable) true applications. It seems reasonable to describe this fusion of the personal and objective as Personal Knowledge. /55/

The following definition, then, is partially a synthesis and partially a personal statement of a theory of knowledge that will be used later in dealing with the questions and problems of fundamental theology.

Knowledge is the result, partially expressible in language, of a complex-interaction of awareness and disclosure between the knower and what is there to be known in the world of both fact and value, characterized by a bodily oriented awareness of symbolic, multi-dimensional particulars and coherent wholes, which integrates rather than di·chotomizes fact-value and subject-object.

As a working definition, however, the above is so all-inclusive that it becomes awkward. The following is proposed as a simplification: experiential knowledge is an encounter with a disclosing other through indwelling in a framework and the integration of its particulars into a coherent whole. Later, in chapter six, both experiential knowledge and religious experiential knowledge will be analyzed more systematically.

Since a firm and renewed epistemological position is so important to fundamental theology, and since, as has been said a number of times already, a theory of knowledge is only as good as its arguments, the next chapter will complement

103

the extensive internal arguments advanced so far
by presenting some of the views of a number of
distinguished contemporary thinkers. Though not
all of them are philosophers or even directly
engaged in what might be called the epistemological
enterprise, their views provide interesting and
valuable convergence and comparisons with the theory
of experiential knowledge proposed here.

NOTES

[1]Plato, The Works. Transl. by B. Jowett (N. Y.: Dial Press, 1936).

[2]Rene Descartes, Discours de la Méthode Texts et Commentaire, E. Gilson (Paris: J. Vrin, 1976).

[3]Ibid., p. 32 and foll.

[4]John Locke, The Essay Concerning Human Understanding (London: C. & J. Rivington, 1924).

[5]David Hume, A Treatise on Human Nature (Oxford: Clarendon Press, 1888).

[6]_____, Enquiries Concerning the Human Understanding and Concerning the Principles of Morals (Oxford: Clarendon Press, 1927).

[7]See especially John E. Smith, The Spirit of American Philosophy (N. Y.: Oxford University Press, 1963)

[8]John E. Smith, Religion and Empiricism (Milwaukee: Marquette University Press, 1967), p. 44.

[9]_____, Experience and God (N. Y. :Oxford University Press, 1968), p. 23.

[10]_____, The Analogy of Experience: An Approach to Understanding Religious Truth (N. Y.: Harper and Row, 1973), p. 33.

[11]Religion and Empiricism, p. 44.

[12]Analogy, p. 31.

[13]Ibid., p. 39.

[14]Maurice Merleau-Ponty, Phenomenology of Perception. Transl. Colin Smith (London: Routledge and K. Paul, 1962).

[15]Experience, p. 24.

[16] Ibid., pp. 24-25.

[17]Ibid., p. 25.

[18]Analogy, p. 33.

[19]Ibid., p. 35.

[20]Ibid., p. 36.

[21]Religion, p. 46.

[22]Analogy, p. 33.

[23] Ibid., p. 36.

[24]Analogy, p. 40.

[25] Experience, p. 33.

[26]Ibid., p. 33.

[27]Ibid., p. 30.

[28]Ibid., p. 31.

[29]Religion, p. 47.

[30]Ibid., p. 48

[31]Personal Knowledge (Chicago: University of Chicago Press, 1958). Other important works to be referred to are: Science, Faith and Society (Chicago: University of Chicago Press, 1946); The Logic of Liberty (Chicago: University of Chicago Press, 1951); The Study of Man (Chicago: University of Chicago Press, 1959); The Tacit Dimension (N. Y.: Doubleday, 1966); Knowledge and Being ed. Marjorie Grene (Chicago: University of Chicago Press, 1969). Michael Polanyi dies on February 22, 1976 in Northhampton, England at 84 years of age.

[32]Plato, Meno. Transl. B. Jowett (Indianapolis: Bobbs-Merrill, 1976 c. 1949), 85d-86b, p. 44.

[33]Tacit Dimensions. p. 24.

[34]Thomas A. Langford and William H. Poteat, "Upon First Sitting Down to Read Personal Knowledge: An Introduction." In Intellect and Hope: Essays in the Thought of Michael Polanyi (Durham, N. C.: Duke University Press, 1968), p. 3.

[35]Study of Man, p. 13.

[36]Tacit Dimensions, p. 6 and foll.

[37]Ibid., p. x.

[38]Robert E, Innis, "Religious Consciousness in Polanyi," The Thomist (XL, 1976) 396.

[39]Friedrich Heer, The Medieval World. Transl. Janet Sondheimer (N. Y.:New Maerican Library, n.d.), p. 183

[40]Innis, op. cit., p. 398.

[41]Ibid., pp. 398-399.

[42]Jerry H. Gill, The Possibility of Religious Knowledge (Grand Rapids: Eerdmans Publications Company, 1971), pp. 131-132.

[43]William T. Scott, "A Bridge from Science to Religion Based on Polanyi's Theory of Knowledge." Zygon (Vol. 5, 1970) 49-50.

[44]Ibid., p. 43.

[45]Ibid., p. 44.

[46]Tacit Dimension, p. 16.

[47]Knowing and Being, p. 133.

[48]Personal Knowledge, p. 57.

[49]Scott, op. cit., p. 52.

[50]Tacit Dimension, p. 36.

[51]Ibid., p. 40.

[52]Ibid., p. 41.

[53]Langford and Poteat, op. cit., p. 18.

[54]Smith, _Experience and God_, p. 23.

[55]_Personal Knowledge_, pp. vii-viii.

DISCLOSURE OF THE ULTIMATE

CHAPTER FOUR

CONVERGENCES

AND

COMPARISONS

In the preceding chapter, arguments for a new
theory of knowledge were examined at length for
their inner consistency and appropriateness to life.
At the end, a definition was proposed. In this
chapter, a selection of eight contemporary thinkers
will be examined for purposes of comparison. They
are from a variety of disciplines: developmental
psychology, social science, history of science,
linguistic analysis, structuralism, symbolic language, and hermeneutics. Many of them are not
consciously epistemological, or at least not directly
epistemological in intent. Nevertheless, as they
develop their positions, they find themselves of
necessity dealing with the problem of human knowledge. Hopefully this chapter will discover a number
of interesting convergences and comparisons with the
theory proposed in the last chapter.

Each author will be presented individually,
since the wholeness of his thought is important.
Whatever theory of knowledge is there, implicit or
explicit, is presented as part of a larger scheme

111

in its integrity in order to properly appreciate
its epistemological aspects. Though the analyses
will be brief, hopefully they will achieve at
least this much.

Jean Piaget

Jean Piaget seems to be an unlikely thinker
to begin this series of studies of contemporary
epistemological figures. He is widely known for
his studies in developmental psychology and, until
recent years, little attention has been paid to
hisepistemological concerns. What studies there
have been have taken his position to be Kantian
because of his emphasis on the subject's activity
in knowing. /1/

In a recent study, however, Louis E. Conn
suggests that a more careful study of Piaget
reveals him to be more of a critical realist than
a Kantian. /2/ Thus he says, "Piaget's epistemological position with its emphasis on the active
subject <u>and</u> on a normative but dynamic 'equilibrium
between assimilation of objects to the subject's
activity and the accomodation of this activity to
the objects' is more accurately understood as a
critical realism than a critical idealism," /3/

To pursue this question of his critical realism, then, two areas of Piaget's thought will be
examined: concrete operations in early childhood
and formal operations in adolescence, emerging
into the adult person's integration.

Early Childhood

It is in childhood, according to Piaget, that
the most important development in cognitive operations occur. It is here that a system of concrete
operations grows and emerges. Earlier in the
child's development, this kind of systematic aspect

112

is lacking in its cognitive activity. Even though
the child can be said to have spasmodic intuitions,
these do not coalesce into coherent wholes. This
wholeness will be a characteristic of the adolescent
years, but the foundations for it are laid in the
childhood years. /4/

According to Flavell, an operation is "any
representational act which is an integral part
of an organized network of related acts. /5/ They
are actions with intuitive or motor sources. In
Piaget's words, operations "result in a correction
of perceptual intuition--which is always a victim
of illusions of the moment--and which 'decenter'
egocentricity so as to transform transitory relationship into a coherent system of objective
relations." /6/

Conn says that Piaget's basic epistemological
perspective is "objectivity through decentration."
This is the key to understanding Piaget's developmental psychology and genetic epistemology as
the explication of a fundamental process of increasing cognitive self-transcendence that begins in
infancy and continues through adolescence to
adulthood. /7/

Adolescence

As for adolescence, Piaget sees its cognitive
developments characterized by the growth of system
and theory building. Though the child can operate
concretely, it cannot build systems. The adolescent is interested in theoretical problems even
when they are not necessarily related to ordinary,
everyday realities. Adolescence is a time of
orientation towards great ideals, towards the
promise of the future, all of which is highly
appropriate to the adolescent's position in society.
The adolescent is able to do this, says Piaget,
because he is able to "free himself from the concrete and locating reality within a group of

possible transformations." /8/

Contrary to the child, the adolescent approaches problems by first considering all its possible permutations and the interrelationships of the data available. He then experimentally combines various aspects and alternatives and by considering various results arrives at a conclusion as to which of these possibilities is in fact the true one. As Flavell says, "reality is thus conceived as a special subset within the totality of things which the data admit as hypotheses." /9/

This can be understood as reversing the roles between the real and the possible. An adolescent can now reach behind concrete operations which relate to objects directly and consider propositions which ne takes to be pure hypotheses. There are obvious similarities between these structures of adolescent thought and those of mathematical and formal logic.

According to Flavell, there are three characteristics that underscore these similarities between adolescent thought and mathematical logic: the hypothetico-deductive, the propositional and the combinatorial. /10/

By hypothetico-deductive he means the drawing of conclusions from pure hypotheses rather than from concrete observations. Though they are hypotheses, they are confirmable by reference to fact. By propositional he means that adolescent thinking deals not only with concrete objects but also with propositions about these objects. The results of concrete operations are cast into propositional form and used for further developments. By combinatorial he means that the adolescent is also capable of combining propositions into affirmative and negative statements. Thus the adolescent deals not only in relational and propositional variables but in combinations of those variables as well. /11/

It is by such operations that the adolescent
improves upon the previous cognitive advances he
has made. He does not lose the wonder of the
operational child, but it is now a controlled and
planned wonder. His concern with order and pattern
frees him from too slavish an obsession with the
empirically real.

In studying the cognitive developments of
the child it was observed that its egocentrism
increased as it tried to deal with new developments
in its cognitive activity and then subsided as a
new equilibrium was established. The same general
pattern reappears in the adolescent. As he begins
a new cognitive stage, he too begins to increase
egocentrism until it diminishes in a new level of
cognitive equilibrium. For a time the adolescent
believes that his thought is unlimited, reaching
out in ever broader plans and combinations. The
adolescent has a balancing orientation towards
future choices, however, that helps to bring his
newly developing cognitive powers back into equilibrium. This is a "decentering process which...
makes it possible for the adolescent to get beyond
the early relative lack of differentiation and to
cure himself of his (egocentric crisis of idealism)
--in other words, the return to reality which is
the path from adolescence to the true beginnings
of adulthood." /12/ And Conn adds, "The overall
direction of decentering on this level, then,
seems to be from the ideal to the real, from the
possible to the factual (where the real and the
factual are no longer the merely empirically real
and factual of childhood but the factual reality
reasonably affirmed within the larger context of
the possible.)" /13/

Self-Transcendence

As Piaget sees it, then, though the structures

of formal thought are powerful and its constructive
hypotheses fascinating, the very nature of cognitive
activity requires them to transcend themselves in a
movement of objectivity towards the real. It is
this direction of Piaget's thought which justifies
understanding him better as a critical realist than
as a critical idealist:

> In conclusion let us point out
> the basic unity of the processes (of
> mental development) which from the
> construction of the practical universe
> by infantile sensorimotor intelligence,
> lead to the reconstruction of the world
> by the phypothetico-deductive thinking of
> the adolescent, via the knowledge of the
> concrete world derived from the system
> of operations of middle childhood. We
> have seen how these successive construc-
> tions always involve a decentering of
> the initial egocentric point of view in
> order to place it in an ever-broader
> coordination of relations and concepts,
> so that each new terminal grouping
> further integrates the subject's
> activity by adapting it to an ever
> widening reality. /14/

Robert Bellah

In a paper delivered at a Symposium on the
Scientific and Humanistic Study of Religion, Robert
Bellah, speaking as a social scientist, says that
the ideological split between science and religion
that has characterized the West since the Enlightenment is unfortunate and that it should and can
be overcome. /15/

During these years of attacks on religion
from a variety of scientifically inspired sources,
the most prominent theological defense, he says,

has been historical realism. The theologians
felt that if they could make use of clear and
distinct ideas as well and show how their conception of the historical past was "the way it actually
was," then they could defend themselves successfully.

Such a defense left many unconvinced. "When
faced with the inevitable question of how something
clearly fraudulent and indeed absurd could have
been so powerful in human history, they answered
that religion was propagated for the sake of political despotism, maintained by an unholy alliance
of priestcraft and political despotism." /16/
This explanation of religion in terms of its functional consequences Bellah calls "consequential
reductionism" and finds that it has been a standard
process of argumentation ever since.

Later on in the nineteenth century, a more
subtle variation developed called "symbolic reductionism." According to this theory, religion was
not all bad; it had some good points. But those
good points had to be discovered or better uncovered
from under the myths and symbols that obscured them.
"one of the great intellectual strategies of the
symbolic reductionist was to treat religion as a
phase in the history of science." /17/ This
meant that it was understood to be primitive man's
attempt to cope with the mysteries of nature. As
these mysteries were gradually cleared up by the
advance of science, religion's role declined.

Another approach was to see religion as a
stage in the development of human morality or
ethics. The hidden nucleus to be uncovered in
religion was man's growing consciousness of ethical
responsibility. Feuerbach saw religion as the
projection of human nature; Marx as the opium of
the people.

In the twentieth century, these reductionist
theories became even subtler. Freud proposed that

117

the hidden key to religion was the Oedipus complex,
which it expressed in symbolic fashion. Since an
Oedipus complex needs a Father, God becomes the
cosmic father before whom man feels guilty. Now
that modern man can face his neuroses directly he
no longer needs to go through these outdated
biblical symbols and they can be discarded. What
Durkheim saw behind the symbols was society and
its morality. Thus religion was understood as
essentially a religion of humanity and its ethics
as individualistic. Social morality, however, can
now be pursued directly in these more enlightened
times and there is no need to confuse things with
religious symbolism, metaphors and rituals. Finally,
Max Weber, without going so far as to propose a
theory of symbolic reductionism for religion, "still
manages to convey the feeling that the scientific
observer cannot take seriously the beliefs he is
studying, even though he must take seriously the
fact that beliefs have profound social consequences." /18/

Bellah then proposes that this cultural impasse
may be eased by looking for another position implicit in consequential reductionism, namely symbolic
realism: "Not only the great social scientists but
many philosophical, literary, linguistic and religious thinkers have contributed to this position
which has been gestating for a long time and has
become increasingly explicit in the last twenty
years." /19/

He sees these two reductionisms, consequential
and symbolic, as expressions of a cognitive bias
which has been extremely influential in Western
thought ever since the scientific method became
strong in the seventeenth century. "This position
has held that the only valid knowledge is in the
form of falsifiable scientific hypotheses. The
task then with respect to religion has been to
discover the falsifiable propositions hidden within
it, discard the unverifiable assertions and those

clearly false, and even with respect to the ones
that seem valid, to abandon the symbolic and metaphorical disguise in which they are cloaked." /20/

Yet Durkheim's lifework largely goes to prove
that symbols are real and that in human life there
are many levels and substrata that cannot be reduced
to scientific hypotheses. And although Freud said
that rationality can gradually increase effective
control over the unconscious, he never said that it
could replace it. Again and again in his writings
he put aside the format of scientific hypothesis
in order to use the language of myth and symbols
such as Oedipus.

In recent years the reality and necessity of
symbols in and for human life has become more and
more acknowledged. Even the role of noncognitive
factors in science has come to be observed and
noted.

What this signals is a shift away
from the mechanical model of early
natural science in which the reality
was seen as residing in the object, the
function of the observer was simply
to find out the law in accordance with
which the object behaves, and "subjective"
was synonymous with "unreal," "untrue,"
"fallacious." For this mechanical
model there has increasingly been
substituted the interactionist model
of social science, or what Talcott
Parsons calls "action theory." Here
reality is seen to reside not just in
the object but in the subject and
particularly in the relation between
subject and object. The canons of
empirical science apply primarily to
symbols which attempt tp express the
nature of objects, but there are
nonobjective symbols which express the

feelings, values, and hopes of subjects,
or which organize and regulate the flow
of interaction between subjects and
objects, or which attempt to sum up the
whole subject-object complex, or even
point to the context or ground of that
whole. These symbols too express
reality and are not reducible to empirical propositions. This is the position
of symbolic realism. /21/

In our modern times, continues Bellah, we have
neglected the heart and the reasons that the mind
knows not of. This neglect of the interior life
of individuals and collectivities has trapped us
in things and structures. But the interior life
cannot be destroyed. It can be blocked but it
will emerge in new ways, some of them very unattrac-
tive. Bellah claims that "just those who feel
that they are most completely rational and pragmatic
...are most in the power of deep unconscious fanta-
sies. Whole nations in this century have blindly
acted out dark myths of destruction all the while
imagining their actions dictated by external
necessity." /22/

One of the results of a theory of knowledge
called symbolic realism is that it permits us to
take noncognitive symbols seriously and to admit
that there are various kinds of reality, that reality
is not a univocal term. Thus we must be open to
the various levels of consciousness and to the
multiple realities of life and be able to move back
and forth among them easily without setting any one
of them up as a ruler over the others.

In a response to the responses of his original
paper, Bellah adds a clarification, "Now what I
have argued is that from both sides of the fence
there has been developing an understanding of
religion which neither explains it away nor attributes to it "praeterhuman" origins. It is this

understanding which I call symbolic realism. Symbolic realism simply holds that religious symbols are not primarily social or psychological projection systems (though they always contain some projective elements) but the ways in which persons and societies express their sense of the fundamental nature of reality, of the totality of experience." /23/

Such an approach does not sacrifice rationality or scientific neutrality. It is not an attempt to fuse science and religion but to adequately differentiate between them. This differentiation is sympathetic, not antagonistic, opening the way for a new integration. This should be acceptable to the theologian because while Symbolic Realism serves as a conceptual scheme to interpret religion, it makes no attempt to deprive religion of its meaning or value. It also can be called "Symbolic Interpretation," in the sense that the meanings of religion are explained without throwing away, playing down, or denigrating the symbols themselves. The historical particularities of the symbols and the individual differences between various historical religious systems are respected and their integrity protected.

In conclusion, says Bellah. "the key to this new integration is the shift from a situation in which the scientific study of religion undermined faith to one in which it may actually help to make it possible." /24/

Thomas S. Kuhn

Thomas S. Kuhn's book The Structure of Scientific Revolutions appeared in 1962 and was followed by a second enlarged deition wherein he replied to the many critics of the book. /25/ Though intended as an essay in the history of science, it touched upon a number of issues with wider cultural and philosophical implications and the book has had

121

a widespread success. At this stage most of the main arguments are well known, and its key word "paradigm" is now so well accepted that most have now forgotten that its current popularity came from Kuhn.

With that in mind, this study will examine only briefly the main lines of his argument, then turn to the 1970 postscript for some further clarifications.

Normal Science

Kuhn is arguing against a concept of science as development-by-accumulation: the constellation of facts, theories and methods collected in current texts. "Scientific development becomes the piecemeal process by which these items have been added, singly, and in combination, to the ever growing stockpile that constitutes scientific technique and knowledge." /26/

In describing the route to normal science he notes that in the early stages facts are accumulated in vast quantities, with no particular principle of selectivity at work. Baconian natural histories of the seventeenth century, for example, can be characterized as a morass. Confronted with such a mass of phenomena it is no surprise that men interpret them differently. Even more surprising is that these differences should ever largely disappear. This is usually caused "by the triumph of one of the pre-paradigm schools." /27/ Finally there is achieved a consensus or paradigm. This is a theory that must "seem better than its competitors, but it need not, and in fact never does, explain all of the facts with which it can be confronted.

Once such a paradigm is established, what can be called normal science takes over. Normal science is occupied primarily with three classes of problems:

"determination of significant fact, matching of
facts with theory, and articulation of theory...
work under the paradigm can be conducted in no
other way and to desert the paradigm is to cease
practicing the science it defines." /28/

The scientist has a complex of commitments,
conceptual, theoretical, instrumental and methodological, and these lead to the understanding of
science as puzzle solving. Confident of what the
world and his science are like "he can concentrate
with assurance upon the esoteric problems that
these rules and existing knowledge define for
him." /29/ Important as these shared rules are,
however, shared paradigms are even more important.

The fact that a paradigm can be identified
without necessarily agreeing on a full interpretation or rationalization of it does not prevent
it from guiding research. "Normal science can
be determined in part by the direct inspection of
paradigms, a process that is often aided by but
does not depend upon the formulation of rules and
assumptions." /30/ In a footnote Kuhn argues
with this method of scientific knowing is a kind
of knowledge that is acquired through practice
and therefore cannot be fully articulated. He
then explicitly compares this to the theory of
tacit knowledge developed by Polanyi and the games
theory of the later Wittgenstein.

Anomaly and Competing Paradigms

The paradigm then provides the background for
the operation of normal science. It also makes
anomaly possible. "Anomaly appears only against
the background provided by the paradigm." /31/
As more and more anomalies accumulate, something
has to happen and this is what he calls scientific
revolution. When such a crisis appears we find
"The proliferation of competing articulations, the
willingness to try anything, the expression of

explicit discontent, the recourse to philosophy and to debate over fundamentals, all these are symptoms of a transition from normal to extraordinary research." /32/

Scientists, when faced with competing paradigms find that the criteria of normal science no longer suffice. For if two schools, supporting two paradigms cannot agree "about what is a problem and what is a solution, they will inevitably talk through each other when debating the relative merits of their respective paradigms." /33/

It is necessary, says Kuhn, to consider scientific revolutions as changes of world view in order to understand them. "Led by a new paradigm, scientists adopt new instruments and look in new places. Even more important, during revolutions scientists see new and dofferent things when looking with familiar instruments in places where familiar objects are seen in a different light and are joined by unfamiliar ones as well." /34/

Perceptual Shift

Kuhn says that the best analogy for this kind of perceptual shift is the shift in visual gestalt where what seem to be two faces, for example, turn into the sides of a vase. This is not merely a reinterpretation of individual and unchanged data: for the data is not unchanging, and the process involved is not interpretative. "How could it do so in the absence of fixed data for the scientist to interpret." /35/ It is not too strong to say then that paradigms are not corrected or changed by normal science but only by a sudden and unstructured event resembling the switch in gestalt.

Why then are these revolutions so hard to discern? Simply because once they occur and are accepted, normal science takes over and produces textbooks that make it appear as if each succeeding discovery flowed normally out of the preceding by a kind of internal, cumulative logic.

"At the start a new candidate for a paradigm may have few supporters...Nevertheless if they are competent they will improve it...More scientists will be converted and the exploration of the new paradigm will go on." /36/

In a final chapter, Kuhn asks if this movement can be simply described as progress coming nearer and nearer to the truth of reality as it really is. He says that he thinks this evolutionary implication may be misleading. The whole sequence "of developmental process marker by an increase in articulation and specialization...may have occurred as we now suppose liological evolution did, without benefit of a set goal, a permanent fixed truth, of which each stage in the development of scientific knowledge is a better exemplar." /37/

Second Thoughts

In the 1970 Postscript to the second edition, Kuhn clarifies and emphasizes more the communitarian nature of the scientific enterprise and more clearly defines the meaning of the key word paradigm.

Thus he says "a paradigm is what the members of a scientific community share, _and_, conversely, a scientific community consists of men who share a paradigm." /38/ In saying this he emphasizes, in response to a number of criticism of his position, that there sharing community can be limited indeed. In other words there are scientific communities and paradigms of various sizes and importance.

Turning to the question of paradigm itself, Kuhn says that a number of the differing meanings pointed out by his critics were due to stylistic

inconsistencies, but that two basic meanings were
insufficiently differentiated.

First "For the present purposes I suggest
'disciplinary matrix': 'disciplinary' because it
refers to the common possession of the practitioners
of a particular discipline; 'matrix' because it is
composed of ordered elements of various sorts, each
requiring further specifications." /39/

He gives four subdivisions of this matrix.
The third is "values" which are "more widely shared
among different communities than either symbolic
generalizations or models and they do much to provide a sense of community to natural scientists as
a whole." /40/ Among these are prediction, simplicity, self-consistency, palusibility, etc. "To
a greater extent than many other components of the
disciplinary matrix, values may be shared by men
who differ in their application." /41/

Finally, there is a fourth meaning of disciplinary matrix which Kuhn says could be called
paradigm in the strict sense, but which, for the
sake of clarity he will call "shared example." For
a student trying to learn science, the laws and
theories he learns will have little empirical content unless he is able to see them in examples
shared by the community...In other words, science
is learned by doing it rather than by learning
rules about it.

All this is close to Polanyi's "We know more
than we can tell." /42/ Kuhn says that he is
making a basic distinction between perception and
interpretation:

We try...to interpret sensations
already at hand, to analyze what is for
us the given. However we do that, the
processes involved must ultimately be
neural, and they are therefore governed
by the same physico-chemical laws that

govern perception on the one hand and
the beating of our hearts on the other.
But the fact that the system obeys the
same laws in all three cases provides
no reason to suppose that our neural
apparatus is programmed to operate
the same way in interpretation as is
perception or in either as in the beating of our hearts. What I have been
opposing in this book is therefore the
attempt, traditional since Descartes
but not before, to analyze perception
as an interpretative process, as an
unconscious version of what we do
after we have perceived. /43/

Maurice Merleau-Ponty

Maurice Merleau-Ponty's philosophical writings
are part of the phenomenological and existential
movement still important in European circles. He
has a man-centered perspective, is extremely sensi-
tive to the complexities of the world and is
determined to deal with this complexity and ambiguity in a concrete way. "What Merleau-Ponty has
contributed to phenomenological existentialism...
is a revised understanding of perceptual conscious-
ness--an understanding that allows perception to
stand as the primary human function and the perceiving human to take his place as central reference
point in philosophy." /44/

It is helpful to understand that, at least in
part, Merleau-Ponty was reacting against claims that
science is the only valid way of knowing. It is not
that he is against science. On the contrary, his
work can be said to contain a philosophy of science
where it is given its full due. But when some claim
that science and especially social science are the
only genuinely valid ways of knowing, his response
is that this is going much too far. He argues

127

against the reductionistic assumption that scientific knowing is a truer account of reality than that based on direct experience.

Primacy of Perception

His main argument is the circularity in science's claim. In order to assert its primacy, science must begin like all other knowing with direct perceptual experience and, even as it progresses, must continually return to it. This unavoidable circularity shows the essential emptiness of claiming too much for science. It also causes Merleau-Ponty to assert the "primacy of perception" and his own version of Husserl's famous phenomenological maxim that philosophy, for its part, must be a return 'to the things themselves.'" /45/

Another major view against which he is reacting is Cartesianism. He felt that Cartesianism in its attempt to separate the subject from his body had isolated both from the objective world and from other human beings.

The main focus of his work then is perception. He sees it as not merely passive, registering data provided by an external world but as itself partially constitutive of the human world. The world is not merely "out there" all by itself, independent of human life and man's ability to know, and the world is not identical with the understanding of it in science, accurate as this is within certain restricted dimensions. On the contrary, the world is given for a perceiving consciousness. "The world is both revealed and shaped by the acts of perception in which it is grasped." /46/

Perception according to Merleau-Ponty can be understood to operate on two levels, the level of intensive analysis and the level of extensive analysis. Take a house as an example. Intensively,

I perceive it only parts as a time. Suppose it is
the first time I see it. It first appears as a
shape on the horizon, squarish, with a roof. As
I get closer I see that it is a two story house with
many windows, including a picture window to the
left of the front door. There is a small porch,
with a set of brick steps; there are shutters beside
the windows; it is painted white. As I walk around
it I see that there is an extension in the back
opening out onto a patio and that in the back yard
there is a pool. The back door has a small porch
as well. In order to really know the house, to
perceive it, I must take time, walk around it, and
observe carefully. I can keep finding out more and
more about it. But there is a sense in which I can
never completely exhaust the knowability of the
house. "If it remains true that Merleau-Ponty is
never a skeptic in the Humean sense--on the contrary, he holds that, in perception, one does
genuinely achieve the object, that in each act of
perception the dualism of the _pour soi_ and the _en
soi_ is overcome--it remains equally true that the
world is never exhaustively given to the perceiving
or knowing mind." /47/

        Extensive analysis spreads out further. In
looking at the house, one can see that it has a
front lawn, that there are houses next door and a
street that runs in front of it. I can see it as
part of neighborhood in a town and the town as part
of a state and country, etc. The extensivity can
be carried out until I reach what can be called a
world, thus making the world a horizon for all
possible things rather than merely a thing.

                        Embodiment

        This brings up Merleau-Ponty's theory of
embodiment. He says that there are two aspects to
a living body. It is a subject opening itself to
the world it preceives and it is also an object

                            129

within th-t perceived world. "The enigma is that my body simultaneously sees and is seen. That which looks at all things can also look at himself." /48/ This implies that one cannot possess the visible world unless one is also possessed by it. He distinguishes between my body for me and my body for others. It is my body that I am situated in the world. It is by my body that I perceive the world. By my body I am part of the world and have a perspective on the world. It is this perspectivity of intensive and extensive perception as described above. "Thus the lived body is that ambiguous reality which is not identical with the subject-- it is not the subject but rather the means by which the subject is a real subject in a real world --but neither is it the same as external objects, for no other object in our experience is lived from within...Each person's body then is kind of third term, participating in the character of subject and object, but being identical with neither." /49/

Intersubjectivity

Also it is through the body and its expressionality that man's behavior is understood to be an expression of the subject. In his works written after the war, Merleau-Ponty explored in considerable depth the human implications of his theory of perception by means of the principle of intersubjectivity.

"It is Merleau-Ponty's contention that a theory of other persons is guaranteed as soon as we describe the subject as an embodied existence." /50/ The problem of other persons is only an extension of the problem of the external world and it is resolvable through the same principles of incarnation. If my own consciousness is embodied, then why should not other persons also be embodied. I am not negated by the existence of another person, nor is his world only a mere hypothetical possibility, inferred from my own world. "His

views and my own are in advance inserted into a
system of partial perspectives, referred to one
same world in which we coexist." /51/

From this point on Merleau-Ponty will develop
his philosophy of language, art and society and
history. "For the lived body is also man's way
of being with others and situated in a societal
condition and a history...each of these modes of
existence shares in the fundamental human condition
by being precisely dimensions of the existence of
incarnate subjects, besouled bodies." /52/

Paul Ricoeur

Paul Ricoeur developed what he himself calls
philosophical hermeneutics and others hermeneutical
phenomenology. From this perspective a number of
interesting epistemological questions are treated
both directly and indirectly.

Hermeneutics

Hermeneutics obviously implies language and
language is at the center of Ricoeur's attention.
For a start, Ricoeur distinguishes between the
logical, abstract level of language and the concrete
language of experience. He feels that there is a
natural tension in language itself between these
two poles. No matter what level of language is
focused upon, therefore, the implications of the
other level demand recognition. Thus "if we start
at the level of the _telos_ and logical level of
meaning at the _telos_ extreme, there is the reference
back to the source and origin. And if we start at
the level of the original as _Ursprung_, there is the
orientation to the _telos_ of rationality." /53/
Lnaguage can be understood to stand in the middle as
an intermediary between these two extremes.

For Ricoeur all this involves difficulties.
First, there is the danger of losing the orientation

131

towards rationality as we deal with the concrete
level of experience. Then there is the danger
that access to the so-called Ursprung cannot be
direct. It is a going backwards to the sources
with all the difficulties that that implies.
Finally there is the danger that comes from our
natural tendency to prefer the logical. It must
needs be balanced by the other linguistic pole, or
it will lose its vitality and its foundation.

This basic level then "is the unity of intentionality and affection which allows for the
movement from the objectivity to the self affected
and does this from the beginning in the language
of myths and of symbols." /54/ A double intentionality is involved here causing a conflict of interpretations. "Ricoeur's interest is interpretation,
finding meaning through understanding and not in
original or even symbolic forms. Thus he is critical
of the short range possibilities of the works of
Cassirer and others...Unlike the reductionism of
much analytical philosophy, behavioristic psychology and functional anthropology, Ricoeur is trying
to establish the myth-ritual complex upon solid
ground worthy of modern investigation, a ground
which is not reductionistic." /55/

Symbols thus can be interpreted in opposing
ways by the pehnomenology of religion and by
psychoanalysis. Trying to deal with this problem
of interpretation is fruitful for it helps tp
develop greater insight. "In working out this
conflict the link or bond that underlies the subject-
object dichotomy comes to light, not simply as such
but as a multidimensioned bond or link, one which
does not immediately reveal itself and one which is
not too quickly grasped in its unity." /56/

Symbols

In order to reach this concrete level, or
level of Ursprung then, it is necessary to deal with

symbols. After giving narrow and broad definitions
of both interpretation and symbol Ricoeur says that
his understanding of them lies somewhere in the
middle, say between Aristotle's analogy and
Cassirer's symbolic functions. /57/

His basic distinction between sign and symbol
is that a sign is an expression communicating some
kind of meaning while a symbol communicates a
double level of meaning. Thus every symbol is a
sign but not every sign is a symbol. The need for
interpretation of symbols arises out of their
double levelled intentionality. Though he distinguishes between these intentional levels, Ricoeur
is quick to add that they are nevertheless closely
linked. The second level builds upon the first
and the first points towards the second. He says,
"I call symbol every structure in which a direct,
primary, literal sense, designates by excess
another sense, indirect, secondary, figures which
cannot be apprehended except across the first."/58/

For Ricoeur symbols build themselves up into
more elaborate patterns, of which he sees principal
ones. The first is the religious pattern. This
is usually cosmic in nature and becomes the basis
for the rites, myths and sacred languages of
religion. The second is found in dreams where
we try to say more and other than what we say in
the harsh light of day. The third is the pattern
of the poetic imagination, with its almost infinite
variety of symbolic invention. All three areas of
patterns, mythic, oneiric, and poetic need interpretation.

Interpretation

Common to all these symbols is of course the
problem of language. "There is no symbolic before
the man who speaks, even if the power of the symbol
is rooted at a more basic level, in the expressibi-
lity of the cosmos, in the _vouloir-dire_ of desire,

133

in the imaginative variety of the subjects." /59/

The need for interpretation then is based
primarily upon its second sense. Or, to be more
precise, in the movement of the first sense towards
the second. Interpretation is not something external added afterwards to a symbol; it is very much a
part of the symbol and of nature. As a paradox it
makes for greater understanding, and, as an enigma,
it illuminates.

It is in the conflict of interpretations that
one can discover the nature of the link between
man and the world. "In working out this conflict
the link or bond that underlies the subject-object
dichotomy comes to light, not simply as such but
as a multi-dimensional bond or link, one which does
not immediately reveal itself, and one which is
not too quickly grasped in its unity. This is the
attempt on the part of Ricoeur to bring out further
the constantly re-affirmed conviction that man,
even on the level of the Cogito and willing, is
receptive, that the voluntary and Cogito as origins
only constitute what they receive." /60/

One such possible conflict of interpretation
is between suspicion and faith. In order to
resolve it successfully, suggests Ricoeur, it is
necessary to understand faith in a new way, "It is
not the first naive faith, but rather the second
faith of the hermeneutist, the faith that has
traversed the critique, the post-critical faith.
It is a reasonable faith because it interprets,
but it is a faith because it looks for, by the
interpretation, a second naivete...To believe to
understand to believe, such is its maxim." /61/
This process can also be called the hermeneutical
circle.

Finally, in exploring the ontological implications of the hermeneutics of interpretation, he
associates it with the phenomenology of the Cogito.

Interpretation is not something restricted to the
exploration of some individual symbol. It extends
itself to the relation between symbols and to the
universal implication involved in mythic symbols.
Thus hermeutics and reflection are closely related.
Individual mythic symbols need to be interpreted
not merely in themselves or in isolation but also
as part of a universe of symbols and interpretations.
It is the relationship implied in this universality
that constitutes the basis of reflection. Interpretation involves reflection and reflection needs
interpretation. This justifies "the detour by
cultural contingency, by an incurably equivocal
language and by the conflict of interpretations."/62/

The Later Wittgenstein

Though it may seem odd to speak of an early
and a late Wittgenstein, the fact is that there
is a generally recognized divergence between his
early and later views wide enough to justify such
terminology. The work of the later Wittgenstein
is opposed to the representational view of language
once held by himself. /63/

Representational View

The representational view of knowledge is
sometimes called the commonsensical view because
what could be more obvious and commonsensical than
saying that words represent objects and statements
represent the relationships among these subjects
on a variety of levels. Such a view of language
is common to both the rationalists and the classical
British empiricists discussed earlier. It is also
presupposed by Kant himself and forms the assumed
basis for much of his discussion of noumenal and
phenomenal knowledge. More recently Bertrand
Russell pursued such a representational theory to
a high degree of refinement. Thus instead of saying

that the world is made up merely of things, this
position says that the world is made up of facts
that have been actualized out of all possible facts.
In this view a fact is not an object but a relationship among objects. It is a fact that the sky is
blue and it is a fact that these books are on the
shelf.

Language then is a collection of propositions
that represent possible facts. Of course the words
in the proposition represent the names of objects
or of their qualities, but the important thing in
the proposition is the relationship, logically
speaking of the words or names in the porposition.
Meaning develops then out of this relationship
between propositions and facts. Meaninglessness
arises when the proposition does not represent the
factually possible. Truth is a further step, a
statement picturing an actual fact, whereas the
picturing of a possible fact is false. /64/

Out of all this the movement called logical
positivism grew, as represented, for example by
A. J. Ayer's <u>Language, Truth and Logic</u>. /65/
Its main point was its insistence upon the necessity
of empirical verification to determine the meaningfulness of a statement. Even though a statement may
be false, if it is empirically confirmable or
disconfirmable, then it is meaningful. Through a
rather lengthy roundabout way, this returns to the
picture theory of knowledge, that is: only what is
comparable to reality is meaningful.

The later Wittgenstein went beyond these ideas.
As he developed he became more conscious of the
complexity of language. He began to see that
language was multidimensional, having more than one
dimensionality of the picture image. Since it is
multidimensional, it cannot be limited by mathematical logic and the formulas of science. This does
not deny that sometimes language names things and
represents facts; it is simply saying that it is a
restriction and distortion of reality to say that

this is the only thing that language does, when
actually it does a considerable number of other
things.

Three Themes

In The Possibility of Religious Knowledge,
Jerry Gill suggests that there are three major themes
in Wittgenstein's mature approach to these questions.

"The first major theme...is that language must
be understood as a human instrument, or tool, for
the accomplishment of various and diverse tasks."/66/
Statements are thus seen to exist not in some kind
of vacuum but in the context of their use by persons
for certain human purposes. If one admits this
orientatation, it is no longer possible to admit
that all statements must be classified as factual
or value-oriented exclusive of any other contextual
consideration. Wittgenstein himself says, "one
cannot guess how a word functions. One has to look
at its use and learn from that." /67/

The examples that Wittgenstein uses are often
instrumental. Thus he talks about the different
uses that tools can be put to depending on the
function intended. A hammer exerts downward force
to drive nails, or upward force to remove them. A
saw exerts horizontal force as it is drawn across
the object being sawed. A screwdriver is turned
in a circle either to the left ot to the right
depending on whether the screw is being driven in
or removed. Just as one can be sure of what these
tools are only by seeing them in action as it were,
so one can be sure of what words "mean" only by
seeing how they are used. As a matter of fact it
would seem wise not to speak of the meaning of
statements at all but rather of what people mean
when they make a statement.

"The second major theme in Wittgenstein's

fresh approach to language is his concept of
'language games'." /68/ This builds upon what
has just been said about the meaning of statements
residing in their context. It pursues further this
idea of context by examining the somewhat larger
backdrop of certain kinds of human activity and
behavior which might be involved. Thus the use
of the word "game" is intended to signify that
the meaning of speech has to be seen against this
background of human activity with its interrelationships and interactions among persons. There
are various games which depend on the various
areas of human activity. Asking questions and
answering them are two different aspects of activity; describing something, asking for help, are
also differing games. Though these areas develop
more or less independently or others, they sometimes overlap just as in ordinary human activity.

One of the more important conclusions drawn
from this is that no language game should be seen
as having priority over others. This criticism
cuts both ways against the empiricist's demand
that scientific requirements are primary and the
existentialist's demand that ethical requirements
come first. One of the presuppositions of such
demands is that the lines between the different
areas or "games" is a hard and fast one. This is
not the case; they interrelate and interact.
Rather than seeking imperialistic dominion for
any one game it makes more sense to look at the
functions of the various languages used.

Another implication is that language game
rules need not be explicit. It is contrary to
human experience and the use of language itself
to demand that we begin with rules and precise
definitions. On the contrary, language games
are like all games: we learn them by trying to
do what other people do. How many people who
can ride a bicycle, for example, can sit down and
write out a set of rules as to how bicycles should

be ridden? And how many people have learned to
ride a bicycle by simply studying a manual which
says, "Hold the bicycle upright and steady, etc."?
Understanding then comes from rule making but by
using language successfully to perform the functions intended in a particular case.

"The third major theme in Wittgenstein's
interpretation of language is his concept of 'forms
of life'." /69/ In each of these three steps,
Wittgenstein is enlarging his horizon, much as a
movie camera that begins with a close-up of a
building or face and gradually pulls back until a
whole street or a whole hillside is in view. In
this case he is pulling back beyond the limits of
the language games themselves, all the way to the
wider patterns of human life. Implicit in this
approach is that language is not something added
to life, a logical supplement as it were, but an
integral part of life, helping to constitute it
what it is.

Such an understanding of forms of life, although not developed at any great length in
Wittgenstein seems to be in agreement with P. F.
Strawson's position summed up in the phrase which
says that language is a "logically primitive"
notion. /70/ The first implication here is that
the term "meaning" is undefinable, though we still
understand it. Finally, as Gill says, "I am trying
to call attention to the fact that meaning is
something that is grasped 'tacitly' or indirectly,
not explicitly." /71/ The ability to handle meaning is the ability to become and be human. This
denies that meaning resides only in a sentence's
logical structure. Definition and logic, useful
and necessary as they both are, are nevertheless
not the ultimate source of meaning. Meaning grows
out of the way people use language and their general
tacit awareness.

Structuralism and Claude Levi-Strauss

The structuralist movement does show certain
similarities to the tendencies and movements examined so far.
        Structuralism has been described
as a method, a movement, an intellectual
fad and an ideology. Each of these
characterizations is in part valid.
For structuralism is a loose amorphous,
many faceted phenomenon with no clear
lines of demarcation, no tightly knit
group spearheading it, no specific set
of doctrines held by all those whom one
usually thinks of a being associated
with it. It cuts across many disciplines
--linguistics, anthropology, literary
criticism, psychology, philosophy. /72/

Structuralism has discovered and is using a
variety of techniques and has achieved a number of
impressive results in the various disciplines and
areas mentioned above. It's not that a concern
for structure is something totally new--it can be
traced back to ancient times--but new interest in
it began growing in the nineteenth century.

Marx, Freud, De Saussure

The conviction shared by nineteenth century
structuralists such as Freud, Marx and DeSaussure
was that the surface of things and events is an
insufficient source of explanation about them. In
order to really understand them it is necessary to
go beneath that surface and explore the hidden and
the implicit. Individual consciousness, in other
words, is not sufficient basis for explaining the
complexities of human life and civilization. There
are other levels and other areas that enter the
picture and which need to be taken into account if
an adequate understanding of what is really happen-

ing is to be achieved.

There is a phrase of Karl Marx's which sums up his position in this regard. He says, "Life is not determined by consciousness, but consciousness by life." /73/ It is necessary to live before one can think and how one thinks is dependent on the way one lives. Thus consciousness is described by Marx as something that developed as man's needs developed. As man's activity grew and diversified, so did his thinking. It was only later on when it was possible to divide labor up among various segments of society that some men were able to become more explicit thinkers. Marx of course goes on to describe how all human or social relations, including philosophy, religion, law, literature and the institutional superstructure of society are determined in an ultimate way by that society's underpinnings.

It is not necessary to follow Marx to these materialistic or deterministic conclusions in order to find suggestive his idea that the conscious life of man is not something totally autonomous, but is dependent upon the raw infrastructure of experience. So structuralists

> seek to explain consciousness by life and not life by consciousness. In general, they give up any claim of consciousness or of the conscious individual. The primacy of the individual ego, which found its most eloquent spokesman in Descartes and which through the history of modern European thought has continued to be a central theme, is denied by both Marx and the structuralists. Foucault, like Marx, is more concerned with the thought of an age than with the thought of individuals in their individuality. Levi-Strauss, like Marx, sees a close relation between man's life and his thought and defends the "savage mind"

which he sees as being as human as that
of the contemporary Western thinker. /74/

Freud is another figure whose approach is
related to the contemporary structuralists. He was
more interested in the consciousness of individuals
rather than of societies. He was really concerned
about the determining factors in the subconscious
or unconscious life of man. He felt that it was
these that influenced man's conduct, rather than
the conscious reasons or rationalizations usually
given. Thus he attempted to explain all human
activity, normal as well as neurotic in terms of
these theories of the unconscious. Though a good
deal of controversy still surrounds his ideas even
among psychoanalysts today, the general thrust of
his thought has been highly influential even in
other fields such as mythology, literature and art.

Following along these lines, then, linguistics
began to treat language as a series of signs.
Ferdinand de Saussure's suggestion that social
customs and rituals could be treated as systems of
signs and studied in linguistic fashion opened up
avenues of approach that have been followed by the
structuralists:

> What is structuralism? Before
> being a philosophy, as some tend to see
> it, it is a method of analysis. Even
> as such its many facets and different
> uses make it a subject of various
> interpretations, debate, even polemics.
> no simple or single definition applies
> to it except in very general terms.
> One could say a structure is a combin-
> ation and relation of formal elements
> which reveal their logical coherence
> within given objects of analysis.
> Although structuralism can hardly be
> subsumed in some overall formula, we
> can say it is first of all, when applied

to the sciences of man, a certain way
of studying language problems and the
problems of languages...It was then
applied to anthropological enquiries
and in particular to the study of myths
which are also of the nature of a
language. The structural method also
extends to the structures of the
unconscious, as they are apprehended
in psychoanalytical discourse, to the
structures of the plastic arts with
their language of forms, to musical
structures...and to the structures
of literature, since literary language,
drawing upon ordinary language, transforms it into language par excellence. /75/

Claude Levi-Strauss

Claude Levi-Strauss is the central figure in
the structuralist movement due to the sweep of his
theorizing, and the broadness and profundity of
his views. He intends no less than the discovery
of the structure of human nature itself, that universal underlying structure which is hidden below
the surface and shows itself in a whole variety of
everyday and some not-so-everyday ways.

One basic presupposition of Levi-Strauss is
that different activities in any given society
will all have the same basic structure. Whether
we are dealing with ways of preparing food, building highways, making chatter at cocktail parties
or arranging for a wedding, these are varied
expressions of the same society and therefore they
should all have something in common. Obviously
such commonality is not to be found on the surface;
these activities are too superficially different
for that. Rather one must go beneath that surface
to lay bare the deep inner structure.

DISCLOSURE OF THE ULTIMATE

A second basic presupposition is that after we have studied two different societies in this fashion and arrived at their basic structures, we can then compare them one to the other and discover certain striking similarities. These similarities, these commonalities, then, are guideposts along the route to discovery of the mysteries of human nature.

This method has been most successful in dealing with mythologies. Levi-Strauss took a tremendous number of myths which previous authors had been content to put into massive compilations and showed how they were to be taken not as discrete, separate stories but as parts of an interconnected system. The myths of certain people, then, are seen as forming an interconnected system, and one such set can be successfully compared to another set from either the same society or another society.

The tool used by Levi-Strauss in making these analyses is structural linguistics since he treats each of these social manifestations as if they were language or expressions of society. Since each system communicates like a language, they can be studied as a language.

One of the results of this kind of study is a blurring of the lines between the various humanistic disciplines. They are all understood as types of human expression, each structured by similar inconscious operations of the human mind. Since these basic structures can now be seen to be common to all men this weakens cultural and historic divisions.

Hans Georg-Gadamer

Hans Georg-Gadamer's principal work Einheit und Methode was published in 1960 but an English translation did not appear until 1975. /76/ That publication brought with it an increased interest in his work. It has been called "One of the few most important books of this century dealing with

144

how understanding occurs." /77/ and "As a contribution to our understanding of understanding it ranks with the work of Pierce, Husserl, Cassirer, Wittgenstein, Polanyi and Lonergan as a highpoint of twentieth century reflection upon the constitutive conditions of knowing." /78/

Hermeneutic

It is important, first of all, to understand what Gadamer means by "hermeneutic." For practical reasons, the publishers did not include that word in the title of the book either in its original German version or in the translation. But in Gadamer's eyes it is a central notion: "From its historical origin, the problem of hermeneutics goes beyond the limits that the concept of method sets to modern science. The understanding and the interpretation of texts, is not merely a concern of science, but is obviously part of the total human experience of the world. The hermeneutic phenomenon is basically not a problem of method at all." /79/ Despite its methodological overtones, then, Gadamer's hermeneutic goes beyond the formulation of rules of procedure guiding us to objective knowledge to the totality of human experience.

There is obviously an intended opposition to an all-demanding scientific method. "The following investigation...is concerned to seek that experience of truth that transcends the sphere of the control of scientific method wherever it is to be found, and to inquire into its legitimacy. Hence the human sciences are joined with modes of experience which lie outside science: with the experiences of philosophy, of art, and of history itself. These are all modes of experience in which a truth is communicated that cannot be verified by the methodological means proper to science." /80/

Gadamer's intention, then, is to affirm that at least in the experience of art, history and of language, knowledge is not a question of a subject confronting an object. Rather, "Understanding belongs to the being of that which is understood." /81/

Tripartite Division

The whole book then attempts to demonstrate this by a tripartite presentation. In part one he examines experience in art; in part two, experience and understanding in the human sciences and in part three the experience of language and its ontological implications. The method he uses throughout these three major sections is partly historical and partly descriptive: in other words, phenomenological. Because of this it has a richness and a complexity that is very fruitful and productive while at the same time difficult to summarize and interpret without actually experiencing it.

In the first part there is an interesting contrast between the subjectivity of the Kantian aesthetic and the non-objectivity of an aesthetic of play (Spiel). "The guiding idea of the analysis is the fact that in a play or a game, the participants do not stand over against the game as an object distinct from themselves and which they confront in the mode of Vorhandenheit. Rather, the participants become part of the event which cverspills their private individual conscoiusness and which has laws and structures governing its own being not reducible to the operations of objectifying subjectivities." /82/

In the second part, Gadamer describes understanding in relation to the texts and documents that record the historical process. Once again understanding is removed from the area of subjectivity, "In the differentiated unities of our experience the world of meaning and objects form

around us in a process that is rather given to us,
that comes to us, then controlled and guided by us.
In fact, we are guided by experience and taken up
in its play, according to Gadamer and in the process,
once again, an event occurs of which we are participants, not directors." /83/

In part three, he takes up the relationship
between language and understanding, repeating many
of the issues and ideas previously developed. What
Gadamer is trying to do is to show that language
is an ultimate horizon for our understanding. "The
hermeneutic object lies at the heart of Gadamer's
operation: the object is a meaning, a sense, which
in the case of writing, having attained a state of
ideality, allows us to meet it without attempting
to transpose ourselves back into the subjectivities
either of the original authors or of the original
addresses. Meeting the object, or uncovering it,
is the work of the interpreter whose job it is is
to relate the unity of sense found in the text to
'the whole complex of possible meanings in which
we linguistically move'." /84/

Finally, there are the ontological implications
of language. For language is understood as a kind
of country or home in which we live and in which
the world comes through to us as it were through
the play of language. In one sense man can be
said to belong to language rather than that language belongs to man.

The Primacy of Meaning

For the general purposes of this book, it will
be helpful to pursue a bit more in depth two aspects
of Gadamer's thought. First, the primacy of meaning. There are various ways of looking at the
world and of giving primacy to different things.
One view gives primacy to "nature" seeing it as
kind of a lump of clay before the potter comes

147

along to give it meaning and form. This implies
a radical split between the human and the natural
world. Another view "locates reality for all
practical purposes somewhere within our being:
thinking, experiencing, symbolic relations, brain
states, a network of perceptions and judgements,
and so forth. Reality, in its meaning, is in some
sense a subjective state. "In here" there is indeed
meaning and light and truth. But 'out there' is
only what can be utilized for our inner systems...
Bifurcation again. Descartes preserved. Two substances linger, one alive and conscious, the other
only measurable and extended." /85/ Without
denying the limited validity of such views, Gadamer
attempts a different approach that does not involve
this deep bifurcation and allows us to include our
experiences of creation and communication in
understanding.

Here is where the primacy of meaning comes in.
"Meaning is not taken to name a mental or experiential structure. The emphasis falls on how things
occur in relations, not on the conditions of their
occurring." /86/

A contrasting name then for these so-called
"structures of consciousness" would be "disclosure."
The meaning of another person is not sought in his
brain structure, but in how he moves, what he uses,
what he says, what he does not say, what things he
does. Like the "tree in the forest," that person
is present quite apart from me. "Disclosure names
the coming forth of beings and their availability
for whatever may happen with them...mental activity
is never found as the primary source of meaning."
/87/

Disclosure implies dialogue and one of the
results of this approach to the process of understanding is to free the scholar, for example, from
being a kind of silent spectator of the past, of
history and from exhausting his skills, ingenuity
and individuality in the search for the perfect

148

reproduction of that past. Gadamer envisions,
rather, a dialogue with the past and even with the
texts of the past. In other words, knowledge does
not begin in a kind of trans-historical state. We
cannot escape history and our immersion in it. We
do all things human, including scholarship, in a
context which discloses to us the complexities of
a history and thus opens up various future possibilities. Our understanding is neither the product
of ourself or of a group of selves, but of a
disclosing reality.

This is a question of world relations. "We
are beings in the world as distinct to beings
outside the world. World relations constitute
always our beginnings. We are world relations and
we never happen outside world relations. So rather
than speaking of consciousness as though it were a
transcendental identity or merely the impressions
created by the senses regarding 'mute' objects,
we may speak of world relations as themselves
constituting an understanding awareness...Change
a world relation within my life's environment and
you change how I am, whether I know it or not." /88/

Since world relations are complex and involve
a whole context or fabric of meanings that can themselves be responded to in a variety of ways, we may
not always be clear as to just what is going on.
It is this complexity or relations out there to be
disclosed that come close to the Polanyian concept
of tacit knowing.

Truth

A second important element in Gadamer's
thought is the relationship between disclosure and
truth. Gadamer rejects the transcendental ego
because it assumes imvolvement with the world
rather than attending to it, and because centering
on the ego misses the non-subjectivity of the world.

DISCLOSURE OF THE ULTIMATE

How then are we to discover truth since rejection of the Cartesian dualism implies a rejection of truth as correspondence?

Truth as correspondence implies that truth is a mental characteristic. However, "When Gadamer says true he means how a being, or being as such, occurs. Truth is disclosure, and a being's truth it is manifest. With this most powerful departure from the modern way, Gadamer re-inherits that part of our tradition which finds in a being's own event. Truth is the mark we try to hit, not our way of shooting the arrow. Or, for those who do not much care for metaphors, truth is how something is present and available for our focused attention..."/89/ Thus human understanding has its own truth; an event as it is. There is no need for attempted reductions to brain states, content analyses or material conditions.

In conclusion, as Scott indicates, the poem by Rilke which appears at the front of <u>Truth and Method</u> sums up much of the book. Rilke is describing a cosmic game of catch. He says that I merely throw the ball to myself from myself I really haven't gained much of anything. But if an eternal woman throws me the ball, having come out on the field without my asking or even my expecting her, then I do gain something, especially if the ball she throws goes to the very center of my being, and is, as it were, on target. Like God's bridging of the eternal and the finite, my receptivity is creative. "The very ability to hear, to be receptive, to be in touch is not mine, though I live it. It is the ability of a world." /90/

Summaries

So much then for the extended analysis of these individual authors. It is clear that they represent a considerable diversity both in their systemic constructions and in their basic fields of special-.

ization. Despite these differences, however, a consensus, or at least a convergence, emerges in support of the basic theory of knowledge developed in the last chapter. In order to pinpoint areas of consensus, their positions with regard to knowledge, will be briefly summarized, then analyzed.

PIAGET Jean Piaget can be described as a critical realist because of his advocacy of a dynamic equilibrium between the assimilation of an object to the activity of a subject and the accomodation of that activity to the subject. Piaget's basic principle is that of objectivity through decentration. He follows this through the concrete operations of early childhood and the system and theory of adolescence. In each case, the direction of activity is from egocentrism to an ever widening reality.

BELLAH Robert Bellah opposes symbolic realism to consequential reductionism and scientific imperialism. /91/ Consequential reductionism tries to explain away the intrinsicity of religion through its functional consequences; scientific imperialism insists that the only valid knowledge is falsifiable scientific hypotheses. Bellah says that symbols and non-cognitive factors in human life are real and support an integrationist model of reality, one that lies in the relation between subject and object. Such a solution does not repudiate science in favor of religion, it simply points out their legitimate differences.

KUHN Thomas Kuhn argues against understanding science as a process of development by accumulation. He distinguishes between normal science and scientific revolution. This involves what he calls paradigm change. Normal science proceeds by puzzle setting and solving through practical reliance on a ruling paradigm. Paradigm change develops through the accumulation of anomaly until a new paradigm appears by a kind of gestalt shift of perception which then competes for dominance with the old

paradigm. Within the communitarian group of scientists, conversions to the new paradigm gradually
occur until it is translated by a kind of consensus
into normal science through shared examples.
Another term for paradigm is disciplinary matrix.

MERLEAU-PONTY Maurice Merleau-Ponty is against
the claim of scientistic imperialism to be the only
valid way of knowing. He emphasizes the primacy
of perception, even in science, which means a return
to the things themselves. He is also against the
Cartesian mind-body, object-subject dichotomy. He
sees the world as both revealed and shaped by perception, which proceeds by intensive and extensive
analysis. This is due to man's embodiment, making
him both a subject, opening itself to the world,
and an object, within the perceived world. And just
as one subject has an embodied existence, other
subjects are also embodies, the foundations of
society and intersubjectivity.

RICOEUR Paul Ricoeur admits the importance
of the abstract, logical level of language, but
insists that it is imperialistic to say that this
is the only valid level. There is the level of
source or ursprung as well. This level is the
level of symbol. And symbol requires interpretation. Various interpretations are possible and
none should be arbitrarily ruled out. One valid
and important interpretation, arising out of the
conflict of interpretations, is that of symbols
as multi-dimensional links between subject and
object. A symbol has a double level of meaning
closely linked one to the other, which is why
interpretation is necessary. The second sense, the
foundation of interpretation, is part of the world.
It can be called a gift of being not merely to
interpretation but also to universa; thought, as
mystic symbols take their place in the universe.

LATER WITTGENSTEIN The later Wittgenstein
opposed the representational view of language

where fact is a relation among objects, and language a collection of propositions representing possible facts. For Wittgenstein, language was multidimensional and not reducible to mathematical logic or scientific formulae. He saw language as a tool for diverse tasks with the implication that context is important. He developed the idea of language games as the larger backdrop for certain kinds of human activity, with no game having priority over any other. He widened the horizon further to include forms of life or the broader backdrop of human life itself. Thus language in all its logically primitive nature is integral to life, not something added to it.

THE STRUCTURALISTS AND CLAUDE LEVI-STRAUSS
The recent structuralist movement is complex with a variety of new techniques. It takes the stand that the surface of things is an insufficient source of explanation for them and that we must turn to their hidden and implicit sides. Life determines consciousness, consciousness does not determine life. The primacy of the transcendental ego is denied. The hidden infrastructure can be studied through language and symbol.

Claude Levi-Strauss projects the discovery of the universal underlying structure of human nature itself. He sees different activities in a given society as having the same basic structures, and he claims that the basic structure of more than one society can be fruitfully compared and found similar. This method has been especially successful in dealing with mythologies as interconnected systems studied through structural linguistics.

GADAMER Hans-Georg Gadamer understands hermeneutics to be a part of the total human experience rather than just an aspect of scientific method. Knowledge is not a question of a sibject confronting an object, but of understanding belonging to the object as well. Game playing is a basic analogy used implying that we know in the same way we play, making

the game by being in it, not by looking at it.
This is applied to art, documents and language.
Gadamer emphasizes the primacy of meaning. But by
meaning he does not intend the subjectivism of
structures of consciousness, rather he means the
dialogue involved in the way things and persons
disclose themselves and make themselves available
to the subject. Such disclosure involves world
relations and their necessarily vague tacitness.
Truth then is not the mental characteristic implied
in correspondence between subject-object, but
rather can be described as disclosure, the mark we
try to hit rather than our way of shooting the
arrow.

Similarities: Negative

There are a number of similarities and convergences in what these authors are against. Piaget
is against a sharp dichotomy between personality
and world; Bellah is against the functionality of
religion principle of consequential reductionism
and the claim of scientistic imperialism to a monopolistic method of knowledge; Kuhn is against an
understanding of science by accumulation of observable fact; Merleau-Ponty is against scientistic
imperialism's monopolistic claim on the only valid
way of knowing and the Cartesian body-mind dichotomy; Ricoeur is against the claim of linguistic
imperialism that the abstract, logical level of
human life is the only valid one; the later Wittgenstein is against the representational theory of
language; the Structuralists and Levi-Strauss are
against the view that the surface or quantifiable
levels of thins is sufficient to explain them;
Gadamer is against an understanding of hermeneutics
as part of the scientific method, the objectivism
of a structure of conscious theory of knowledge
and truth as mental characteristics in a correspon-
cence theory of truth.

154

Similarities: Positive

Then there are a number of similarities in
what they are for, even though their areas of
concentration, goals and directions otherwise
differ considerably; Piaget is for dynamic equilibrium between developing personality and the
world, achieving objectivity through decentration;
Bellah is for the importance of the non-cognitive
factors in human life leading to an integrationist
model of reality; Kuhn is for a model of science
where an anomalously produced shift in perception
is more important for its advance than the factual
measurement and problem solving of normal science;
Merleau-Ponty is for the primacy of perception
which implies a return to the things themselves
through man's embodiment as both subject and object;
Ricoeur is for a level of source or symbol in
human knowing which rests on a multidimensional
link subject and object; the later Wittgenstein is
for language as multidimensional building upon the
ever rippling out contextuality of human activities
and human life itself; the Structuralists and Levi-
Strauss are for the hidden and implicit structures
of life which determine consciousness and can be
studied through language and myth; Gadamer is for
Hermeneutics as part of the total human experience
and for meaning and truth as primarily dialogical,
with persons and things disclosing themselves to
the subject.

Comparison with Definitions of Knowledge

At the end of chapter three, a definition of
experiential knowledge was proposed, namely, that it
is "an encounter with a disclosing other through
indwelling in a framework and the integration of its
particulars into a coherent whole." As the above
listing of positive abd negative similarities among
the contemporary thinkers indicates there is remarkable agreement among them and with the basic thrust

155

of our definition despite the other obvious systemic differences.

One final thing remains to be done with regard to the theory of knowledge developed, and that is to give it a name. Several are possible: critical realism, radical empiricism, symbolic realism, interpretative realism, dynamic realism, integrationism, integral realism, dialectic or dialogical realism, disclosive realism, intersective realism. The first two are well known. But that in itself creates a problem. "Critical realism" has had so many meanings attached to it over the years, especially after the internal discussions of the American Critical Realism School earlier in this century, that it becomes confusing. "Empiricism" in "Radical Empiricism" still carries much of the weight of classical empiricism. "Symbolic" also retains a number of subjectivistic connotations. The remainder stress in various ways the integrationist character of experiential knowledge. Of these the two that seem most suggestive are "disclosive realism" and "intersective realism."

Disagreement

Of course, there are undoubtedly many, especially among those who continue to support the monistic view of science, who do not accept such a theory of knowledge.

In an interesting exchange at the 1969 American Academy of Religion Convention in Cambridge, Mass., several members responded to Robert Bellah's paper on Symbolic Realism, to which he then responded in turn. A brief examination of this exchange may be helpful as an example of the kind of objections such a position raises. /91/

The objectors claimed that Bellah's symbolic realism: rejects the separation between subject and object; brings religion out of its proper area of

the intrapsychic; is contrary to cognitive rationality and the scientific study of religion; tries
to bring moral subjectivism and emotional paroch-
ialism into the neutral zone of the university; and
tries to make what is acceptable as a cultural
system acceptable as an action system.

To all of this Bellah responded in part:

> Now what I have argued is that from
> both sides of the fence there has been
> developing an understanding of religion
> which neither explains it away nor
> attributes to it "preterhuman" origin.
> It is this understanding which I call
> symbolic realism. Symbolic realism
> simply holds that religious symbols
> are not primarily social or psycho-
> logical projection systems (though they
> always contain some projective elements)
> but the ways in which persons and
> societies express their sense of the
> fundamental nature of reality, of the
> totality of experience. Recognizing
> this fact requires no sacrifice of
> cognitive rationality or scientific
> neutrality whatever. What it does
> require is the sacrifice of scientific
> hubris, of what Turner calls the
> "implicitly theological position" of
> the old stance in which science is held
> to be superior to religion. In one
> sense symbolic realism implies less
> a regressive fusion of science and
> religion than a more adequate differ-
> entiation between them, but precisely
> because this differentiation is unlike
> the old one, non-antagonistic in principle
> it allows the possibility of new
> integration. For symbolic realism
> can also be accepted by the theologian,
> not as a substitute for his religion
> but as a conceptual scheme for the

157

interpretation of it which does not
attempt to deprive it of its value
and meaning. /92/

A theory of knowledge called dialogical realism may also seem strange to many Roman Catholics,
whose theology, epistemologically speaking, could
be characterized as Thomistic, or, in more recent
times as neo-Thomistic. Also the extremely important and massive theological systems developed by
such contemporary Roman Catholic scholars as Karl
Rahner and Bernard Lonergan have become more familiar since the Council. Without wanting to get into
a debate with either of these formidable figures,
I feel it true to say that just as their theories
of knowledge move considerably beyond what could
be called classical Thomism without surrendering
a number of important elements of the Catholic
heritage such as a paradoxical interest in both
rationality and realism and a sense of deep spirituality, imagination, ritual and mystery, /93/ so
dialogical realism moves in a different direction
still, all the while maintaining a similar kind
of basic continuity, and should be accorded its
dur rights in the increasingly pluralistic world
of theological discourse.

In these two chapters both the internal
coherence of a dialogically realistic theory of
knowledge, its cultural support among a variety of
important thinkers and its basic continuity with
the Catholic spirit have been proposed and demonstrated in various ways. /94/ As it is used as
a tool for further theological reflection, it will
produce results that may seem controversial to
some. It is important and only fair that any
consideration of these positions make an effort to
take into account the theory of knowledge that
undergirds them.

And now, at long last, we turn in the next
chapters to the problems of religious knowledge,
revelation and God.

NOTES

[1]John Flavell, <u>The Developmental Psychology</u> <u>of Jean Piaget</u> (N. Y.: Van Nostrand and Reinhold Company, 1963).

[2]Louis E. Conn, "Jean Piaget as Critical Realist," <u>Angelicum</u> (54, 1977) 67-68.

[3]Ibid., p. 68. Quote from Piaget's <u>Psychology</u> <u>and Epsitemology</u> (N. Y., Grossman, 1971), p. 108.

[4]Jean Piaget, <u>Epistemologie des Sciences de</u> <u>l'Homme</u> (Paris: Gallimard, 1972).

[5]Flavell, op. cit., p. 166.

[6]Jean Piaget, <u>Six Psychological Studies</u> (N.Y.: Vintage Books, 1968), p. 46.

[7]Conn, op. cit., p. 71.

[8]Jean Piaget, <u>The Psychology of the Child</u> (N. Y.: Basic Books, 1969), pp. 130-131.

[9]Flavell, op. cit., p. 204.

[10]Ibid., pp. 205-206.

[11]Piaget, <u>The Psychology of the Child</u>, pp.135-136.

[12]Jean Piaget, <u>The Growth of Logical Thinking</u> <u>from Childhood to Adolescence</u>, transl. by Anna Parson and Stanley Milgram (N. Y.: Basic Books, 1958), p. 346.

[13]Conn, op. cit., p. 87.

[14]Piaget, Six Psychological Studies, pp. 69-70.

[15]Robert Bellah, "Christianity and Symbolic Realism," The Journal for the Scientific Study of Religion (9, no. 2, Summer, 1970) 89-96. This was given at a joint session of the American Academy of Religion and the Society for the Scientific Study of Religion, in Cambridge, Mass., October 25, 1969. The paper was reprinted in Bellah's book Beyond Belief (N. Y.: Harper and Row, 1970), as part 2 of Chapter 15.

[16]Ibid., p. 89.

[17]Ibid., p. 70.

[18]Ibid., p. 91.

[19]Ibid., p. 92

[20]Ibid., p. 92.

[21]Ibid., p. 93.

[22]Ibid., p. 94.

[23]R. Bellah, "Response to Comments on 'Christianity and Symbolic Realism'" Same issue of Journal pp. 113-114.

[24]Ibid., p. 114.

[25]Thomas S. Kuhn, The Structure of Scientific Revolutions. International Encyclopedia of Unified Science, Vol. II, no. 2. Second Edition: Revised

and Enlarged (Chicago, University of Chicago Press, 1970).

[26]Ibid., pp. 1-2.

[27]Ibid., p. 17.

[28]Ibid., p. 34.

[29]Ibid., p. 42.

[30]Ibid., p. 44.

[31]Ibid., p. 65.

[32]Ibid., p. 91.

[33]Ibid., p. 109.

[34]Ibid., p. 111.

[35]Ibid., p. 122.

[36]Ibid., p. 159.

[37]Ibid., pp. 172-173.

[38]Ibid., p. 176.

[39]Ibid., p. 182.

[40]Ibid., p. 184.

[41]Ibid., p. 185.

[42]Kuhn cites him explicitly in this connection on page 91.

[43]Ibid., p. 195.

[44]John F. Bannon, The Philosophy of Merleau-Ponty (N. Y., Harcourt-Brace and World, 1967), p. vii.

[45]Alden L. Fisher, ed., The Essential Writings of Merleau-Ponty (N. Y.: Harcourt-Brace and World, 1969), p. 9.

[46]Ibid., p. 10.

[47]Ibid., p. 11.

[48]Merleau-Ponty, The Primacy of Perception and Other Essays. Ed., by J. Edie (Evanston: Northwestern University Press, 1964), p. 162.

[49]Ibid., p. 12.

[50]Robert M. Friedman, "Merleau-Ponty's Theory of Subjectivity," Philosophy Today (XIX: 3/4, 1975) 231.

[51]Merleau-Ponty, The Visible and the Invisible; followed by Working Notes. Transl. by Alphonso Lingis (Evanston: Northwestern University Press, 1968), p. 82.

[52]Fisher, op. cit., p. 13. Cf. also Mary Rose Barral, Merleau-Ponty: The Role of the Body Subject In Interpersonal Relations (Pittsburgh: Dusquene University Press, 1965).

[53] Patrick Bourgeois, "Hermeneutic Sumbols and Philosophical Reflection: Paul Ricoeur," Philosophy Today (XV, 4/4, Winter, 1971) 233.

[54] Ibid., p. 234.

[55] John Henry Morgan, "Religious Myth and Symbol," Philosophy Today (XVIII, Spring, 74) 74.

[56] Bourgeois, op. cit., p. 235.

[57] Paul Ricoeur, Le Conflit des Interpretaions: Essai sur l'Hermeneutique (Paris: Ed. du Seuil, 1969), p. 16.

[58] Ibid., p. 16.

[59] Bourgeois, op. cit., p. 237/

[60] Ibid., p. 235.

[61] Ibid., p. 239.

[62] Ibid., p. 241.

[63] George Pitcher, The Philosophy of Wittgenstein (Englewood Cliffs, N. J.: Prentice-Hall, 1964) Justus Harnack, Wittgenstein and Modern Philosophy (N. Y.: New York University Press, 1965); Garth Hallett, A Companion to Wittgenstein's "Philosophical Investigations," (Ithaca: Cornell University Press, 1977).

[64] Irving Adler, Thinking Machines (N. Y.: New American Library, 1961).

DISCLOSURE OF THE ULTIMATE

[65]Alfred Jules Ayer, <u>Language, Truth and Logic</u> (N. Y., Dover Publications, 1952).

[66]Jerry Gill, <u>The Possibility of Religious Knowledge</u> (Grand Rapids: W. B. Eerdmans, 1971)

[67]L. Wittgenstein, <u>Philosophical Investigations</u> (N. Y.: Macmillan, 1953), p. 109 (n. 340).

[68]Gill, op. cit., p. 102.

[69]Ibid., p. 104.

[70]P. F. Strawson, <u>Individuals</u> (London: Methuen, 1959).

[71]Gill, op. cit., p. 108.

[72]Richard T. DeGeorge and Fernande W. DeGeorge, ed., <u>The Structuralists: From Marx to Levi-Strauss</u> (N. Y.: Doubleday, 1972), p. xi.

[73]Karl Marx, <u>The German Ideology</u>. Transl. from German; Edited by S. Ryazanskaya (Moscow: Progress Publications, 2 vols. in 1, 1968)

[74]De George, op. cit., p. xv.

[75]Jacques Ehrmann, ed., <u>Structuralism</u> (N. Y.: Doubleday, 1970) p. ix.

[76]Hans Georg Gadamer, <u>Truth and Method</u> (N. Y.: Seabury Press, 1975)

[77]Charles E. Scott, "Gadamer's 'Truth and Method'" <u>Anglican Theological Review</u> (LIX, n. i, January 77)

63.

[78]Robert E. Innis, "Hans Georg Gadamer's 'Truth and Method': A Review Article," The Thomist (50, 1976) 319.

[79]Gadamer, Truth and Method, p. xi.

[80]Ibid., p. xii.

[81]Ibid., p. xix.

[82]Innis, op. cit., pp. 314-315.

[83]Ibid., p. 316.

[84]Ibid., p. 317

[85]Scott, op. cot., p. 65.

[86]Ibid., p. 66.

[87]Ibid., p. 66.

[88]Ibid., p. 67.

[89]Ibid., p. 74.

[90]Ibid., p. 76.

[91]Bellah does not use this term. It is used in this book as a convenient name-summary for an attitude that is harmful to genuine science and to the understanding of man. It is only quasi-scientific, hence scientistic, in the sense that it extrapolates scientific method into a basic philosophy of life

and it is imperialistic in that it demands that all other disciplines and even religion conform to the scientific method or run the risk of being declared meaningless. Though generally on the decline and obviously not found in pure form in any individual, it nevertheless remains strong enough, especially in the mass culture, to warrant serious attention.

[92]Referred to earlier, Journal for the Scientific Study of Religion (9, n. 2, Summer, 1970). The discussion occurs in pp. 97 through 115.

[93]Ibid., pp. 113-114.

[94]If this combination seems paradoxical, it is helpful to point out that the world of the Hobbit, The Lord of the Rings and the Silmarillion was created by the English Roman Catholic imagination if J. R. R. Tolkien, influenced in part by the works of Francis Thompson, medieval sagas and the Fathers of Newman's Birmingham Oratory. It is interesting to note as well, in connection with the theme of this chapter, that Humphrey Carpenter in the authorized biography Tolkien (Boston: Houghton-Mifflin Company, 1977) quotes Tolkien as saying that in the Silmarillion he was doing more than writing a story "He wrote of the tales that make up the book: 'They arose in my mind as "given" things, and as they came separately, so too the links grew. An absorbing, though continually interrupted labour....; yet always I had the sense of recording what was already "there", somewhere; not of "inventing".'," p. 92.

CHAPTER FIVE

FAITH AND REASON

IN

AQUINAS AND AUGUSTINE

Introduction

At the end of chapter two's discussion of the
religious dimension of experience, it was noted
that though the arguments for the reality of that
religious dimension seemed overwhelming, many
people remained unconvinced. It was further suggested that the basis for much of the difficulty
lay in the general epistemologies presupposed. For
if one has a theory of human knowledge, implicit
or explicit, religious knowledge will be taken up
and interpreted in the same way. That chapter
then concluded, "For if, as such modern psychology
and philosophy hold, knowing is a thoroughly subjective experience; or if, as much current scientism and secularism hold, only what is factual is
real; or if, as some linguistic analysts hold,
religious language is meaningless or at best private,
then the arguments in this chapter do not suffice.
They must be supplemented and, if possible, supported by a third method, namely a more general or
epistemological examination of human knowledge.
That is the subject of the next two chapters."

DISCLOSURE OF THE ULTIMATE

So the third chapter examined in considerable depth two complementary modern theories of
knowledge, the radical empiricism or critical
realism of the american pragmatist school of Pierce,
James and Dewey and the Michael Polanyi heuristic
system called personal knowledge. Building on
these foundations, then, a definition of knowledge
or experience was proposed that seemed reasonable,
coherent, balanced and appropriate for our more
psychologically sophisticated times.

In chapter four a number of contemporary
thinkers' views on knowledge were examined briefly.
In the course of this examination, a number of
points of comparison and consensus were discovered,
epistemologically speaking.

In returning to religious knowledge, we will
attempt a two-staged approach. The first stage,
this chapter, will examine the classic positions
on faith and reason in St. Thomas Aquinas and St.
Augustine. It will balance these with critiques
and commentary from John Hick and Michael Polanyi.
Then, the second stage, chapter six, will try to
present a more systematically developed theory of
religious knowledge.

Since with Aquinas and Augustine we are dealing
with two main pillars of Western christian thought,
such an analysis needs to proceed with seriousness
and respect. Yet that same respect precludes our
leaving them as mere historical figures, with little
or no dynamic relevance to today's christian thought
and life. It seem even more respectful to try to
integrate them, with due modifications, into the
contemporary scene.

Given the current state of Roman Catholic
thought, such an enterprise can be especially helpful. For while there have been in recent years a
tremendous number of developments in Catholic
thought and life, in spirituality, liturgy, canon
law, religious orders, ethics and scripture, an

overarching theological synthesis encompassing all
these changes in a reasonable and systematic way
has not yet been fully developed. It is the lack
of such a synthesis that causes a certain malaise
among many educated Catholics. The development of
such a synthesis remains an urgent theological
task, and this book is an attempt to move at least
partially in that direction. In this effort Catholic theologians can be grateful to those Protestant theologians who have been struggling for some
time with these problems and with considerable
success. Yet much remains to be done on all sides
and certainly this is an area where it is important
that the ecumenical spirit express itself theologically.

This chapter will analyze the classical theory
of Aquinas and Augustine because the Thomistic
understanding of faith as propositional remains
influential today among many Christians, Catholic
and Protestant and even among many who argue
against Christianity itself. This analysis will
be in the terms of a sympathetic British churchman
and philosopher of religion., John Hick, and will
be followed by an exposition of Hick's own theory
of religious knowledge. Then Augustine's position
on faith and reason with its emphasis on believing
in order to understand will be examined as well as
parallels with and differences between this system
and that of Michael Polanyi examined in detail in
chapter two. Hopefully, then, through a dialectical
process of thrust and counterthrust, a number of
areas connected with this difficult question of
the relation between faith and reason will be
clarified.

Faith and Reason in St. Thomas Aquinas

Meaning of Faith

In the introduction to his book, <u>Faith and
knowledge</u>, /1/ Hick makes clear that the word
"faith" which he is about to explore has two basic

meanings. The first is epistemological or cognitive while the other is not. Cognitively speaking Faith (fides) is "a state, act or procedure
which may be compared with standard instances of
knowing and believing." While faith as trust
(fiducia) is an attitude "Maintained sometimes
despite contrary indications, that the divine purpose toward us is wholly good and loving." Faith
as trust presupposes faith as cognition and it is
this logically prior notion that is taken up in the
investigation.

Hick then suggests the following as the widely
accepted classical understanding of faith derived
from Thomas Aquinas, "Faith thus consists of believing strongly various propositions of a theological
nature, which the believer does not and cannot know
to be true." He goes on to say:

> To know here is taken to mean
> either to observe directly or to be
> able to prove by strict demonstration.
> Where this is possible, there is no
> room for faith. It is only that which
> lies beyond the scope of human knowledge
> that must be taken, if at all, on faith
> or trust. When in such a case we do not
> adopt some belief, the lack of rational
> compulsion to assent is compensated by
> an act of will, a voluntary leap of
> trust, so that the man of faith comes
> to believe something which he cannot
> prove or see. /2/

This general understanding of faith is one
which is still widely accepted and influential today,
for it represents the main way in which Western
christianity has been speaking about it since medieval times. This is not to say that there are
not important movements away from it in both Protestant and Catholic circles, but more of that
later. For the moment, we are concerned with the

Thomistic synthesis itself.

Tripartite Division

Basing himself upon Thomas' thorough discussion of faith in the <u>Summa Theologica</u>. /3/ Fick finds that it falls into three main divisions.

The first division deals with the fact that faith is understood as propositional, that it consists, in other words, in assenting to propositions. This obviously intellectualistic interpretation comes from a theory of human knowing based on composition and division. What is immediately known in faith then are propositions about God. "Faith," says Aquinas, "occupies a position between knowledge (scientia) and opinion (opinio) and accordingly falls on a common scale with them; and since they are both concerned with propositions, so also is faith." /4/

This propositionality of faith was influential at Vatican I. That Council described faith as "a supernatural virtue by which we, with the aid and inspiration of the grace of God, believe that the things revealed by him are true, not because the intrinsic truth of the revealed things has been perceived by the natural light of reason, but because of the authority of God himself who reveals them, who can neither deceive nor be deceived." /5/

The second division says that the porpositions which are thus believed in faith are special in the sense that they are mysteries, "they are propositions whose truth can never (in this life) be directly evident to us and which therefore have to be accepted on authority." /6/ Chief among these of course are the Incarnation and the Trinity.

In order to explain this further, Thomas proposes two kinds of assent. The first kind of

assent is the assent of _scientia_ which is compelled
by self-evidence or the demonstration that has led
to it. Faith differs from _scientia_, however, according to Thomas, in that here "the intellect assents
to something, not through being sufficiently moved
to this assent by its proper object, but through an
act of choice, whereby it turns voluntarily to one
side rather than to the other." /7/

Because of these basic differences, it is impossible for one person to have knowledge and faith
at the same time with regard to the same object.

As for opinion, though this too is not compelled by its object, it is accompanied by doubt
and anxiety, whereas with faith there is certainty
and no such confusion or anxiety. Faith as distinct
from opinion involves commitment and peace.

The third division concerns faith's voluntary
character. If faith is something which is not
compelled by the evidence of its object and therefore requires an act of the will on the part of the
believer, then what lies behind this decision to
believe, what motivates it? Is it arbitrary or is
it reasonable? According to Thomas it is a reasonable decision because it is based on the knowledge
and acceptance of the existence of God and the
further fact that he has made known the matter
believed. This is a description of the "preambles
of faith." We have already examined in an earlier
chapter how these preambles form a logical whole
if certain presuppositions are accepted.

Preambles of Faith

But, continues Hick, "If we now ask more particularly whether these _preabula fidel_ are held
to be rationally compelling, so that anyone who
examines them and who is not prejudiced against
the truth must acknowledge them, or whether on the

contrary, some degree of faith enters their acceptance, no satisfactorily unambiguous answer is
forthcoming." /8/

The answer is ambiguous first because it says
that these revealed truths are provable by reason.
It is argued that faith must prove itself in some
way before the court of reason. Thus it must needs
be proven that God exists and that the doctrine of
faith does as a matter of fact come from him. It
assumes that both of these are provable. As Canon
George Smith says:

> The human mind, then, is able to
> learn with certainty the existence of
> God; is able by the proper investigation
> of the facts, to conclude that Christ is
> the **bearer** of a divine message, that he
> founded an infallible Church for the
> purpose of propagating that message; and
> finally, by the process indicated in
> apologetics, to conclude that the
> Catholic Church is that divinely
> appointed teacher of revelation. These
> things, I say, can be known and proved,
> and by those who have the requisite
> leisure, opportunity and ability, are
> actually known and proved with all the
> scientific certainty of which the
> subject is patient. The preambles of
> faith, therefore, rest upon solid
> ground of human reason. /9/

Second, it is ambiguous because it emphasizes
that faith is not compelled, that it is free.
Reason can provide motives for believing but these
motives are not so overwhelming that anyone is
forced to believe. And because there is no force
involved, only freedom to accept or not, then the
act of believing is worthy and meritorious.

Hick summarizes thus Thomas' position on faith:

"His teaching, is, then, that Christian faith is
a voluntary acceptance of the Church's doctrine,
not because this can be directly seen by our intel-
lects to be true, but because the historical
evidence of prophecy and miracle, leads (without
coercing) a mind disposed toward goodness and truth
to accept that teaching as being of divine origin."
/10/

The primary appeal here is to reason. The
teachings of faith are to be believed because the
Church's claim to present them can be supported by
historical evidence that can be seen and accepted
by reason. "But this virtue carries with it the
danger that the court to which the church thus
appeals, the court of human reason, may not return
a favorable verdict." /11/ The fact is that the
greater part of humanity does not accept that
reasonable verdict and if pressed too hard, such an
argument can turn into an appeal for private
judgement, which itself runs counter to the communitarian thrust of the Church.

Hick continues, "We now have the Thomistic-
Catholic analysis of faith before us. To introduce
labels which will draw attention to the three main
aspects of it which we have noted, we will say that
it is intellectualistic, in that it regards faith
as a propositional attitude: fideistic, in that it
regards faith and knowledge as mutually exclusive;
and voluntaristic, in that it sees faith as the
product of a conscious act of will." /12/

Summary of Points of Agreement and Disagreement

The following is a summary of the relative
positions of Thomas and Hick. In many ways they
are not as far apart as they seem at first sight:

1. For St. Thomas Aquinas, faith is seen to be
a form of assent to porpositions. For John Hick,

revelation, while it does not exclude propositions
as statements of faith, is primarily a total interpretations of experience.

2. For Aquinas revelation is constituted by
propositions. For Hich it is constituted by events
or actions.

3. For Aquinas the assent of faith is whole-
hearted and untentative, and, though voluntary,
has a rational basis. For Hick, the voluntariness
of faith is also rational.

4. For Aquinas, the rational basis of faith
lies partly in the fact that some truths about God
can be demonstrated. For Hick its rationality
does not come through this possibility of prior
cemonstration because such demonstration would
coerce man' freedom.

5. For Aquinas, faith and knowledge are exclusive (natural and revealed theology). For Hick
faith and knowledge are not exclusive since man
knows that God exists through experience (plus, and
this is an argument that has come to be particularly Hick's own, through eschatological verification).

6. The points of agreement then are many and
are the following:

a. Both consider faith to include adher-
ence to porpositions (through events).

b. Both see faith as voluntary.

c. Both see faith as rational.

d. Both agree that there is an ongoing
tension of some sort between the voluntariness of
faith and the rationality of faith. Even Aquinas
would agree that the rationality of faith does not
mean that its whole content is demonstrable, for
he refuses to admit that one and the same person

can have faith in a proposition and learn it from philosophical demonstration. (The limitation of natural theology.)

7. The main disagreement then seems to be the following:

Aquinas tries to establish the rationality of revelation by proving the rationality of its credentials or preambles. Hick criticizes Aquinas for saying that man is a free agent in accepting revelation and yet holding that revelation's credentials are establishable.

There is an assumption underlying both Hick and Aquinas that helps tp explain their disagreement. The assumption is that the voluntariness of faith depends on the unprovability of its propositions.

Terence Penelhum disagrees with that presupposition saying that faith is independent of the provability or non-provability of its propositions. In order to support this argument he undertakes a lengthy and complex analysis of "provability" which shall not concern us here. He says:

> Faith and Knowledge, then are not exclusive. The voluntariness of faith is not inconsistent with a man's knowing its propositions to be true, since he could have refused to accept them, either from proof, had such existed, or from revelation. ...The fact that revealed propositions can be rejected does not, however, show that they cannot be proved as well as revealed, or that they cannot be known to be true. ... I would argue that the compatibility of faith and knowledge could extend equally to propositions that have been proved from non-theistic premises, since men could still, even it such proofs existed, refuse to accept them

176

and the knowledge that they had if they
did accept them would still need to be
maintained through faith. Human freedom
could still coexist with successful
proofs of God; and one can still wonder
why it does not do so. /13/

Thus the argument with Aquinas's proofs of the
existence of God lies not in the fact that admitting
them as preambles to faith would destroy the voluntariness of faith, but rather in the fact that the
preponderant weight of philosophico-religious
thought since Descartes. through locke, Hume and
Kant, has been that they do not logically do what
they try to do, namely prove conclusively by inference the existence of God.

There are others who disagree, says Penelhum,
with this trend and find in a modified version of
the ontological proof or in a reductive argument
of all the proofs that could be called cosmological,
that there are indeed arguments for the existence
of God. But even when this is admitted, all that
has been proven is a _truth_ about God's existence.
His existence itself is not grounded on such theistic
arguments, for he needs no ground. But more of this
later.

Finally Penelhum concludes that all this is why
an emphasis on revelation as event and encounter is
a sounder way for modern man to approach these
questions, for it is experientially supported rather
than logically concluded, and brings God much
closer to man and his world.

Revelation as Proposition and as Event

To return to John Hick. His own proposal concerning religious knowledge rests on two basic
elements. The first is an understanding of revelation as event rather than as proposition:

177

"According to this alternative view revelation consists not in the divine communication of religious
truths, but in the self-revealing actions of God
within human history." /27/, /14/ The second is
his stand on the intimate relationship between
ordinary human knowledge and religious knowledge,
or the claim that there is an element of continuity
between faith and reason. In this book, Faith and
Knowledge, Hick does not develop the first pillar
of his theory, namely the non-propositional nature
of revelation. Whatever the reason, whether because
he is primarily a philosopher or whether he feels
that this is now so accepted in Protestant circles
that it needs no elaboration on his part, he assumes
it sufficiently to reduce it to analytical principle
in his examination of the faith-reason relationship
in Aquinas.

Roman Catholic Understanding

The situation in Roman Catholic circles is not
so simple, The modern biblical movement was later
in developing there than in Protestant circles, so
there has been less to assimilate all its implications. Also though there is a very broad consensus
now among Roman Catholics about revelation being
understood as event rather than as proposition, and
though this general understanding is seen constantly
at work liturgically, homiletically, spiritually
and practically, it has still not fully replaced
the older more theoretical synthesis of faith and
reason as a working theological or religious tool.
As was said above, the resolving of these differences remains one of the urgent theological tasks.

Rather than presupposing the non-propositional
nature of revelation, as Hick does, we will pause
to examine the present understanding of revelation
in Catholic circles. And the simplest, most representative way of doing this is to examine Vatican
II's position on revelation.

FAITH AND REASON IN AQUINAS AND AUGUSTINE

The Council issued a Dogmatic Constitution on Divine Revelation. /15/ The history of that document is irrelevant here beyond saying that the original proposals for it aroused so much controversy that they required the direct intervention of Pope John XXIII and extensive revisions that did not come to fruition until four years later in the final 1965 sessions of the Council. All these discussions and revision are significant because they mean that this Constitution is very much a product of the Council itself and accurately reflects the consensus of the Fathers.

Chapter I is of special interest. It is entitled "Revelation Itself." Article 2, then defines revelation;

> In his goodness and wisdom, God
> chose to reveal himself and to make
> known to us the hidden purpose of His
> will...Through this revelation, therefore,
> the invisible God, out of the abundance
> of his love speaks to men as friends and
> lives among them so that he may invite
> and take them into fellowship with Himself.
> This plan of revelation is realized by
> deeds and words having an inner unity;
> the deeds wrought by God in the history
> of salvation manifest and while words
> proclaim the deeds and clarify the
> mystery contained in them /16/

In his commentary on this section, Joseph Ratzinger says that this gives much more emphasis to the personal and theocentric starting point of revelation than Vatican I, for "it is God himself, the person of God, from whom revelation proceeds, and to whom it returns, and thus revelation necessarily reaches--also with the person who receives it-- into the personal centre of man, it touches him in the depth of his being, not only in his individual faculties, in his will and understanding. ...Thus we can see how the idea of revelation also outlines

179

a conception of man as the creature of dialogue who,
in listening to the word of God, becomes contempor-
aneous with the presentness of God and in the
fellowship of the word receives the reality which
is indivisibly one with this word: fellowship with
God himself." /17/

As the historical documents of the council show,
the Fathers were concerned about going beyond the
traditional neo-scholastic understanding of revelation as a series of mysterious propositions. They
were more interested in the wholeness of revelation,
one which sees both word and event as important,
the two of them together constituting the whole.
Thus they considered it as a dialogue dealing with
the whole man as a person not merely addressing
his reason.

Article three touches on the historical nature
of revelation, showing that it comes to man not as
a series of timeless ideas or propositions but as
God operating hisotrically in our own day.

Article four shows the christocentrism of
revelation:

> For he sent his Son the eternal
> Word, who enlightends all men so that
> he might dwell among men and tell them
> the innermost realities about God.
> Jesus Christ, therefore, the Word made
> flesh, sent as "a man to men" "speaks
> the words of God" and completes the
> work of salvation his Father gave him
> to do. ...For this reason Jesus
> perfected revelation by fulfilling
> it through his whole work of making
> himself present and manifesting himself;
> through his words and deeds, his signs
> and wonders, but especially through his
> death and glorious resurrection from the
> dead and final sending of the Spirit of
> truth. /18/

FAITH AND REASON IN AQUINAS AND AUGUSTINE

As Ratzinger says, "Thus the perfection of revelation in Christ is here removed from the domain of
positivist thinking: God does not arbitrarily cease
speaking at some point in history...Christ is the
end of God's speaking, because after him and beyond
him there is nothing more to say, for in him God
has, as it were, said himself. In him the dialogue
of God has attained its goal; it has become a union."
/19/

Intellectualism and doctrinalism have difficulty with revelation because revelation is not a
talking about something outside the human, outside
the personal, it is rather a concern with the fulfillment of man's existence and the relation of the
human I to the divine thou. "The purpose of this
dialogue is ultimately not information, but unity
and transformation." /20/

In article five, the Council presents its own
definition of faith which differs from that of
Vatican I. The text says:

> The obedience of faith must be
> given to God who reveals, an obedience
> by which man entrusts his whole self
> freely to God, offering "the whole
> submission of intellect and will to
> God who reveals," (Vat I) and freely
> assenting to the truth revealed by him. /21/

There are three significant differences in
this text and its concluding paragraph from the
related passage in VaticanI. First, there is the
omission of one of three elements in the genesis
of faith which had been presented by Vatican I,
namely the external arguments for revelation.
This Council limits itself to the grace of God and
the illumination of the Spirit. Thus faith is
presented as more inwardly directed and less dependent on external proofs.

181

Second, instead of using Vatican One's phrase on faith as "believing as true what has been revealed by God," the Fathers of Vatican II simply speak of "revelation given by him." In this context, the phrase "entrusts his whole self" is important. As the pertinent footnote in Documents says, "The Council desired to get away from a too intellectualistic conception. Christian faith is not merely assent to a set of statements; it is a personal engagement, a constituting act of loyalty and self commitment offered to man by God..." /22/

The third difference lies in the emphasis on the constant perfecting of faith through the gifts of the Holy Spirit. There is an openendedness, a dynamism here which is absent from the earlier statement. This takes nothing away from the action with man through revelation.

Finally, in Article six, Vatican II modifies the text of Vatican I by substituting "to show forth and communicate himself" for "reveal." "Through divine revelation, God chose to show forth and communicate himself and the eternal decision of his will regarding the salvation of men." /23/ This emphasizes once again that revelation goes beyond the doctrinal or propositional and can be considered a continuing salvationa; dialogue. "The development from Vatican I, however, is seen again in a different context. In 1870 people had started with the natural knowledge of God and had moved on from this to 'supernatural' revelation. Vatican II has not only avoided the technical term supernaturalis, which belongs too much to the world of physical thinking...but followed the reverse procedure. It develops revelation from its Christological center, in order then to present the inescapable responsibility of human reason of the whole. /24/

FAITH AND REASON IN AQUINAS AND AUGUSTINE

Historical Explanation

Gabriel Moran, writing shortly after the Council, offers an historical explanation of the above developments that includes four main elements. /25/ First is the Scriptural movement in Catholic circles, where new methods of exegesis and hermeneutics have been developing by quantum leaps through this century. Such intense and widespread interest in Scripture naturally has led to a reevaluation of revelation itself as the most fundamental question associated with scriptural interpretation.

The second influence he sees is that of contemporary philosophy. "The student of the Bible will find himself on ground not entirely unfamiliar when he meets the body-subject in Merleau-Ponty, encounter in Buber, truth as unveiling in Heidegger, freedom in Sartre, or transcendence in Jaspers."/26/ Since a narrowly conceived neo-scholasticism seems to be fading rapidly into the past, a whole number of contemporary philosophical influences are contributing to this new synthesis of theology and revelation.

A third influence is ecumenism. With the contemporary breaking of inteconfessional barriers and greater communication and understanding among Christian scholars, there has been a great interchange of ideas between groups and churches that had previously led lives quite consciously apart. Thus Catholic scholars have discovered that Protestants have developed a considerable body of literature on revelation and that this immediately projects them into the middle of an ongoing discussion. One common element of that theology has been the rejection of a propositional idea of revelation.

Finally, Moran cites the Catechetical movement as influential here because of its emphasis on the pastoral nature of catechetics or religious instruction. To do so it needs to return to the deepest sources of theology's power "to enrich with the best human reflection, and to bring theology into a dynamic unity that would take account of the personal, historical and social." /27/

Summing it up, Moran continues, "Since it is the very notion of revelation that is now challenged and called into question, Catholic theology faces a crisis in its foundation. Such a crisis presents both grave dangers and at the same time great possibilities....Theology as well as philosophy is an eternal beginning, moving outward from its starting point only far enough to reground its original position....a richer understanding lies in the future precisely because of the eternal beginning." /28/

John Hick: The Nature of Faith

It is time than to return to John Hick, whose systematic analysis of faith and revelation is extremely suggestive, even if, as will be suggested, it may need to be slightly modified or supplemented. In our earlier discussion in this chapter it was mentioned that there were two main pillars to John Hick's theory, the first being the understanding of revelation as event rather than as proposition, the second his affirmation of the close relationship between ordinary human knowledge and religious knowledge. The first he presupposes, the second he develops as great length in the chapter entitled "The Nature of Faith." /29/

Towards the end of the book he offers the following description of faith: It is "the interpretative element within religious experience," with the "function of preserving our cognitive freedom in relation to God," expressible in language that is "cognitive in character." (p. 200) In

184

chapter five itself he sees faithm like the significance found in the natural and human orders to be
"a primary and unevidenceable act of interpretation
...directed toward God. /30/

He arrives at this understanding of faith only
after an extensive analysis which we will now pursue in some detail.

Hick begins by asking some basic questions
concerning man's knowledge of God and the relationship of that knowledge to man's knowledge in general. "What manner of cognition is the religious
man's awareness of God and how is it related to
his other cognitions?...Can God be known through his
dealing with us in the world which he has made?" /31/

Hick's basic answer to these questions is the
assertion that religious knowledge's epistemological pattern is the same as that of all other human
knowledge even if its object is unique. One of the
characteristics which it shares is common with all
other human knowledge is its mediated structure;
"'Mediated' knowledge, such as is postulated by
this religious claim, is already a common and accepted feature of our cognitive experience." /32/

Significance and Interpretation

By mediation he understands an interplay of
significance and interpretation. These are key
elements of his thought and need careful delinea-
tion. First of all, by significance he means
something at first extremely broad which later
focuses more specifically: "By significance I mean
that fundamental and all-pervasive characteristic
of our conscious experience which de facto constitutes it for us the experience of a 'world' and not
of an empty void or churning chaos." /33/ This
broad sweep is the primary locus of significance
but it can be logically separated into smaller

divisions. "We may accordingly draw a provisional distinction between two species of significance: object-significance and situational-significance." /34/

Object-significance has to do with the naming of things and is the foundation of language, whereas situational-significance is more personal and contextual. Needless to say, we are not able to apprehend significance in the abstract, only significant objects and situations.

Significance has a correlative subjective factor that can be called interpretation. Interpretation arises out of the possibility of ambiguity in the given. "Two uses of 'interpretation' are to be distinguished. In one of its senses, an interpretation is a (true or false) _explanation_, answering the question, why? We speak, for example, of a metaphysician's interpretation of the universe. In its other sense, an interpretation is a (correct or incorrect) _recognition_, or attribution of significance, answering the question, What?...These two meanings are interconnected." /35/

All explanations deal primarily with recognition. Thus when we are puzzled by the meaning of something we try to place it in a meaningful context and then finally are able to see what it means by relating it to that context. Unfortunately this process does not work for the universe as a whole, for it is the context of everything else and cannot be itself placed in a context. This poses unique interpretative problems, involving both recognition and explanation. For the moment, interpretation, including religious interpretation, is understood as a recognition of significance.

Such acts of recognition are of course complex, dealing as they do with two types of ambiguity in the given. "There are, on the one hand, interpretations which are mutually exclusive (e.g. "That is a fox." and "That is a dog." refering to the same

object), and on the other hand interpretations
which are mutually compatible (e.g., "That is an
animal," and "That is a dog.").. Of two logically
alternative interpretations, only one (at most)
can be the correct interpretation. But two compatible interpretations may both be correct." /36/

One further point about Hick's theory of
significance-interpretation that needs to be taken
into account is that it is basically oriented
towards action. As we pursue our lives, we are
surrounded by influences among which we need to
choose so that we can act in our own vital interests.
We live on macroscopic rather than microscopic
levels because we select from our environment only
what we need in order to act. Also "Interpretations which take the dispositional form of readiness
for action, instead of immediate overt activity,
borrow this feeling of 'reality' from concrete
interpretations which are being or are already confirmed in action." /37/ Thus one interpretation,
confirmed, suggests another, and so on, forming a
network of interpretations as the substructure of
life.

Situational Significance

A good deal of this can be summed up in the
term "situational-significance." According to Hick,
"A 'situation' may be defined as a state of affairs,
which when selected for attention by an act of
interpretation, carries its own distinctive practical significance for us." /38/

Such situational-significance should not be
considered in isolation. We can, as a matter of
fact, be involved in a number of different and
differently related situations at once. "We may
be involved in many different situations at the
same time and may move by swift or slow transitions
of interpretation from one to another. There may

187

thus occur an indefinitely complex interpretation
of situations." /39/

Two persons, for example, may be riding in an
automobile going down an interstate highway. They
are obviously related to each other, all the more
so as they are deep in conversation. The automobile
in which they are riding is controlled by automotive,
physical and chemical laws. Their travel itself is
conditioned by highway laws. As they drive along
they come upon an overturned tractor trailer in the
median strip, surrounded by rescue vehicles and
police cars. The driver has apparently long since
been removed and salvage operations have begun.
Such accidents are absorbed into a complex system
of law enforcement officials and rescue equipment.
The truck itself is part of the widespread and
enormous network of commercial U. S. trucking,
itself part of the world economy. And so the
circles go, ever-interconnecting, ever-widening.

Hick presents three such orders of situational
significance, "corresponding to the threefold division of the universe, long entertained by human
thought, into nature, man and God....In the case
of these three realms, the natural, the human and
the divine, a basic act of interpretation is required which discloses to us the existence of the
sphere in question, thus providing the ground for
our multifarious detailed interpretations within
that sphere." /40/

To take the physical world first, our conscious
experience of the physical world contains an
element of interpretation of which we are not normally aware and which we cannot justify by argument.
Even so, we have no reason to doubt the existence
of that physical world. Even Hume indicates that
nature has not left this as a matter of choice to
us, "We may well ask, What causes us to believe
in the existence of body (i.e. matter)? but t'is
vain to ask, Whether there be body or not? That

is a point, which we must take for granted in all our reasonings." /41/

Then there is the human world.. We live not merely in a physical environment, but also in a community of personal relationships with mutual responsibilities. "And so we find that presupposing consciousness of the physical world, and supervening upon it, is the kind of situational significance which we call 'being-responsible,' or 'being-under-obligation.' The sense of moral obligation, or of 'oughtness' is the basic datum of ethics." /42/ A precondition of moral obligation is "that there should be a stable medium, the world with its own causal laws, in which people meet and in terms of which they act." /43/

Hick points out that in this relationship between the physical world and the moral we are dealing with an epistemological paradigm, namely "one order of significance superimposed upon and mediated through another." /44/ He then goes on to ask whether the two first orders, the physical and the moral, mediate and interpenetrate the religious and whether, in turn, the religious interpenetrates the both of them? His answer to this question is that yes, they do.

Religious Significance

What exactly does Hick mean by religious significance? First, he sees it as "the believer's experience as a whole," /45/ a total interpretation that has nothing beyond itself. He offers the example of someone who wanders into a large room and hears a group of people planning a violent revolution and murder in loud screeching voices. Then just as he is about to run from the room to seek help, he notices that there are bright lights up in the ceiling and that off to one side can be seen a set of movie cameras. He has wandered into a movie set. Though at first he thought he was in a real situation, by comparing this to the context in which it is placed, namely the lights and stage of a movie set, he is able to switch what was a judgment about one kind of reality to another. In the case of religious interpretation, however, this is not possible, for life is not a movie set and there are no lights shining in upon it, or cameras photographing what is happening in the universe as a whole. There can be no context for what itself is context. In that sense religious interpretation is total interpretation.

Hick goes on to correlate this with the monotheistic faith. "The monotheist's faith-apprehension of God as the unseen Person dealing with him in and through his experience of the world is from the point of view of epistemology aninterpretation cf this kind, an interpretation of the world as a whole as mediating a divine presence and purpose." /46/

Just as moral living presupposes the physical world, religious significance presupposes the moral and physical worlds. Religion is not merely cognitional; it is a way of life _in_ the world. A clear vision of the divine purpose brings about obedience to the divine will in the whole of our lives.

This does not mean that we are in a constant state of religious awareness. Like moral perception, it arises only occasionally. In the earlier example of two persons riding in a car, it was pointed out that they were at the center of ever widening circles of significance. But widening circles cannot widen forever. They must eventually reach a limit and that limit is the religious, for it gives an ultimate significance to all the others. And because of this dimension of ultimacy it is perceived only from time-to-time as circumstances and personal sensitivity permit.

Hick concludes by saying, "The theistic

believer cannot explain <u>how</u> he knows the divine
presence to be mediated through his human experience. He just finds himself interpreting his
experience in this way. He lives in the presence
of God, though he is unable to prove by any dialectical process that God exists." /47/

Commentary

Hick's system is a powerful one, carefully
worked out. It merits the very serious consideration and interest that it has received in both
philosophical and theological circles. Excellent
as it is, however, there are certain areas where
it could be improved by following through a bit
more in depth.

It would have been helpful, for example, first
of all, to have made more of a distinction between
the awareness-limit as a religious experience and
revealed religion. Towards the end of the exposition there is a sudden shift from epistemological
and philosophical analysis to an explicitly theistic, even christian one. Though this is by no
means illegitimate, it does as a matter of fact
proceed so quickly that some helpful steps have
been omitted.

Second, though the epistemological position
presented is in line with that developed earlier
in this book, it is disappointing to find that
Hick's justificational arguments are presupposed
rather than developed. A case could be made of
course, that given the context of this section,
such a development would have led from the main
argument. But since the epistemological issue is
so absolutely basic, it would have been helpful
to have had it pursued a bit more in detail.

Third, though there is explicit stress upon
the experiential or non-cognitional in experience
and faith, the terms used, "significance and

interpretation," still retain strong cognitional and even intellectualistic overtones. While these terms have the advantage of clarity and Hick does explain their meaning carefully, once again it would have been helpful if this non-cognitional element had been presented a bit more fully.

Fourth, hough Hick's idea of mediation is promising and is close to the "multidimensional" discussed earlier, its rich connotations and connected questions are not pursued. It could legitimately be asked, for example, whether mediation is the same thing as interpenetration, and, if it is, how does this process work?

Faith and Reason in St. Augustine

After this extensive discussion of the Thomistic theory of faith and reason and its alternative proposed by John Hick, it is time to turn to that other towering figure in Christian intellectual history, St. Augustine. It is common knowledge that Augustinianism dominated Christian intellectual life until the turn of the millenium when it was gradually replaced by the medieval synthesis influenced by Aristotelianism and the gradual rise of the new science and the new society. This is not to say that its influence disappeared. It continued to be extremely important as the strongest intellectual alternative to scholasticism and its influence in the spiritual life of monasticism and other elements of church life continued strong. The Spiritual Excercises of St. Ignatious of Loyola, for example, written in the sixteenth century, are deeply impregnated by Augustinianism.

Michael Polanyi suggests that in dealing with the relation between Thomism and Augustinianism, we are dealing with a massive cycle of historical and intellectual change. He says that Augustine in his early years was interested in science as is clear

from the Confessions, but that the intellectual
pride of the science of his day led him to a negative attitude towards it. This negativity towards
natural science was influential in the Christian
community for centuries up until the early middle
ages. At that time, natural science in the West
began to stir itself into vigorous new life that
picked up momentum as the years went by. By the
time of the Renaissance, says Polanyi, "Augustine's
spell (was) broken in its turn by a gradual change
in the balance of mental desires. The secular
spirit, critical, extrovert, rationalist...revived
the scientific study of nature." /48/ Polanyi is
not belittling or bemoaning this change. He feels
it was a necessary and important turn in the broad
movement of cultural history. But he does add that
he feels that today the strength, vigor and origin-
ality of the rationalistic spirit has itself become
almost exhausted and that now a balance needs to be
restored so that there will be a harmonious coexis-
tence of man's volitional and cognitive faculties:
"I think that today, we can feel the balance of
mental needs tilting back once again" /49/ towards
Augustinian insights and foundations.

Aristotelian Intellectualism

Before turning directly to Augustine's theory
of knowledge, we will begin by summarizing the
Aristotelian intellectualism that characterized the
medieval and subsequent periods and which is assumed
in the Thomistic understanding of faith discussed
in the first part of this chapter.

In Aristotelian intellectualism, Being has
primacy over Good; the theoretical mind is more
important than the practical. Aristotle doesn't
totally rule out affection from the mind; on the
contrary, it is there, but it is there as a consequent not a prior determinant;

For Aristotle this is as it ought

to be, for the ideal of objectivity
is served if all preferences regarding
good or evil do not in the least direct
but rather are derived from antecedent
cognition of Being. Thus all desire of
appetition follows upon sensation,
opinion or thought (See <u>De An</u>, 431a 11
and <u>Met</u>.1072a 30). Aristotle safeguards
"pure truth" by rendering its acquisition
independent of "practical" considerations.
This is the ground of the subordination
of the practical to the theoretical
reason in Aristotle and generally in
Western thought. /50/

What is involved here is an ideal of knowledge
as the pure contemplation of Being. For Aristotle
the speculative mind is involved with the theoretical and interacts with the practical only insofar
as the practical offers objects to it for choice.

As we shall see, Augustine held for a dependency of
theoretical reason on practical reason, the reverse
of the above. In this he was following the Socratic-
Platonic tradition of sophia-wisdom, which integrated
the functions of practical and theoretical reason.
To Aristotelian intellectualism, including its
Thomistic version, <u>scientia</u> triumphs over <u>sophia</u>,
science over wisdom. "The will is in all cases
subservient to the intellect--the practical to the
theoretical reason. Here is the triumph of the
true over the good, of Being over value." /51/

Will is not of course completely excluded by
Aristotle. But its proper place is in what he
calls belief. "Not so with knowledge or even
opinion. In knowledge, Being is apprehended (or
not apprehended), and there is no place for preference or consent of will. When there is knowledge
or true opinion, it is because Being <u>prescribes
itself</u> necessarily." /52/ When this is applied
to faith and reason, it results in "a knife edge
distinction...locating them in noncommunicating

compartments." /53/

Augustinian Merger of Reason and Faith

Faith Factor in All Knowledge

Augustine, when faced in his own day with the burning question as to whether faith or reason provided the most helpful interpretation of the whole life and human existence, developed a solution, which all the while that it supported the faith standpoint as primary, nevertheless did not repudiate reason, philosophy or the universal. He felt that the classical ideal of <u>scientia</u> was insufficient for man's continued meeting of the meaning and trials of life and that for these <u>sophia</u> or wisdom was necessary.

His basic principle is that there is more to knowledge than logical abstraction:

> The principle may be stated simply.
> It is the doctrine of the primacy of the
> will in all knowledge. What is known
> cannot be divorced from what is loved.
> At the very minimum, all cognition is
> directly dependent on interest, and
> nothing is fully known to which the
> consent of the will has not been given.
> Yet there may be awareness of reality
> without completed cognition of that
> reality. The completion of cognition
> lies with affection. Thus full cognition
> is re-cognition. /54/

It is clear that in Augustine faith then does not take the place of reason; it serves reason. It sees reason as basically neutral or passive and needs to be directed towards recognition by the will or the mind's affections. Inadequate love means inadequate knowledge.

195

DISCLOSURE OF THE ULTIMATE

Reason and Illumination

Augustine never considers the mind in total
isolation. He sees it as part of a God created
universe in which the illuminating activity of
God is central. Because of this he speaks of
reason as that which makes man the image of God,
a phrase that finds particular favor among the
Fathers of the Church. It makes him into God's
image by allowing him to partake in some way in
God's nature.

> By it (reason), God has left a
> witness to Himself among the Gentiles.
> For even in man's fallen condition,
> his reason is exalted by the divine
> informing, so that God is the light
> by which are known whatsoever things
> are known, temporal or eternal. The
> Platonists are right: "the light of
> our understanding, by which all things
> are learned by us, they have affirmed
> to be the self-same God by whom all
> things were made. /55/

As the above quote indicates, Augustine is
heavily influenced by Platonic theories of illumination. He compares God as the inward illuminator
to the sun which lights up the world around us and
makes possible our certainties in daily life and
in the sciences. He talks of foundational categories of knowledge as being in his heart even
before he learned about them. "Inasmuch as the
(Platonic) forms constitute things what they are,
and yet are found only imperfectly in things, the
Platonists are correct that their apprehension
cannot be from experience; rather their apprehension
is the precondition of experience. /56/

This Augustinian dependence on Platonic categories need not be pursued further, though important

in itself. Augustine hurries to add that though we
may be enlightened by God, we may have difficulty
acknowledging this enlightenment. The light of
nature may as a matter of fact not clarify God for
us as much as obscure him.

St. Paul said, "Ever since the creation of the
world his invisible nature, namely his eternal
power and deity, has been clearly perceived in the
things that have been made." /57/ "But Augustine
does not interpret Paul as teaching that a knowledge of God may be had by a direct inspection of
the outward world. Rather he understands St. Paul
to mean that reflection upon nature has theological
value only for those 'who compare that voice
received from without by the senses, with Truth
which is within.'" /58/ Thus Augustine sees God
as abiding in man's mind or, to take a broader
term, his heart. He cannot be known or recognized
except by those who turn within themselves. Observing the external world in not enough. This
observation indicates that things are true, but by
turning inwards, man is able also to see that they
are good.

Reason Needs Faith

In Thomas Aquinas reason is autonomous, in
Augustine it is continuously illuminated by God.
But if this is so, then where in Augustine's
thought is there any need of faith. If God is
already there, who needs faith?

"The answer is that in spite of all he has
said to exalt the role of reason, Augustine's
pervasive insistence is that Jesus Christ, the
eternal Word incognito, disguised in the flesh, is
the principium or the beginning point of knowledge." /59/

He begins by saying that though man's reason
(God's image) may be weakened or defaced, it never

totally ceases to be. It is always there in man's
life. So when he urges a turn to Christ as a
source of authority, a historically conditioned
source for the universalistically inclined domain
of intellect, he is not demanding blind obedience
to authority:

> The function of authority is not
> primarily that of providing an impreg-
> nable ground of certainty for the
> doubting intellect. Nor is it that
> of propounding a datum which, because
> ex hypothesis it is unamendable to
> comprehension, must therefore command
> uncomprehending aquiescence of the mind.
> It is not that I must believe because
> reasoning is inherently incompetent.
> It is rather that my reason is incom-
> petent in virtue of the perversion of
> my will, so that I cannot understand
> until my pride and sinful will to
> independence is submissive to the
> Mediator--the eternal Word in the form
> of the Servant. /60/

The Incarnation for Augustine is not a universal truth that can be reached by rational reflection or deduction. It is a historical reality,
a datum. And it is a datum of the past. As such
it can only come to us by transmission through
something or someone, in this case Scripture and
the Church.

This dependency of reason on faith arises from
Augustine's conviction that reason depends on the
will and that the human will is corrupted in
practice. The implied order of progression, therefore, is not something superfluous. It is not a
question of believing and understanding it is
rather a question of believing in order to understand. The will is the determinative factor in
knowledge and since it is Christ who heals and
moves the will, Christ becomes the prime principle

198

of knowledge, the beginning place for a total interpretation of life and experience.

Knowledge and the Will

The last important element of Augustine's
thought in this area, is the relationship of the
will to knowledge and particularly the relationship
between faith and knowledge.

"Augustine perceived in the merely rational
approach to God an internal contradiction; it cannot reach God because it does not want to have God.
It withholds commitment until it has sight; but it
cannot achieve sight until it yields commitment.
The rational approach to God does not perceive that
it founders upon the original sinfulness of the
human heart." /61/

Augustine diagnoses this sinful condition as
a kind of ingratitude born of pride. It is out of
a love of domination and dominion that men use the
light that is given them by God to exploit creatures through an unbridled _scientia_ without bothering to give thanks to the light in return.
Idolatry for him is an awareness of God that does
not turn into a submission due to a perversion of
will. The paradoxes involved are explored in
depth in his _Confessions_ where he says that we do
not will fully enough to be with God and are content
to remain with creatures, and thus with ourselves.
But "In the case of God, as in the instance of all
other cognition, full knowledge waits upon desire
or love, It is appetition, love or will which
turns diffused awareness into true cognition." /62/

Thus Augustine holds, in contrast to Aristotelian intellectualism, that theoretical reason is
dependent upon practical reason for its operation
and direction. He integrates these two aspects in
sophia or wisdom, rather than dichotomizes them in
scientia.

DISCLOSURE OF THE ULTIMATE

The immoderate love of creatures, which turns men away from God rests upon self-pride. "Pride is the beginning of all sin," he says, "and the beginning of man's sin is a falling away from God." /63/ This pride means that he desires to be like God and this ultimately transformed into an attempt to be independent of God. Man would not flee from God, he claims, if he did not secretly love him, for he is aware deep down that to acknowledge this love and to develop it would be to him a loss of autonomy to God. This fear is groundless, concludes Augustine, for the Gospel teaches us that it is only by losing one's life that one finds it.

Finally, since the will and its sinfulness is the key problem, an emancipator is needed, and that is Christ, the Word made flesh. Because Christ moves the will to goodness and love, he becomes the source and principle of purification and knowledge. Once purified and humbled, the will is open to the truth and goodness of God that has always been present to reason. And all this happens in history, which becomes the "medium of revelation and instrumental to the fulfillment of knowledge. Time and change become, by the Incarnation, the vehicle of the eternal....What is _fides_? It is acknowledgement (_agnito_) of the Word in the form of the Servant. Pre-eminently, it is love awakened by the lowly form of the historical. It is fundamentally a motion of the heart. It is the conversion of the will through the crumpling of pride." /64/

Some Helpful Distinctions

John Smith suggests some helpful distinctions for understanding Augustine's position in the area of faith and reason. He says:

> Two pairs of distinctions are called for. To begin with, we must distinguish between understanding or intelligibility on the other hand

and proof or demonstration on the other.
Second, we must take note of the difference between activity or reason within
faith and that same activity as it
appears prior to faith. /65/

First with regard to the function of reason
within faith, Augustine clearly considered understanding a quest of intelligibility where finite
things lead the mind ot grasp things that transcend. This is not a question of inference or
rationality demonstrative proofs wholly founded in
the human. Augustine, as we saw, builds upon the
doctrine of illumination, where all understanding
is conditioned and made possible by the Uncreated
Light. Rather it is an emphasis on symbolism, or
the way these uncreated things can be signs of the
divine. Since the divine is beyond us, the only
way we can grasp it is to find likenesses and
similarities in our own experience. "This reflective and meditative approach, carried on by each
individual for himself, in which propositions are
related to each other, stands in contrast to
logical demonstration in which propositions are
related to each other in accordance with explicitly
stated principles quite apart from reference to
the experience of any individual person." /66/
This is the method used extensively, for example,
in Augustine's De Trinitate.

Yet if we do achieve understanding, this
understanding combined with faith must constitute
an advance over the previous state. The first
element of this advance is that it serves as a
spur for seeking after God. In other words, this
search after understanding is not one which leads
away from the faith object into a barren landscape
cf desolate speculation, it allows one not only
to remain in contact with this living power, but
to deepen one's appreciation and love. It is a
search for what, in one sense, Augustine says, we
already know. Understanding then, is not a

distraction away from God, but a stimulus towards him.

A second advance is that the believer discovers that there is an intelligibility to his faith. It allows a deeper penetration into life and the divine reality and keeps the believer from a mere acquiescence in authority.

Looking beyond the borders of faith, Augustine does, in one or two earlier works, speak of the priority of reason to faith, but this seems to mean nothing more than that man is a rational being to begin with and thus is able to understand the meaning and the process of "credo ut intelligam." In any case it is clear from the massive totality of Augustine's writings, that his fundamental conviction is that faith is necessary for understanding and not vice versa.

Some Qualifications

Smith goes on to evaluate this Augustinian position, assessing its strong points as well as its weaknesses. He says first that Augustine was "essentially correct," in his "insight that, while faith precedes reason, a living faith aware of itself in the world cannot remain dogmatic but must seek understanding." /67/ All faith is an understanding that is only beginning. There is much room for it to grow and deepen. The quality of faith is not changed, but there is much that can be added and interwoven into it to make it more aware and developed.

Second, he says that Augustine was correct in his view "that understanding means the discovery of the intelligibility of faith through similitudes, analogies and counterparts drawn from finite experience of the world and ourselves." /68/ There is more involved here then than mere clarification. It is an attempt to see how far faith and our extended experience coincide with or touch each other.

Also it is an attempt to show faith's relationship
to the rest of our knowledge. Faith is not purely
arbitrary; it does have its own inner logic and
consistenct; it is not unrelated to the rest of
man's life.

Inadequacies

Smith also points out that there are inade-
quacies in this approach. First Augustine never
"fully grasped the historical character of both
faith and reason, the historical character of the
revelatory content and the historical situation
in which it was received. Consequently, (his)
conception of reason was too narrow and not sufficiently responsive to change and development." /69/
As our cosmological view of the universe has changed,
so our understanding of reason has changed. We
no longer see reason as a kind of independent force
removed from the travail and dust of history. Even
Logic itself has changed considerably from the time
of Augustine. These changes need to be taken into
account.

A second difficulty is that Augustine did not
take seriously the full range of human experience.
One should not press this argument too much to his
disadvantage, since he obviously did not have the
cultural developments at hand that have characterized the Western thought since the period of the
Enlightenment and which came to a focus in the
classic Britich empiricists. For Augustine, experience remained very much an individual meditation
confined to the mind. He neglected the fact, so
well understood by modern culture that "Experience
has a social as well as a personal dimension.
Experience means being in the world; it involves
interacting with the world and it embraces all that
is ingredient in human community and history." /70/
This does not exclude reason. On the contrary,
without reason, experience cannot really speak.

It emphasizes rather that experience is the prior setting within which all understanding takes place.

With regard to the general problem at hand, the position of Augustine can be regarded as less precise that the later medieval developments on faith and reason exemplified by Thomism. There is undeniably a certain ambiguity present, and, as numbers of critics, particularly those with Thomistic inclinations, have pointed out, there are elements of both fideism and rationalism in Augustine's view of the relation of reason to the non-believer. Yet despite this ambiguity, from our contemporary perspective we can see that his position offers important advantages. By not dichotomizing reason and faith, they are kept in a state of living tension, a dynamic tension prevents one from being sequestered in the "natural" sphere and the other in the "supernatural."

When faith and reason are compartmentalized, "faith is awarded the mysteries of revealed theology beyond the competence of reason to discover or criticize, and to reason is awarded secular knowledge and the metaphysic of the natural intellect." /71/ These two spheres are related to each other in Thomistic thought by the fact that they are considered to have the same source in God who is truth and therefore cannot conflict with each other. However that may be, it cannot be denied that in this process sight has been lost of the believing self, reflecting. meditating and praying. It was this self, interpenetrated by faith and reason that was central to the Augustinian vision and which is obscured by the other. To make an analogical comparison, Temporal experience was replaced by spatial relationships. Logical hierarchy is clear, but the searching believer is obscured

At the same time, the criticism noted above indicates that it is not enough to resurrect the

Augustinian position in its pure form and expect it to be applicable today. If its basic vision is appreciated, it still requires considerable adapt- ation and modification.

Similarities between Augustine and Polanyi

Such an adaptation has been done by Michael Polanyi, whose theory of knowledge was discussed earlier. This is not to say that Polanyi was a theologian or that the main thrust of his work was Augustinian or a specific attempt to modernize Augustine's point by point. But the fact remains that Polanyi does refer to Augustine many times, indicating points of inspiration and agreement, even when he is presenting his own position. He says for example, "that although the critical movement, which seems to be nearing the end of its course today, was perhaps the most fruitful effort ever sustained by the mind...yet we must now go back to St. Augustine to restore the balance of our cognitive powers." /72/ In the same place he explixitly cites Augustine's maxim "Nisi cred- ideritis, non intelligitis," several times, thus confirming his own commitment to an Augustinian type of fiduciary epistemology." "A modern return to Augustine,"as he explicitly says," will restore the balance of our cognitive powers after three hundred years of skepticism: 'belief must be rehabilitated.'" /73/

The Premises

Polanyi, through the influence of modern psychology, is more aware of man's less articulate processes of learning based in our bodily nature. Precisely because this foundation of knowledge is physical, it can never be totally articulated. Embodiment, as was seen earlier, has a number of ramifications. It can be understood as primarily phys_cal in relation to the skills that we acquire. It can be understood as linguistic in the sense that we inherit a meaningful language. And it can be understood as systemic in the sense that we inherit coherent systems of thought which enable us to go on to new discoveries.

While Augustine uses the more traditional terms from faculty psychology, man's will and its quality of charity, Polanyi prefers the term commitment. He understands this commitment to be the force which directs us to seek satisfying and meaningful coherences in our lives. For both Augustine and Polanyi, truth implies desire and all our assertions have a passionate nature.

Learning

As was stated, Augustine describes the learning experience through two basic metaphors: illumination and recognition. Illumination he understands to mean a sudden sense of emerging coherence; and recognition for him means that this new sense of coherence occurs within a person who somehow "knew" it beforehand.

For Polanyi "human learning is also rooted in the function of an irreducible and active center in man which enables the illuminating integration of particulars into satisfying wholes." /74/ Here appears Polanyi's acknowledged debt to Gestalt psychology which sees meaningful integration occurring through a kind of sensible equilibrium. In discussing earlier the principle of marginal control, it was indicated that this integrative power of man cannot be reduced merely to a sum of parts. Account must be taken of the operational principles of the whole, which somehow surpass the sum of the parts.

Polanyi also speaks of the joy of illumination. This occurs when after wrestling with a problem the pieces suddenly fell together in a new way and a

206

solution or combination appears which shortly before
had gone unnoticed. This is a discovery and it
brings with it a certain satisfaction or joy.
It is both the driving impulse and the reward of the
quest for discovery. This is an example of what
Polanyi calls "tacit awareness". Because we go
from subsidiary clues to tacit awareness, "we know
more than we can tell."

Though, like Augustine, Polanyi stresses the
need for commitment and belief in order to know
and though this involves a reliance upon other
persons and the society of which we are a part, this
does not imply any kind of craven dependence. Blind
authoritarianism is held in check by the reality
which is the basis of subsidiary awareness and which
sends out its own authentic impulses.

While Augustine speaks of the need for "conversion" in order to really know, Polanyi speaks of
"the mental crises which may lead to conversion
from one set of premises to another" and which are
often "dominated by strong impulses of will-power."
/75/

Augustine speaks of aversion from good based
on the weakness and sinfulness of the will. Polanyi
speaks of "moral inversion". Due to historical
developments, moral inversion has led man "to deny
the reality of man's moral passions and of his transcendent aims and ideals." /76/ It is because man's
basic impulse cannot be crushed, only diverted,
that they turn to other objects with often tragic
results. Thus philosophical skepticism can be
"ultimately demoralizing." /77/

The Journey of Life

For Augustine life is a voyage home. The
contents of our knowledge find their significance
by referral to God in whom alone they find full

meaning. Thus he contrasts Jerusalem with Babylon.
Though the heavenly city of Jerusalem will not be
realized in time, yet one can belong to it spiritually. It is possible to live in Babylon and
belong to Jerusalem. "True citizenship is determined by the quality and direction of our lives."
/78/

Polanyi speaks of "the theological character
of learning" which is derived from the from-to
character of our knowledge, from the tacitly known
subsidiaries to the focal. "All meaning tends to
be displayed away from ourselves." /79/ All this
points "towards a deeper coherence which comes
only when individual meanings are subsidiary within ever-higher integrations." /80/ We go on
from them to higher and more absolute truths or
values which involve our commitment. The correca-
tion with religious knowledge is evident.

Polanyi also speaks of the ethical aspects
of the human community's pilgrimage through life.
It that society refuses to dedicate itself to
transcendent ideals, it leaves itself open to
servitude and decay.

Final Word

Incomplete as is this comparison between
Augustine and Polanyi, it does demonstrate at least
two things. One is the latent resourcefulness of
the thought of one of the greatest Christian
thinkers, which makes it possible for him, with due
allowances and modifications, to be relevant for
a new day and a new age. The other is the way that
Michael Polanyi, while undoubtedly influenced by
the Augustinian vision, has developed a highly
original heuristic approach of his own.

FAITH AND REASON IN AQUINAS AND AUGUSTINE

Conclusion

This chapter has moved dialectically. It
began with the classical Thomistic position on
faith and reason with its understanding of faith
as propositional. It then went on to the sympathetic but strong critique of John Hick, who developed
a theory of his own centered around an understanding of revelation as event. Then some criticism
of both Aquinas and Hick were offered. In the
second part of the chapter, an overall balance
was offered to Aristotelian Thomism through the
historically prior but still relevant system of
Augustine. It was suggested that the cultural
cycle has now swung full circle and that it is
time to revitalize the Augustinian approach with
its emphasis on belief. Such a resurgence implies
a number of developments and changes corresponding
to the cultural and spiritual developments of the
intervening years and especially of the twentieth
century. Michael Polanyi was seen as an example
of someone who is influenced by the Augustinian
system while at the same time developing a system
of his own particularly apt for our contemporary
situation.

This dialectic between Aquinas and Hick,
Augustine and Polanyi on the one hand and between
the first pair and the second is helpful in clarifying the very difficult relationship between faith
and reason and the lengthy history of theories
dealing with it. These theories have been incorporated into brief formulae which are well known
and which may serve as a helpful summary. It begins
of course with Tertullian's phrase, "Credo quia
absurdum," "I believe because it is absurd." This
is rejected by Augustine who says "Nisi credideritis
non intelligitis," "Unless you believe, you shall
not understand." In later centuries, especially
with St. Anselm of Canterbury, this same position
was refined to "Credo ut intelligam," "I believe

in order to understand." When it came to Thomas
Aquinas, it is difficult to turn a summary phrase
this neatly, but it has been suggested that "Intelligo et credo," "I understand and believe," is
a fair statement but that "Intelligo ut credam,"
"I understand in order to believe," is going too
far. Paradoxically enough, at the very moment
that the greatest emphasis is being placed on the
rationality of the preambles of faith, faith is
being described in terms with echoes oi Tertullian
(non provability). What this chapter and this book
is suggesting is that the earlier Augustinian
tradition with its emphasis on the priority of
faith, if properly adapted, can provide us with
the solution to a number of theological problems
that have become intrac_table in the light of
modern intellectual and cultural developments.
If it is not too presumptuous, I would like to
suggest an adaptation of the Augustinian formula,
influenced by Paul Ricoeur, that would go, "Credo
ut intelligam ut credam," "I believe in order to
understand in order to believe."

In the next chapter, we will try to gather up
these many threads concerning religious knowledge
and weave them together in somewhat more systematic
fashion.

FAITH AND REASON IN AQUINAS AND AUGUSTINE

NOTES

[1] *Faith and Knowledge* (Ithica: Cornell University Press, 1957070).

[2] Ibid., pp. 11-12.

[3] IIa IIae, QQ. 1-7.

[4] *Faith and Knowledge*, p. 13.

[5] K. Rahner, ed., *The Teaching of the Catholic Church*. Transl. G. Stevens (Staten Island, N. Y.: Alba House, 1966). "Vat. I: Dogmatic Constitution on Catholic Faith," Chapter III, 35, 3008: Faith, pp. 32-33.

[6] *Faith and Knowledge*, p. 14.

[7] *Summa Theologica*, IIa IIae, Q. i, art. 4.

[8] *Faith and Knowledge*, p. 17

[9] Canon George Smith, ed., *The Teaching of the Catholic Church* (N. Y.: Macmillan Company, 1949) Vol. I, p. 13

[10] *Faith and Knowledge*, p. 21

[11] Ibid., p. 21.

[12] Ibid., p. 23.

[13] Terence Penelhum, *The Problem of Religious Knowledge* (N. Y.: Herder and Herder, 1971)pp. 143-44.

[14] _Faith and Knowledge_, p. 27.

[15] Walter Abbott, ed., _The Documents of Vatican II_ (N. Y.: Guild-America Press, 1966), pp. 111-132.

[16] Ibid., p. 112.

[17] Joseph Ratzinger, _Commentary on the Documents of Vatican II_, transl. Doepel, Jakubiak, Simon and Erika Yound (N. Y.: Herder and Herder, 1969), p. 171.

[18] _Dogma. Const. on Divine Revelation_, p. 113.

[19] Ratzinger, op. cit., p. 175.

[20] Ibid., p. 175.

[21] _Dogm. Const._, op. cit., p. 113.

[22] Ibid., p. 113.

[23] Ibid., p. 114.

[24] Ratzinger, op. cit., p. 180

[25] Gabriel Moran, _The Theology of Revelation_ (N. Y.: Herder and Herder, 1966).

[26] Ibid., p. 34.

[27] Ibid., p. 37.

[28] Ibid., p. 24.

[29] Faith and Knowledge, op. cit., pp. 95-119.

[30] Ibid., p. 97.

[31] Ibid., p. 96.

[32] Ibid., p. 96.

[33] Ibid., p. 98.

[34] Ibid., p. 100.

[35] Ibid., pp. 101-102.

[36] Ibid., pp. 102-103.

[37] Ibid., p. 104.

[38] Ibid., p. 106.

[39] Ibid., p. 106.

[40] Ibid., pp. 107-108.

[41] David Hume, A Treatise on Human Nature (Oxford: Clarendon Press, 1888), Bk. I, pt. IV, sec.2.

[42] Faith and Knowledge, op. cit., p. 111.

[43] Ibid., p. 112.

[44] Ibid., p. 113.

[45] Ibid., p. 113.

[46] Ibid., pp. 114-115.

[47] Ibid., pp. 118-119.

[48] _Science, Faith and Society_ (Chicago: Chicago University Press, 1970), p. 26.

[49] Ibid., pp. 26-27.

[50] Roy W. Battenhouse, Ed. _A Companion to the Study of St. Augustine_ (N. Y.: Oxford University Press, 1955), "Faith and Reason," Chapter XI, p. 302. Aristotle reference: _De Anima_, 431a 11; _Metaph._, 1072a 30.

[51] Ibid., p. 303.

[52] Ibid., p. 303.

[53] John Smith, _The Analogy of Experience_ (N. Y.: Harper and Row, 1973), p. 3.

[54] Battenhouse, _Companion_, p. 289.

[55] Ibid., p. 292. Augustine quote: _De Civitate Dei_, VIII, 9.

[56] Ibid., p. 293.

[57] Epistle to the Romans, 1:20.

[58] Battenhouse, _Companion_, pp. 293-94. Augustine quote: _Confessions_, X, 6, 9.

[59] Ibid., p. 295.

[60] Ibid., p. 297.

[61] Ibid., p. 301.

[62] Ibid., p. 302.

[63] Augustine, In Johannis Evangelium Tractatus, (Opera Turnholti, Typogr. Brepols.), Vol. VIII, XXV, 15.

[64] Battenhouse, Companion, op. cit., pp. 307-309.

[65] John Smith, op. cit., p. 6.

[66] Ibid., pp. 6-7.

[67] Ibid., pp. 21-22.

[68] Ibid., p. 22.

[69] Ibid., pp. 22-23.

[70] Ibid., pp. 23-24.

[71] Ibid., p. 4.

[72] Polanyi, Personal Knowledge, op. cit., pp. 265-268.

[73] Patrick Grant, "Michael Polanyi: The Augustinian Component," New Scholasticism (48, Autumn, 74) 444. Polanyi quote: The Logic of Liberty (Chicago: Chicago University Press, 1951), p. 22.

[74] Grant, "Aug. Component," op. cit., p. 449.

[75] Polanyi, Science, Faith and Society, p. 67.

[76]Grant, op. cit., p. 454.

[77]Ibid., p. 455.

[78]Ibid., p. 457.

[79]Michael Polanyi, "Meaning: A Project," Draft for a lecture, 1961, p. 13.

[80]Grant, op. cit., pp. 457-458.

CHAPTER SIX

DISCLOSURE
OF THE ULTIMATE
AS LIMIT AND LOVE

Over the course of the preceding five chapters,
a number of methodological principles have been
discussed, some at length, some briefly. In this
chapter we propose to pull these together in a more
systematic fashion. This will give us as opportunity both to clarify some individual points and
to show how these principles are integrated among
themselves. We will proceed by offering three
major definitions followed by their analysis:
experiential knowledge, religious experiential
knowledge and Christian revelation. Though a
definition always leaves something to be desired
in the sense that it falls short of the fullness
of what is being defined, nevertheless it does
serve a useful purpose by delimiting a discussion,
offering some precision in terminology and allowing
point for point agreements and disagreements to be
noted more precisely. So that is how we will
proceed.

DISCLOSURE OF THE ULTIMATE

First Definition: Experiential Knowledge

This first definition, that of experiential knowledge, will be the briefest because it has already been treated at considerable length in our study of intersective realism. What we will not do is merely summarize the main points of the theory as an introduction to our definition and discussion of religious experiential knowledge. This then is the definition of experiential knowledge: <u>an encounter with a disclosing other through indwelling in a framework and the integration of its particulars into a coherent whole</u>.

The Name Itself: Experiential Knowledge

The word "experiential" can be understood on two levels. First, all our concrete experiences are specific, detailed and individual. We meet this person, we see this building, we walk on this street, we have this feeling. On the second level, however, the theoretical one, we are dealing with the abstract rather than with the concrete. Theories of experience are attempts to explain the nature and meaning of the specific, individual experiences. It is important to remember that theorizing about experience, such as we are doing here, can take place only by building upon the concrete experiences. The concrete and individual are paramount. They both precede and outlast theories about them. Nevertheless theorizing does have its usefulness in allowing us to gain added perspective and insight into what is limited by its very individuality.

The word "knowledge" is taken here in its general sense of cognitive awareness. By combining the two words then, the title experiential knowledge makes explicit two otherwise implicit aspects. It makes clear that experience is not to be considered as the domain of sense in contrast to thought, any

more than knowledge is to be considered the domain
of thought in contrast to sense. Experiential
knowledge is the knowledge of a living, human
person. It has a wholeness to it. It goes beyond
reaction to response.

Encounter

The term encounter refers to the <u>intersection</u>
in experience between reality and a self conscious
knower. Obviously it demands the co-existence of
a knower with the known and the ability of the
knower to stand over against it. It also refers to
the existence of a reality which is there to be
known or experienced. Such a view of experience
is closer to that of Piaget than to that of Descartes
as was disclosed earlier. The encountering movement
is not of an isolated consciousness moving out to
a public world. What begins in private ends in
private. At the pre-theoretical level, the distinction between subject and object is not operative.
Only after there has been encounter after encounter
does the self, through reflection, begin to discover
itself.

Experience at every stage of its
development from the simplest to the
most complex retains its basic nature
as <u>encounter</u>; and encounter always
involves the one who experiences and
the what of experience. Experience
is at the very least a dyadic affair
and it is even possible that it is
irreducibly triadic in character, but
it is certainly not monadic in the
sense of being bare, sensible content.
Unless experience is understood as
relation to a world encountered beyond
the self at the outset, there is no way
out of the closed circle or mental life
to a reality beyond. /1/

Encounter should not be discussed or analyzed too atomistically. In practice it functions through repetitiveness. The world is not totally lucid; there is a quality of opaqueness about it and life. This opaqueness cannot be pierced all at once. Time is needed. Only repeated encounters in time allow us to see the many faceted fullness of things. This temporal, cumulative aspect of encounter has to be considered very much a part of it. As a matter of fact, when we use the term "experienced" to describe a person, what we usually mean is that that person has done or experienced something frequently enough to have refined it, clarified it and made its repetition in the future both feasible and reliable. Having done or seen something many times, that person is said to be experienced.

This does not imply that all encounter is done on a purely individualistic basis, any more than the experienced person can be said to be one who has learned what he knows entirely by himself. An experienced person is also very much the one who has been able to learn from the accumulated experience of others in an intersubjective process.

Disclosure

Disclosure is the other side of the coin of encounter. The process of knowing involves both encounter and disclosure as two partners. Encounter refers to man's role, disclosure refers to the role of what is known. There is even a way in which this disclosive aspect of reality can be called transcendent, for the known transcends the individual attempting to know it. It has its own capacities and qualities and these enter into the dimension of experience. This does not mean total passivity on the part of the knower, as is sometimes implied by scientifically inclined theories, but rather an openness by means of which the self acknowledges these aspects of the known. The

differing aspects in what is encountered can be
called dimensions of reality. These are the different ways of understanding what is encountered.
These dimensions of reality are very much a part
of experience. "Experience is...an _intersubjective_
way of meeting reality which issues in the funded
result of many encounters, whereby it is disclosed.
That funded result, in the form of qualities, relations, events, purposes, meanings is a genuine
disclosure of the real world." /2/

Other

This one word "other" sums up the dialogical
or intersubjective nature of experience. It emphasizes that experience is a disclosure-encounter
from/with a reality which is there to be known.
The word other is chosen as deliberately ambiguous.
It does not distinguish between things and persons,
or between relations and meanings. All of these
are others which involve a disclosure or encounter
with an experiencing person.

Indwelling as a Framework

This second half of the definition, influenced
by Polanyi's theory of personal knowledge, goes
deeper into how the encounter-disclosure process
takes place.

The word "indwelling" adapts "the traditional
epistemological axiom that all knowledge comes
through the senses, by modifying it slightly to say
that all thought has a bodily basis. This implies
that all articulations by men are dependent upon
inarticulate powers or faculties." /3/ Another
way of describing this inarticulateness is to say
that we knowmore than we can tell. Man is dependent upon personal criteria that he cannot fully
define.

DISCLOSURE OF THE ULTIMATE

Through our bodies, then, we gain a measure of control over our environment. Our bodies integrate the internal experiences of objects outside themselves into a focal comprehension even when we are not aware that this is happening.

Indwelling can be pursued a step further to our use of tools. Just as we dwell in our bodies and integrate particulars into wholes, so we can indwell in a tool. By our focusing on the activity which the tools was designed to accomplish, the tool begins to function as an extension of ourselves. As we use it, we can be said to indwell in it.

Pursuing this one step further, we can also be said to indwell in intellectual frameworks. In order to understand history, we dwell in the conceptual framework of history. In order to deal with the world, we indwell in a conceptual framework of the world. The process is the same as the indwelling in our bodies or in a tool. Through it we are able to interiorize certain elements of our experience in order to arrive at a focal awareness of them as a whole.

All this can be compared to a skillful performance. All skillful performances involve the whole person and not merely a part of him. Thus we are involved as a whole in our knowing because knowing is something we do rather than something we have. Encounter, as above, is another way of putting this activity of the whole person. Though there may be rules involved, in the performance of a skill, the one who is acting does not avert to these rules. As a matter of fact, attending to the rules of a skill while performing it can have disastrous results, as any over-self conscious golfer can testify. A skill is best performed when awareness shifts from the particulars or the details to the overall action, from the details of "keeping you eye on the ball," to just jetting close to the green with a nice smooth swing.

DISCLOSURE OF THE ULTIMATE AS LIMIT AND LOVE

There is a tacit ground of particulars operative
in such skillful performance and, in principle,
this tacit ground underlies all our knowing.

Above and beyond the personal involvement of
the knower in the shaping of his knowledge, there
are social ramifications in the acceptance of an
articulate framework of indwelling. This is so
because articulate frameworks are not ethereal
abstractions, but expressions of concrete societies.
A framework involves the acceptance, sharing and
cultivation of common cultural passions and ideals.
All our efforts at communicating with other people
are based on sharing a common framework. This is
true even when it has not developed into articulate
language. And if this is true of the relationship
between individual persons, it is equally true of
the relations involved in general cultural activity:

> The acceptance of a cultural
> framework thus operates in much the
> same way as the recognition of a
> problem. In the latter case our
> heuristic intimations of a new reality
> are activated by our tacit awareness of
> the particulars on which we are beginning
> to rely in order to strain our imagin-
> ation for an eventual focal and explicit
> coherence leading to insight and dis-
> covery. So too, a novice in the cultural
> life of a society tacitly relies on the
> premises, standards, values, andoptions
> implicit in that culture in order to
> make them a part of himself and by so
> doing to view reality from that vantage
> point. /4/

While all this may clarify the fact that both
the one who encounters and the disclosing other
have to be seen in the broader context of their
situations in the world with all the multiple
relations involved, the further point added here
is that many of these relations and subsidiary

elements are necessarily operative in all acts of knowing because the knower cannot help indwelling in them any more than he can help indwelling in his own body and its largely unnoticed processes.

Second Definition:

Religious Experiential Knowledge

With the meaning of experiential knowledge briefly restated, the following is a working definition of religious experiential knowledge: <u>it is an encounter through indwelling and integration with an ultimate other which discloses itself both as the limit of all knowledge and of all life and thereby as the holy object of supreme worth to be worshipped and as the revealer through history of its reality and nature</u>.

Structure of the Definition

Before examining the definition in detail, it is important to point out the integral logic of its structure. It has two main parts: the first dealing with the process of encounter, the second with the object of encounter and the way this object, the ultimate, doscloses itself. The second part has three divisions of its own, or better, three disclosures. The first is the disclosure of the ultimate as the limit of all knowledge or the condition for all knowledge. The second is the disclosure of the ultimate as the limit of life, or that towards which man tends as he searches for a meaning to human existence and in so doing focuses upon a supreme object worthy of worship. Taken together, these two form what is called the religious dimension of experience. This is as far as man can go by himself. The third part is the disclosure of the ultimate as the revealer of itself in history. This is revelation and the basis of concrete, historic

224

religion. It takes place on God's initiative and is the response to the only partially satisfied quest involved in the religious dimension of experience.

As will be discussed later a bit more fully, there is both continuity and discontinuity implied among the three disclosures in the second part of the definition. There is continuity in that the human process of encounter through experience is the same for all three disclosures, for experience is the only medium through which men can know. There is discontinuity in the sense that the religious dimension of experience is a quest for an ultimate which is forever beyond its grasp. In revelation, the ultimate responds to that search by making itself known as concerned and loving. Though even this last is known through the same kind of encounter thatman generally experiences, this does not mean that revelation is thereby diminished, cheapened or humanized. It still comes from beyond man.

First Part of the Definition

After the brief review of experiential knowledge above, there is no need to go over these same elements in the first part of the definition of religious experiential knowledge. The perspective remains the same.

Second Part of the Definitions: The Disclosures

First Disclosure:

The Ultimate as the Limit of All Knowledge

We shall examine three aspects of this first disclosure of ultimacy: the cultural framework and commitment through which we know the world. the intellectual passions which give us a drive to understand which is objective and universal in intent, and the tacit foreknowledge of reality which grounds every judgement.

The Cultural Framework and Commitment

As was explained above, our knowledge functions through the use of intellectual frameworks which "provide the conditions for our application of explicit methods, norms, axioms and the like. They form the general ontological conceptions implicit in any given intellectual inquiry. We know this world in an explicit way by thinking <u>through</u> them, not <u>about</u> them. As such they are not, indeed cannot be, the subject of explicit, formal demonstration." /5/

Implicit in all this is an element of limit on the knower. It is a place where the personal and the universal meet.

> We have seen that the thought of truth implies a desire for it, and is to that extent personal. But since such a desire is for something impersonal, this personal motive has an impresonal intention. We avoid these seeming contradictions by accepting the framework of commitment, in which the personal and the universal mutually require each other. Here the personal comes into existence by asserting universal intent, and the universal is constituted by being accepted as the impersonal term of this personal commitment. /6/

Thus the personal act of knowing includes an element of limit. This is found in the responsibility that the person must excercise in judgements about reality. A framework selects certain elements from the chaotic flow of experience. Acceptance of a framework's premises is a commitment to them

226

that allows them to function. Such a commitment
involves responsibility towards the framework's
"truth". That is, they are being relied upon as
adequate for the understanding of those aspects of
reality that are being examined. The flow of
reality is thus limited by the need to affirm the
truth of those particular aspects of it that are
seen in the light of an intellectual framework to
which the knower is committed. This can be called
truth "even when the truth affirmed is contingent
and provisional, not absolute or necessary," for
all demands of rationality have been met, /7/

The Intellectual Passions

and Their Universal Drives

The second aspect of this first disclosure of
ultimacy is what can be called our intellectual
passions. These are the forces which drive us
to try to understand objectively and universally.
Acting heuristically, they lead us to select certain
things and values, and, alternately, to avoid
others. As such the are cognitive, part of man's
constant drive towards universality in knowledge,
not all is possible and not all is knowable. The
intellectual passions both limit and open up man's
way of knowing. For they limit as they focus upon
certain aspects in a framework, but also open up
in that the framework itself can lead us in universal directions.

The Tacit Foreknowledge of Reality

Grounded in Every Judgement

The third aspect of the first dimension of
ultimacy is the tacit foreknowledge of reality
which grounds every judgement. It is also the most
important. To understand the dimension of ultimacy
functioning as the condition for our being able to

227

know, it is necessary to begin by returning to the idea of knowledge as discovery, for as was said earlier, the knowledge of a good problem leading to a new discovery is the paradigmatic example of knowledge.

Any searcher, scientific or otherwise, is urged on by a vague knowledge of coherence ahead. This impetus of a dynamic intuition or potentiality is usually described as a problem, not in the work-stopping, negative sense of that term, but in the positive, work-inducing sense. To put it another way, what we are dealing with is a tacit foreknowl-edge of things as yet undiscovered. In this sense, it is cognitive.

The searcher or discoverer comes into contact with the dimension of ultimacy as the condition of knowledge through this foreknowledge of the reality he is after. Such a process has been described earlier, as a "from-to" process, which presupposes just such a tacit foreknowledge of the real.

How does all this apply to the religious dimension? By linking religion with this dimension of ultimacy as the foundation of knowledge. As was seen, this dimension is not comprehended as an object in the way that we would comprehend some specific object. It is experienced rather as a condition allowing us to affirm the truth of any-thing. As we dwell in an articulate framework and strive towards something, we have a tacit foreknowl-edge of it. Because it is very much a part of the way of human knowing, all men can come to a provis-ional understanding od specific entities through this dimension of ultimacy, it can be said that in a broad and very general sense, all men are relig-ious. This meaning obviously is wider and deeper than the general sense of the term. But what is being referred to is the general human situation, the overall way of human knowing, and not to any specific actualization of this capacity for the ultimate. If history is understood as an ever

228

more comprehensive discovery of reality, then there
must be a term towards which man is drawn. Since
this dimension of ultimacy overarching the world
of specific events is understood as sustaining
every act of understanding of the real, then it can
be said to be operating religiously.

Such an equation of the religious or sacred
with the real is found throughout the history of
religion. "In any concrete historical religious
tradition, the sacred, no matterhow it is conceived,
is that which is real un the ultimate sense and that
from which all other actions and entities derive
their meaning and reality." /8/

How does this operate? Its structure can be
better perceived by returning to the idea of framework. As has been said, the knower reaches what is
known through indwelling in a framework. This makes
it possible for him to integrate its particulars
into a coherent whole. When the knower has to deal
with a reality on a higher level of existence, say
going from a rock to a machine, he has to go to a
higher level of indwelling as well.

"Religious faith is to be understood as that
form of indwelling which has as primary goal the
breaking out toward the transcendent source of the
experience of ultimacy. It strives to break out
of the limited horizons which any form of indwelling imposes in order to contemplate directly that
which is experienced tacitly in ordinary acts of
knowledge as the dimension of ultimacy." /9/

The efforts of the mystic are focused precisely
in this direction, to somehow bypass the world of
limited objects and come in direct contact with the
unlimited ultimate. As any perusal of mystical
literature shows, such a process is largely negative in method and achievement. It is by "peeling
the onion" of created objects, that one begins to
get closer to the uncreated core of all. Such a
process has been described as a "via negativa."

Both the experience of the mystic and the explanation of the way the human mind unfolds in its tacit reliance on the dimension of ultimacy lead us to a non-knowledge, a lack of positive signification of this dimension of ultimacy.

The reason why we arrive at this negative result lies in the very nature of the cognitive process we have been describing. If our tacit foreknowledge of the real which urges us on in the process of discovery is what provides a concrete foundation of our specific judgements, then that real itself cannot become an object of understanding. Though the analogy limps a bit, this is like being able to see something only through a special kind of glass which is itself totally transparent. We cannot see anything outside without it, yet we cannot see it in itself.

We dwell in a framework whose ultimate horizon is reality. Since it is our reliance on this horizon that makes our understanding possible, and since this horizon is experienced as a dimension of ultimacy, than it can be known only tacitly and never focally. All this is another way of saying that man's conceptual systems are limited to this world as the only commonly shared object of experience. The sacred is something which transcends our world and therefore it cannot be taken up into a human conceptual system in the way that other things in the world can. It is not a thing and does not share "existence" with them in the same sense. More of this in chapter seven.

Marechal and Rahner

Much of the above is undoubtedly unfamiliar language for many Roman Catholics. It might be helpful, therefore, to supplement the discussion by looking briefly at the ideas of two influential Roman Catholic thinkers, one a philosopher, Joseph

230

DISCLOSURE OF THE ULTIMATE AS LIMIT AND LOVE

Maréchal, the other a theologian, Karl Rahner, both
of whom deal with the problem of the relationship
between the intellect and the absolute. Though
their works are, for the main, engaged in a dialogue with the Kantian tradition, their theories,
especially those of Maréchal, make a helpful comparison to our considerations so far.

Maréchal's first criticism of Kant deals with
Kant's two antinomies between sensibility and understanding and between understanding and reason.
"According to Maréchal, the human intellect is both
an empirical faculty and a possibility for the
absolute." /10/ While it is true, he claims, that
every judgement does, as Kant says, express a synthesis of the sensibly given, this should not be
restricted to the purely categorical. The human
intellect has a relationship to the absolute. And
if the human intellect has this possibility of
reaching the metaphysical order of the absolute,
then it must already be in that order. That is the
reason why he titled his major work,"Le Point de
départ de la métaphysique." /11/

A second criticism of Kant by Maréchal is the
way Kant ignores the dynamic aspects of human knowing and places too great an emphasis on its static
aspects. For Kant, human knowledge is comprised
of motionless forms regulating sensible matter and
their constituting objects. Whereas for Maréchal,
the starting point is quite different. "He begins
with the object-oriented act of knowing, the imma-
nent unity of subject and object in the act of the
knower in terms of being." /12/ Maréchal is not
confusing the intentional and real orders, he is
merely trying to show how the representational
order sinks its roots into the real through an act
of knowing which has a finality to it. This finality is a dynamic relationship to the whole of
being. Thus the mind is directed not merely to
space and time, but to the wholeness of being, all
the while that it is dependent on the sense given

231

through the a priori operation of the understanding on the phantasm. This dynamism of the human mind towards the totality of being is called by Maréchal, "une sorte d'anticipation metaempirique." /13/ Though this totality of being cannot be conceptualized, it can be reached through analogy.

Maréchal's third difference with Kant is that he cannot accept Kant's characterization of such an intellectual dynamism as merely a subjectively postulated ideal. Maréchal sees it rather as an objective reality, necessary and absolute. Rather than dichotomizing the object of knowledge, Maréchal looks upon it as a whole containing both intellect and will, theoretical and practical reason in a unified human knower. "Because willing depends for its goals on understanding, intellect maintains a priority. But because understanding depends on the subjective human dynamism, the will has its own priority. And in the order of willing it is impossible to desire a pure abstraction," /14/ For Maréchal then, the total goal of such intellectual dynamism is nothing else than transcendent, infinite, absolute being.

Comparing Karl Rahner briefly to Maréchal, we see that there are strong resemblances, with some individualistic differences. Rahner too is dialoguing with the Kantian tradition and one of his major concerns is to reach in some implicit way being itself.

Rahner's basic principle is the unity of knowing and being or being as self-presence. He too begins with the knowing subject, "The question is a metaphysics of knowledge is not that of a bridge between the subject and the object of knowledge, the problem of 'intentionality', but rather the conditions of possibility for human knowledge of the 'other'." /15/

DISCLOSURE OF THE ULTIMATE AS LIMIT AND LOVE

Maréchal emphasized the act of knowing and the
lived out implications of the mind's activity, whereas Rahner analyzed "performance knowledge" (Wissen-
svollzug) rather than concepts. Both deal with the
pre-conceptual world of experience and see the task
of knowledge as making what is implicit explicit,
of thematizing what is unthematically "known". Noth
see the implicit affirmation of being in judgement:
Marechal by "metaempirical anticipation," Rahner
by "Vorgriff" cr the pre-apprehension of being itself, simultaneously affirmed in the knowledge of
the concrete object. Marechal proceeds by means
of a transcendental analysis of human knowing, Rahner
through a phenomenological description of the relationship between being and knowing. Though there
are important differences in their starting points,
there are startling similarities in their conclusions and though they approach these questions from
the point of view of transcendental analysis, we
find an interesting convergence with the conclusions
reached earlier concerning the ultimate as the
condition of all knowledge.

Second Disclosure:

The Ultimate as the Limit of Life

The Whole Person

This bring us to the second aspect of the first
part of the disclosure of ultimacy as stated in the
definition: the ultimate as the limit of life. This
is an enigmatic and cryptic statement and needs elu-
cidation. A preliminary remark is that when we talk
anout religious experiential knowledge, we are
talking about the experience of the whole person.
One of the important elements of a stress upon the
experiential in these matters is that it allows as
to go beyond the merely conceptual to what is truly
human and comprehensive. The human person, in the
old psychology, had two major faculties, the intellect and the will. Though an oversimplification

233

in the light of the complexities of the human psyche uncovered by modern insights, it nevertheless remains true to say that man has a cognitive and a conative side, and that both, with their attendant complexities, are necessary for the fullness of the human.

When we spoke above about the ultimate as the limit of knowledge in the sense that it was the condition for all knowledge and that religion was to be understood as a reaching out or a breaking out towards that dimension of the ultimate, we were speaking about man's cognitive side. Without implying that such a dichotomy exists that man's conative side has no cognitive aspects, or vice versa, we must look at the dimension of ultimacy also from its conative side if we are to be true to the reality of human existence and the nature of the ultimate itself.

The Searching for Meaning

Only man can ask about the purpose of life. Only man can look at the wholeness of existence and ask what it means. This is both man's glory and man's pain. Down through history, this fundamental question about the purpose of life has occurred and reoccurred both for individuals and for communities. It is a question that stays with man. Sometimes it slumbers beneath the surface. Sometimes it is drowned in materialistic excesses, but, inevitable, it creeps to consciousness during those quiet moments of life that can be no more avoided than breathing. It is a question about the quality of existence rather than its quantity. It is not a theoretical question such as a scientist might ask about the relative weight of two substances, it is an agonizing existential question about the meaning of yesterday, today and tomorrow. It is the kind of question that demands an answer, no matter what shape that answer may take.

234

DISCLOSURE OF THE ULTIMATE AS LIMIT AND LOVE

The Holy and the Profane

In the second chapter of this book, the holy
and the profane were discussed along with a number
of historical and symbolic expressions of the holy.
It is now time to consider the holy once again from
the point of view of the ultimate as limit in man's
search for meaning.

We continue to use the words holy and profane
in preference to sacred and secular because over
the years sacred and secular have been forced to
carry a heavy freight of valuational implication
which makes them less useful. Secular is often
seen as a fighting word used by religious apologists engaged in attacking certain aspects of
contemporary society. Sacred, on the other hand,
can mean at times little more than that something
is highly valued. The words holy and profane are
less touched by these shortcomings.

"The key to understanding the holy in experience is to be found in the contrast between the
ordinary activities of human life-waking, nourish-
ing ourselves, working, replenishing our energy
through taking rest and recreation, and those
special times or junctures in life that are set
apart from the ordinary course of events and
'celebrated' as having some peculiar significance
about them." /16/ Those special times that are
set apart are not hard to find: being born, initia-
ted into adulthood, growing up, choosing a way of
life, being married, having children, being sick,
having birthdays, dying.

The word celebration in relation to these
"set-apart" events is not meant in the sense of
merry-making, though this does accompany some of
these occasions. It is meant in the broader sense
of being "awed, fascinated, and even overpowered
by the special events as a result of acknowledging

235

that they are times when a sense of the mystery of all being and of one's own being is forced upon us." /17/

Through such celebrations we mark off the event in our lives, retain it in our memories and provide ourselves with the elements for re-celebrating it ritually at some later time. Even though they have a once-and-for-all character, which is what impresses them upon us in the first place, they have such a universal dimension, such a depth of meaning and importance that they call for a kind of memoralizing which allows them to continue their unique influence in our lives even after the actual occasion itself has passed.

Another word for such an occasion is "crisis". For it is through crises that the purpose of human existence comes to the fore. At such moments we are forced to pause amidst the myriad details of our daily routine in order to take a look at life as a whole. Even the most joyful of these crises involve an element of judgement, or overarching importance, leading us to become aware of both our personal limitations and the limitations of mankind. Such limitations involve, conversely, dependence upon one another and our mutual dependence upon something ultimate beyond ua all. In certain primitive religions these moments of crisis are considered "dangerous" times, for these are moments when our lives come close to the vast precipice of the ultimate.

Profane life, on the other hand, even when it is exciting, such as a football game or a battle, holds no such aura of wholeness, awe or mystery. It is just ordinary day-to-day experience such as going to work, shopping, eating, etc. It is the profane which makes up most of our lives. Like the Bourgeois Gentilhomme, we have been "living profanely" all our lives without being aware of it. This is in no way derogatory, for we cannot look down

236

upon what constitutes the bulk of our lives.

In these ordinary times we are not bothering about the meanin, of our lives as a whole. We are not experiencing a sense of mystery, or looking for an answer to the riddle of life. We are simply going about our daily business.

"The basic relation between the holy and the profane may be summed up by saying that the holy provides the final purpose, giving point and poignancy to all the details of profane existence, while the profane is the body of life and the medium through which the holy is made fully actual." /18/ Profane life without the holy would be materialistic, with our attention focused upon limited horizons and objects. And the holy without the profane would become a kind of "spirit" world inconnected with the human realities of life. Thus life consists of an interrelationship between the holy and theprofane. The autonomy of ordinary life must be protected, while the crucial events of life cannot be allowed to be bypassed if they has no wider significance.

In conclusion, then,

At such times /man/ is led to ponder the purpose of existence as such. The crucial times, moreover, force an awareness that man is a dependent being, that he is not self-sustaining, and that he needs to find an object of supreme worth to which he can devote himself if he is to achieve self-realization. This threefold awareness to which we are led represents, from the side of purely human experience, the material of the religious dimension. /19/

237

DISCLOSURE OF THE ULTIMATE

The Holy as God

In our discussion so far, we have been attempting to show that man experiences the ultimate as limit not merely on his cognitive side as the condition for all knowledge, but also on his conative side as holy object of supreme worth on which he is dependent.

For, as we saw, the experience of crisis leads man to an awareness that he is not self-sustaining, that he is limited and dependent upon the holy as an object of supreme worth to which he must devote himself in order to achieve full self-realization. Man is attracted towards a vaguely understood absolute while remaining acutely aware of the intrinsic limitations and weaknesses that keep him from getting closer to the ultimate. Man is standing on a plain looking towards the snowy heights of a sacred mountain, knowing both that he is irresistibly drawn to the top yet cannot reach it by his own forces.

Knowing that he is called to the top despite the difficulties, man expects a deliverance. He is like a prince carried off in childhood, who knows from deep within himself and from the actions of those with whom he dwells, that his dim aspirations for a return to a kingly home can be realized only if help can come, and he is sure it will, from across the distant planes of time and space.

What we are dealing with here is the question of the meaning of life. It is important to point out that methodologically speaking, before we can say that God is the answer, we have to say that the answer is God. For God is perceived precisely as an answer to man's limitations and problems, as the holy who can somehow make up for man's deficiencies. One reason why so many people have difficulty handling the God-question is that they deal with

238

God primarily as a concept and do not see him in this intensely experiential context. All of which raises questions of course about the "existence" of God, and we shall take these up in the next chapter.

So far, then, whether we look at man from the cognitive side, where the ultimate is perceived as the necessary ground of all knowledge, or whether we look at man from the conative side, where is the crises moments of life, man experiences both his own limitations and his need for deliverance with the help of a holy who as God is the answer to man's quest and worthy of worship, we remain within what we have called the religious dimension of experience. This somewhat vague experience needs something more. And that more can be known only through an initiative from the supreme object of worship, from God himself. The initiative is what is known as revelation and its result as revealed religion. This we shall examine shortly in detail, but before doing so, we need onefurther conceptual clarification of all this.

A Natural Desire for the Supernatural?

We have examined in some detail man's quest for the ultimate both as the ground of all knowledge and as the limit of life focussing upon the ultimate as the supreme object of worship. We have suggested and will develop shortly the idea that the revelation that underlies positive religion is God's response to this quest. Both the quest and the revelational fulfillment are such vast and complex realities that it is easy to skip over the further question of clarifying their mutual interrelationship in some conceptually satisfying way. Would man still be man, for example, if his striving towards the ultimate did not have some genuine possibility of fulfillment? Would man still be man if his quest for the ultimate could never be achieved because there was no

239

response of any kind? If God does respond to man's search across the barriers that divide man from God, is God diminished? If man has this need, does this need diminish him? Would not man be greater if he could stand totally on his own two feet and not have the slightest dependence on something that seems to be greater than he? If God is seen as responding to man's real needs, does this reduce a God to something merely humanistic or psychological?

The Roman Catholic theological tradition, particularly of the last century or so, has been highly influenced by the massive theological architectonic of St. Thomas Aquinas. In more recent years it has been more accurately called neo-Thomism.

There are many problems and difficulties connected with dependence on one theological thinker or tradition, no matter how great, but there is no need for going into those now. There are advantages as well. Among them are historical continuity, a certain juggernaut courage in tackling the most complex and paradoxical questions and a precision of conceptual language. When faced with the contemporary existentialist claim, for example, that man must be completely autonomous and is at his greatest when asserting his integrity in the face of a meaningless universe, few theological systems try to tackle this theoretical question head on: is man greater for being dependent for his fulfillment on the infinite, or is he greater if he tries to find total fulfillment in himself, even if this means the fulfillment of despair?

Surprisingly, St. Thomas did not hesitate to plunge right into this question, though the cultural framework and terminology needs some adaptation to the modern problematic. The first translation needed concerns the terms "natural and supernatural". A whole treatise could be developed on the history and meaning of these terms. But for our purposes we can prescind from the medieval cosmology that is imbedded in them and see them as equivalent to "human and ultimate." The thrust of the argument remains the same when the terms are used in that sense.

A contemporary Thomist scholar sums up St. Thomas' position in this area in the following way:

> The teaching of the Doctor Communis can be summed up in the following way. On the one hand, St. Thomas maintains with remarkable vigor and clarity the supernatural and gratuitous character of the end towards which man is ordained. He often repeats that man's natural forces do not suffice for his attaining that end, or even to know and desire it. On the other hand, in several places he affirms with no less vigor and precision the existence of a natural desire to see God. /20/

If we phrase the question in Thomistic terms as that of a "natural desire for the supernatural," we find that a number of theologians or Thomistic commentators of the Renaissance period denied that there was any such natural desire in man. And despite the fact that for several preceding generations of commentators, Thomas had been interpreted as saying that there was. The main opposing figure was Cajetan and his argument ran thus: a natural desire calls for a natural object, so if nature plants a desire in man then man must be able to satisfy it. Since the supernatural is obviously beyond man's powers, then nature cannot give man a desire for it. The underlying concern of this argument is to protect the supernaturality and gratuity of grace or God's relationship to man. In other words, at this period they were more concerned about protecting the greatness of God and his ways with the world than in pursuing an in-depth analysis of the implications of all this for

241

Christian anthropology. Their concern is a legitimate one, but St. Thomas himself, as we shall see, felt that it could be met just as well without overnarrowing man's powers of openness or man's dignity.

Thomas was quite aware of the problem. This is how he poses it to himself in the Summa: "Man's natural desire does not reach out to a good surpassing his capacity. Since then man's capacity does not include that good which surpasses the limits of all creation, it seems that man can be made happy by some created good. Consequently some created good constitutes man's happiness." /21/

In another of his works, The Trinity and the Unicity of the Intellect, St. Thomas poses the same problem in a somewhat different way,

> Anything that is naturally
> ordained for some end possesses
> certain predisposing principles by
> which he is able to arrive at that
> end, for nature is the principle of
> all natural motion; but man is by
> nature ordained to a knowledge of
> immaterial substances as to an end,
> as is affirmed by the holy prophets
> and by the philosophers. Therefore
> he possesses within himself naturally
> implanted principles of this cognition. /22/

In his answer to the objection in the Summa, St. Thomas says that man is capable of something more than created good. In the answer to the objection in the De Trinitate he says that though man tends naturally towards this ultimate end greater than natural good, he cannot obtain it by himself but must be aided by grace.

> Answer: Created good is not less
> than that good of which man is capable,

as of something intrinsic and inherent
to him; but it is less than the good
of which he is capable as of an object,
and which is infinite. /23/

There are inscribed upon our minds
certain inherent principles by means of
which we can prepare ourselves for
perfect cognition of separate substances
even if (in this life) we cannot attain
to it by means of them. For although
man naturally tends toward his ultimate
end, he cannot gain possession of it by
purely natural means or powers, but only
by grace. And this is so because of the
(supernatural) experience of that end. /24/

An Opposed Text

To try to clarify this matter even further, it
is helpful to consider briefly an apparently opposed text in St. Thomas, one of a number which have
been cited by supporters of a "pure nature" theory.
He is discussing whether man can obtain merit by
desiring the happiness of God. He says, "When
therefore by his own reason with the help of divine
grace he grasps as his happiness any particular
good in which his happiness really does consist,
then he merits, not because he desires happiness,
(which he naturally desires) but because he desires
this particular good (which he does not naturally
desire), for example, the vision of God." /25/

This text seems to deny his earlier affirmations
about the natural desire of the vision of God. The
solution lies in his distinction between two meanings of natural desire. For Thomas it means an act
of the will following upon the action of the intellect and tending naturally towards the good. And
it also means an inclination or relation between
something which can be perfected and that which can

perfect it, all quite independent of any action by the will.

> It is this distinction which allows us to reconcile the double series of texts which the commentators have had so much trouble explaining. For when St. Thomas affirms the existence of a natural desire to see God in the reasonable creature, he is referring to the natural 'ontological' appetite, which preceded all conscious activity of the mind or will. On the other hand, when he clearly denies that there is a natural appetite of the will directed towards the vision of God, he is certainly referring to the willed natural desire and not to the "ontological" natural desire. What he is denying then is the natural wish and not the natural appetite which is prior to all willing. /26/

The Autonomy of Man

This brings us back to one of the original aspects of the problem, namely that even if one admits that there is in man a natural desire for the supernatural, as does St. Thomas, isn't it still true that man would be greater if he did not have this kind of dependence and were totally autonomous? The answer to this in part, of course, depends on whether or not one is prepared to accept the reality of a religious dimension of experience. But even apart from this, the question of human autonomy remains.

Some theologians developed a theory of pure nature in an attempt to resolve the problem. Thus according to this theory, man, left to himself, would be perfectly complete, content and fulfilled.

244

But since God decided to open up the possibility
of communion with him, in order to make this work,
he had to give man the power to hear and reach him.
To the proponents of this theory of pure nature
later graced by God, this seemed to preserve both
man's autonomy and native dignity and the supernaturality and gratuity of God's grace.

St. Thomas, while no less concerned about the
supernaturality and gratuity of God's grace, does
not accept an understanding of man in which theoretically at least he would have no relationship
at all with God.

Starting with the idea that
Thomas very clearly taught the existence
of a natural ontological desire of the
intellect for the vision of the "quid
est" of God, (i.e. a knowledge of God
that is strictly supernatural since it
partakes of God's own knowledge of
himself), we would like to show that
this idea does not compromise either
the supernatural character of that
vision or its gratuity. /27/

St. Thomas simply denies the existence of a
dualistic separation between a totally sufficient
natural human order and one with a supernatural
orientation. The basic principle upon which he
bases that denial is that it is better to attain
a superior good, even if help is needed to do so,
than not to attain it at all.

This is summed up in the following passage
from the _Summa_:

Obj. Since man is more noble than
irrational creatures, it seems that he
must be better eqipiied than they. But
irrational creatures can attain their
end by their natural powers. Much more
therefore can man attain Happiness by

245

his natural powers...

Answer: The nature that can attain
perfect good, although it needs help from
without in order to attain it, is of
more noble condition than a nature which
cannot attain perfect good, but attains
some imperfect good, although it need
no help from without in order to attain
it, as the Philosopher says (<u>De Caelo</u>
ii, 12). Thus he is better disposed
to health who can attain perfect health,
albeit by means of medicine, than he
who can attain but imperfect health
without the help of medicine. And
therefore, the rational creature, which
can attain the perfect good of happiness,
but needs the divine assistance for the '
purpose, is more perfect than the
irrational creature, which is not capable
of attaining this good, but attains
some imperfect good by its natural
powers. /25/

In order to save man's inherent dignity and
worth in the face of existence, St. Thomas does
not invoke a purely natural order in which man
would be self sufficient and would be able to
reach his ultimate goal by the sole forces of his
own nature. Man's dignity and value remain whole
even when he needs the help of grace to achieve
what the depths of his nature draw him towards
achieving. To go too far down this road of pure
nature, even as a theoretical hypothesis, can lead,
as St. Thomas apparently foresaw himself, to
postulating the possibility of an order where man
could reach his ultimate goal without any help at
all. This would deny the necessity of the supernatural order and clash with those deep instincts
of the human soul which constantly cry out for
deliverance from those chains that keep it from
reaching that towards which it is irresistibly
drawn.

DISCLOSURE OF THE ULTIMATE AS LIMIT AND LOVE

In direct response to the basic objection that nature, if it gives a desire cannot not also give what is necessary in order to achieve it, St. Thomas responds that "Nature provides necessities according to its own capacities; with regard to those things that do not surpass man's faculties, man has from nature not only passive principles but active ones. With regard to those which exceed the powers of the faculties of man's nature, man has from nature a capacity to receive." /29/ What he is saying is that nature gives beings different faculties for fulfilling the desires which is part of them.

> Would one say, for example, that /nature/ leaves man deprived of the means of preserving his life and that of the species because she does not furnish him with clothes, means of defense and habitation like other animals? It would be ridiculous to say this. For she gives him all this virtually in giving him his reason and his hands. In the same way, one can say that she has not left him helpless with regard to beatitude, since, without giving him those active powers necessary for obtaining it--something absolutely impossible--she nevertheless furnished him with the powers of receiving the divine help when she gave him a free will. /30/

According to St. Thomas, then, man is not totally powerless before God. He can prepare himself and dispose himself after a fashion. He can be said to have a certain "capacity" or a certain "aptitude" for God. /31/ This passive ability to receive which exists between a better-able subject and that which makes him better, protects both man's dignity and the supernaturality and gratuity of God's action. Thus the pure nature theory is not rejected, but it is modified

247

considerably. /32/

Though the terminology may be remote, there is
nothing remote about the boldness with which St.
Thomas raises and then deals with a surprisingly
modern problem, the relationship between the religious dimension of experience on the one hand and
revealed religion on the other, both set in the
context of man's autonomy and dignity.

Third Disclosure: The Ultimate as Self-Revealer

Let us pause for a moment to see where we are
now in this chapter. We began with a summary
definition of experiential knowledge based on the
epsitemological theory of intersective realism,
then attempted a definition of religious experiental knowledge in that same context. Three major
disclosures of the ultimate were contained in that
definition: first, as the limit of all knowledge;
second, as the limit of all life and thereby the
holy object of supreme worth to be worshipped;
and, third, as the revealer through history of its
reality and nature. So far in this chapter we
have been discussing the first two of these disclosures and are about to turn to the third.

But before doing so, it is important to indicate again the basic continuities and discontinuities that exist between the first two disclosures
taken together and the third disclosure. The first
two are part of what we have described as the
religious dimension of experience, while the third
is revelational.

Three Continuities

Analysis shows that there are three continuities between the first and second disclosure on
the one hand, and the third on the other. The

248

first continuity lies in the fact that all of the disclosures are received experientially by man, since there is nothing that man can receive or know except through experience. Speaking of experience also raises the need for interpretation. For just as experience in general is in need of interpretation, and the first two disclosures as well, so the third, the revelational, requires man's experiential interpretation.

A second continuity lies in the way the third disclosure is seen as the answer or response to the quest contained in the first two. Through the religious dimension of experience it is possible to arrive at both the question and the solution, dimly perceived, of the meaning of human existence. This is another way of putting the God-question. It is possible to see that a supremely worshipful object is the goal of life. At the same time, because of the limitations of human knowing and living, man realizes that he can go only so far in seeking this ultimate which attracts him while transcending all human categories. Crossing that barrier requires an initiative on the part of the ultimate. It requires a response to the search. It requires the action of a concrete and concerned God. This bridging of the gap between man and God is what is called revelation. Insofar as it is a response to a quest, revelation is not something totally alien to man. One of the reasons revelation is at times neglected or misunderstood is that it has been separated too far from the existential human need to which it is responding. Answering a real need, it comes to man in the same way other experiences do, with its symbolism and analogies in need of interpretation.

A third continuity lies in the application of the analogy of the experience of another self to God. "A self has precisely the character of being directly present in experience and thus of not needing to be inferred, and yet a self is not

249

immediately known in encounter, because it must express itself through various media that must be interpreted before their meaning is delivered."/33/

When we are dealing with another self or person, we do not first become aware of words, actions, signs by means of which we infer the presence of a person. On the contrary, we are aware of the presence of that person from the start. Then we go on to a further understanding of the person: qualities, abilities, characteristics, looks, actions, value system, etc. This is done especially through that person's use of language. By interpreting his words we get to know him much better. Yet these media of communication, including language, do not exhaust the richness of that self or person. In a sense the person can be said to transcend these signs; to be larger and deeper than they.

The disclosure of God in revelation can be compared then to a relationship between two persons. God is experienced in revelation but not inferred. He is known directly but not immediately. The next chapter will examine this question in more detail. Suffice to say now that though the mind experiences the elements in the inferential chain, it does not experience the reality of the ultimate through inference, since God is the very ground of knowing.

It is the mystic who claims immediate knowledge of God. For the mystic, God is known immediately through a negative process of purging the mind more and more of all created things in order to approach closer and closer to the ultimate. Thus it should be possible, according to the mystic to reach a state where nothing then remains between the mystic and God, or an immediate experience og God.

Such a claim needs qualifications. Though the role of the mystics in the religious history of

mankind and of christianity is an important one
and we have much to learn from them, it does no
one any good to push their legitimate achievements
farther than they can go because of the very
nature of things. The mystics do give closer
experience of God; they pull our eyes away from
beautiful distractions so that we can see the
purity of the limit which bathes them; they give
us a sense of great intimacy with God. But this
immediacy has to be understood as only a relative
kind of immediacy. It is relative because the
human mind can approach the ultimate only so far
and no further. Even the mystic must make use of
some medium of understanding, no matter how refined
that may turn out to be. And for the Mystical
experience to be understood by the mystic personally, as well as for its communication to other
people, it needs interpretation in the same way
that ordinary experience does. Witness the
flowery fields of St. John of the Cross.

These then are a number of the similarities
and connections between the first two kinds of
disclosure and interpreted through human experience
and the process involved can be compared for all
of them to the relationship between two selves.
Yet there are essential discontinuities as well.

Two Discontinuities

The first area of discontinuity is the content
itself of what is revealed. Because of the nature
of God, just what that is and his full relationship
towards us are beyond man's limited powers to grasp.
In this sense we can be said to be dealing with
mystery. Lest that term be used in exclusively
obscurantist fashion, however, it is necessary
to say that that which is revealed is fully compatible with human life and nature and is that
towards which man strives and seeks without knowing
exactly what it is he is striving for. What is

mysterious is not necessarily absurd, pace Tertullian. On the contrary, in genuine revelational experience, one experiences the shock of recognition, of peace, of oneness with the universe and God, which would not be true if the revelation of what was beyond us was at the same time incredible to us. Since what we are ultimately searching for is an answer to the dilemma of existence, to receive an answer from God about this must mean that when we receive it we understand it in the sense that it quiets our search and gives a fuller meaning to our lives. None of this is to say that the divine is merely humanized or psychologized or diminished in any way, only that in its very differentness it is genuinely understood by man after his own fashion.

Experiential religious knowledge then, in its revelational dimension, does not differ from ordinary knowledge in that it takes place through a medium. Like all knowledge, it is based on experience. But the experience of God is doubly unique. It is unique first in that as the ultimate ground of knowing, God cannot be known in the way that other things are known and must be approached through an analogical medium. It is unique secondly in that that analogical medium is historical with a transcendent dimension. Though the problem of the one and the many may be an abtruse philosophical question, it becomes very real and urgent in the paradoxical combination of historical particularity and ultimacy that is found in the revelational situation.

A revelational event can be said to be one in which God is present and which points beyond itself. It obviously is not God, but it directs us towards God. In this sense it is a sign and signs have to be carefully distinguished from that which they signify. Always present is the danger of idolatry, of confusing the sign for what is signified, for taking the sign to be God. Down through the centuries there have always been warnings about this danger.   But man has always managed to deal with it.

The second discontinuity lies in the fact that
revelation takes place in history.   The medium
through which revelation is experienced is historical.   Certain special occasions, which include
both persons and events, are understood as containing the divine presence in a special way.   This
involves the paradoxical situation whereby the
concretely historical has an ultimate transparency.
These historical occasions of revelation become
normative for individuals and for communities.

Another way of clarifying the uniqueness of
this historical dimension is to say that it is
illusory to claim that the same ideas, insights
or conclusions could have been arrived at by
sufficiently intense abstraction or mental concentration.   As has been seen, God lies beyond man's
limits; he cannot be reached directly by man's own
efforts.   He must make himself known to man, and
he does so through the events of history.

All this implies, or course, a belief in the
value of historical time itself.   Temporality is
something that is taken seriously by Christianity.
It does not understand time to be too fragile, too
unsubstantial to be able to support the divine
presence.   It does not demand a tearing away of
the historical, temporal veil in order to reach
the intense purity of the infinite.   If it is a
veil, then, there is nothing man can do about it.
Man and the world are historical and it is only
in that historical world that we live and move and
know what we know of God and it is through that
world that he makes himself known to us.   A
contrast with non-Christian religions in this
regard should not be pushed too far, however, for
a close analysis will show that though their
description of historical differs somewhat from
the Western and though their language tends to the
more abstract, yet there is a greater similarity

253

there than is generally realized.

Third Definition: Christian Revelation

It is clear that our discussion so far has already begun to take us beyond the kind of revelational disclosure described in the proposed definition of religious experiential knowledge. It says there "an ultimate other which discloses itself...as the revealer through history of its reality and nature." That description is deliberately vague and is intended to be applicable to various concrete religious traditions. It might be objected that it already contains a Christian optic, but even if it did it remains sufficiently generic to be broadly applicable. Our concern here, however, is not with questions of comparative religion, but with the Christian religion and Christian revelation.

In the light of what has been said so far about this third type of disclosure and in the light of our continuing analysis of Christian religious knowledge, a fuller, more specific definition of this third kind of disclosure is needed to develop it in Christian terms. I therefore propose the following definition: Its explanation and development will occupy the last portion of this chapter:

Christian revelation is the fulfillment of man's quest for the ultimate through God's disclosure of himself as love, in events in history, in the life and person of Christ and in the records, life and worship of the church.

The Fulfillment of Man's Quest for the Ultimate

There is no need to repeat once again the analyses through which we have tried to indicate the continuity between the religious dimension

254

of life as a quest for the ultimate and the response to that quest by God in his revelation of
himself and the meaning of life for men.

Through God's Disclosure of Himself as Love

As was said above, the relationship of a revealing God to man has to be understood as the
experience of a self communicating himself to
other selves. Although this is a comparison or an
analogy, like all attempts to understand God, it
is an essential one. The highest kind of personal
relationship that can exist, the one that seems
most likely to fit the kind of ultimate quest that
dwells in man's heart and the greatness of God's
personality itself, is the relationship of love.
God's love for man and man's fulfillment of himself
in loving God in return is the absolute core of
Christian revelation. It penetrates it, sustains
it, clarifies it and distinguishes it.

In Events in History

God reveals himself in love through events in
history in the Old Testament especially. A great
historical sequence goes from the call of Abraham,
the Exodus from Egypt and settlement of Palestine,
the exile and return, through the many years of
faithfulness and unfaithfulness on the part of
the people of Israel.

Great spiritual leaders arose who heard more
acutely the call of God and who were able to discern and interpret his message of love in these
great events. First there is Abraham, called by
God to become his friend and who willingly leaves
his homeland to follow God's call into a strange,
new land. His faithfulness and generosity prompt
God's promise that there will follow him a vast
progeny of children for whom God's love and pro-
tection will be special. Then there is Moses,

255

the great leader of his people through the mysterious events in Egypt and the desert, where he is
able to point out God's loving hand. He is the
intermediary between a loving, caring God and a
grateful, wavering people. Moses grows in intimacy
with God, speaking with him as with a neighbor and
experiencing his great tenderness without losing a
sense of his holiness and greatness.

Then there are the prophets. They too are
God's confidants, personally loved by a God who
seizes them, frightens them at times, but encourages
them, steels them with a mission and fills them
with joy. They are witnesses of the drama of the
love and anger of Yahweh with his people. Hosea,
Jeremiah, and Ezechiel all reveal that God considers
himself Israel's spouse, even when Israel is unfaith-
ful to that relationship. God's love overcomes
that unfaithfulness and sinfulness, creating in
Israel a new heart capable of love. The prophets
speak of God as the Shepherd and the Vine. And it
is in Deuteronomy (6:5) that this tradition is
codified in the great commandment of love,"You shall
love the Lord your God with all your heart, and
with all your soul, and with all your might."
Though there are difficulties and human weakness
involved in Israel's response to God's call of love,
God strengthens them and makes them capable of over-
coming these shortcomings and loving him in return.

After the exile, this tradition of God's
revealing himself as love becomes even more person-
alized. God is seen as addressing himself not
merely to the people of Israel as a collectivity,
but to the heart of each individual as well. The
poor in spirit, the meek, the just, the weak, all
are objects of God's love. The dialogue of love
between a man and God is expressed strongly and
poetically in the Song of Solomon. Also about this
time, the idea that the love of God is so deep, so
strong and so great that it extends to all men
begins to spread.

DISCLOSURE OF THE ULTIMATE AS LIMIT AND LOVE

As the time of the arrival of Christ grows near, the pious Jew knows that he is loved by a God whose faithfulness and mercy, whose goodness and graciousness he experiences and praises. So strong is this conviction and experience that it survives even the fire of martydom as in the case of the Maccabees.

In the Life and Person of Christ

When we arrive at the New Testament, we find that the focus concentrates on one person, Jesus Christ, who is seen as both the author and object of the revelation.

Without developing a christology, we would like to examine two questions about Christ that may be illuminating. The first is a look at the use and meaning of the title "Son of God", as it is found in the New Testament. The second is a brief examination of the theoretical problem posed by Jesus as a medium of the revelation of God.

Jesus as the Son of God

It is in Jesus that God reveals himself especially and fully, "who, though he was in the form of God, did not count equality with God a thing to be grasped, but empties himself, taking the form of a servant, being born in the likeness of man. And being found in human form he humbled himself and became obedient unto death, even death on a cross. Therefore God has highly exalted him and bestowed on him the name which is above every name, that at the name of Jesus every knee should bow, in heaven and on earth and under the earth, and every tongue confess that Jesus is Lord, to the glory of God the Father." /34/ (2: 6-11)

In the Synoptic Gospels the title Son of God is frequently used with regard to Jesus. At first

this seems to have overtones of an earthly messiah.
Jesus is quick to disclaim any such meaning. In
the temptation scene in the desert the title Son
of God means great power and strength for Satan;
for Jesus it means finding sustenance in doing the
will of the Father. When Peter says "You are the
Christ, the Son of the Living God," /35/ Jesus
accepts it bud adds as Son of Man he will have to
die to reach his glory.

He accepts the title in answering the Sanhe-
drin's question, "And they all said, 'Are you the
Son of God then?' And he said to them, 'You say
that I am'". /36/ And yet this takes place in
the paradoxical situation where it brings about
the process of condemnation and execution. Several
times during his life he speaks to himself as
"Son" in relation to Abba, the Father. There is
always a sense of great intimacy and communication
between the Son and the Father.

It is through his death and resurrection that
the Apostles finally understand the mystery of
what this Sonship meant. As St. Paul sees it,
God has sent his Son that we might be reconciled
to him by his death. It is through this that he
has been established in power and we are called
to communion with him. The christian life is a
life of belief in the Son of God who loved us as
the Father loved him and who gave himself up for
us. In St. John's Gospel the theme of divine
Sonship becomes a dominant one. God has sent his
beloved Son into the world to save the world. He
is the unique Son and revealer of the Father, and
he brings to men the eternal life that comes from
God. And he who believes in him has eternal life.

So central is this theme of Jesus as the Son
of God, that it is seen as influencing the condition of mankind. Human beings are understood to
be adopted sons of the Father through Christ. To
those who believe in Christ, says St. John, God

gives the power to become children of God. Through
Jesus the Son, then, man is so loved by God that he
participates in some mysterious fashion in the life
of the Father.

The Special Role of Christ

In the course of our discussion on revelation,
we indicated that because of the nature of the
ultimate, God cannot be known immediately, but has
to disclose himself to us through the medium of
experience, since the only way we can know things
is through experience. There is a gap between man
and God, which, even when he takes the initiative
to bridge it, requires the use of a medium of com-
munation. The great events of Exodus, for example,
are the medium through which Moses and the people
of Israel were able to experience God as Savior and
Preserver. With regard to Christ, however, a
special problem arises. Can we continue to maintain
a distinction of this kind between God and the medium of revelation when we are speaking of Christ
as the central revelation of christianity? "At
first it would appear that it is impossible to
maintain the distinction at this point, for is it
not said that Christ is identical with God and is
it not claimed that Christ, as the final disclosure
of God, is the presence of God without qualification
o' diminution." /37/

The answer to the difficulty is of necessity
nuanced. On the one hand, Christ is a medium like
other mediums. Even a superficial reading of the
Gospels will quickly disclose how often and empha-
tically Christ points away from himself. He says
that he is the obedient servant of God, that he
comes from the Father and that he prays to him.
He then goes so far as to empty himself of all self-
will and submits to the will of the Father in the
total obedience that will mean his death. On the
other hand, Christ is understood as the fullness

of the presence of God, "Being the full and final presence of God, Christ cannot, like other media, merely point beyond himself since he is the embodiment of the very being to which he would point." /38/

This seems to present us with an unresolvable dilemma: how can Christ be a medium and not a medium at the same time? The answer lies in the direction of a better understanding of the nature of a symbol or medium. A symbol cannot substitute itself for the thing signified, but if it is to be genuinely meaningful, it must have some internal connection with it, it must participate in some way in what it is.

Christ is a symbol who stands for and participates in God. But he does this by self-negation. Building upon the Suffering Servant Symbolism of Isaiah, Christ is the obedient servant of God par excellence. It is by his emptying himself completely that God is made manifest. In setting himself aside he indicates at the same time that God is essentially scrificial love. "A self-negating medium that reveals God in the very act of setting itself aside is precisely the sort of reality required for solving the dilemma posed by Christ... The nature of the medium, or since in this case, the medium is a person, the mediating person, becomes identical with God without ceasing to be the means whereby God is made known to man. What Christ reveals is that God is to be understood as sacrificial love that exists in a concrete and personal form. /39/

in the Records, Life and Worship of the Church

Like any community, the christian church remembers the past, develops it in the present and projects it into the future. It may be helpful to examine briefly the role of the church both with regard to past revelation and to what we shall try to explain as present revelation.

The Church as Preserver, Interpreter

and Transmitter of Past Revelation

The relationship of the church to past revelation can be considered from the point of view of the nature of religion and from that of the nature of revelation itself.

From the viewpoint of religion, the church needs to be understood as an expression of religion's societal dimension. As we saw earlier, religion is not something which is confined to the psyche of the private individual. The contact which the human person makes with the religious object is a contact with reality. The contact he makes with other persons, all of whom have their own relationship to the religious object, is a contact with reality. Without repeating what has been said earlier, the following passage may be helpful,

> The whole riddle of intersubject-
> ivity must be posed and solved on the
> initial level of perceptual experience.
> Neither ontology nor epistemology can
> possibly begin with the notion of the
> ego and its mental representation and
> then hope to synthesize or constitute
> the original world of perception and
> the other perceived subjects...Prior
> to thinking...I believe that I live
> outside myself among objects which show
> themselves to everybody. I believe
> that we all see the things themselves
> (les choses mêmes) and the same things
> (les mêmes choses). Everything rests
> upon the insurpassable richness, the
> miraculous multiplication of percep-

tible being, which gives the same things
the power to be things for more than
one perceiver. /40/

The social dimension of religion is also emphasized in the idea of framework discussed earlier.
In order for a person to understand the reality
which a framework claims to explain, it is necessary
for that person to accept the particular framework
involved. This is a more modern way of putting the
Augustinian, "Nisi credideritis, non intelligitis."
It is not a question of blind authoritarianism
since what we are dealing with is an encounter, or
a dialectical relationship between the individual
and the framework, where change is always possible
and actual.

Intellectual frameworks do not float in mid-
air as empty abstractions. A framework is embodied
in some community, the community accepts it and even
advocates it. Thus "the condition for recognizing
the sacred...can be actualized by an individual
person only if he opens himself to the guidance of
a specific religious tradition." /41/ Like all
creative breakthroughs, this requires the oncome of
a crisis of some kind, upon the occasion of which
a breakthrough occurs. This breakthrough, in religious terms, is called a conversion, though the
term conversion is not entirely inappropriate for
other creative breakthroughs even in science.

The role of the church with regard to past
revelation can also be considered from the point of
view of the nature of revelation itself. Revelation is given by God in history to the people of
God, not merely for those to whom it comes directly,
but for their brethren and successors. Given in
history, evelation has a necessarily historical
dimension. It had to be understood and set down
in writing so that it could be operative in the
future. Thus the Bible became the primary record
of revelation, containing God's Word as accepted
and expressed by his people through various

cultural and historical frameworks. Christ of course was the revealer of God par excellence, and the biblical records of the New Testament are focused primarily on his life, death and resurrection.

The Apostles of Christ were the primary preservers and interpreters of his revelation. They transmitted it to the generation that succeeded them and by their efforts influenced untold generations to come.

Down through the centuries, the christian community has preserved, nurtured, clarified, developed and passed on the revelation which is has received. It is this activity of the christian community which underlies the understanding of the church as an institution. In order to safeguard the transmission and interpretation of revelation there are needed communal structures which foster this. Among such are persons in positions of authority who are able to speak with decisiveness and finality in interpreting the revealed word.

This involves a danger of course. For it is possible for such leaders to judge revelation rather than to be judged by it. But just as God has so loved man as to reveal himself to him and to send his own beloved Son to save him, so he watches over his community and its leaders and sends the Spirit to lead them in the way of faithfulness to what has been revealed in history by him.

Another important group for the preservation and interpretation of revelation in the christian community is that of biblical scholars and theologians. Their textual and historical studies, their conceptualizations of the revealed in the developing cultural forms of each age are also improtant to revelation. For not only does it need to be understood by each age in its own way, but it has an inner life and vitality that demands that it not be transmitted as a merely passive, lifeless object.

DISCLOSURE OF THE ULTIMATE

Looking at the matter from the point of view of what is "recorded", a community's records embody the framework of its traditions. They contain the recounting of the great events through which the religious insights of the community were communicated. They also contain the cultural framework in and through which these communications were interpreted. In the course of time, some of these events and interpretations become especially privileged as they are handed down from generation to generation. This is the role that the Bible plays in the Judaeo-Christian tradition. We can be said to be dealing with a set of "data" which are for understanding the implications of faith in the world. "In this sense religious belief can be fostered or impaired by the understanding of empirical evidence which corroborates or contradicts the data sustaining its heuristic vision." /42/

The Church as Receiver and

Developer of Present Revelation

This last point raises the question of the possibility of revelation in the present. God has revealed himself in the past, but does this mean that he no longer reveals himself in the present? Is God's active presence or disclosure of himself confined exclusively to the past as refracted through a continuing historical process of human interpretation or does God continue to actively reveal himself today?

Normative Revelation

The first thing that needs to be said is that the revelation of God in history is normative for Christians. God has revealed his fullness, especially in the life and person of Jesus Christ. In revealing himself as loving creator and lord, God gave us an understanding of the greatness and fullness of himself.

This normativeness of past revelation should not be interpreted in static terms, however. We should not compare the revealing God to the deistic God. It is not as if God the great clockmaker who made the world and then let it go off to tick away by itself also included some instructions as to how to wind the clock so that it could be kept going all by itself without having to bother him again. A deistic revealer is as cold, remote and improbable as a deistic creator.

So normativeness has always included the possibility of interpretation, of further understanding just what it was that God revealed and how it helps us to live our lives today. God's revelation is not historical in the sense that the clay tablets of Sumer are historical. These tell us of the achievements of a past civilization and carry no internal life giving force beyond whatever further understanding we have of man's past accomplishments.

So there has always been a great tradition of interpretation of God's revelation, especially as that is set down in the biblical texts preserved in the ongoing life of the christian community. There has always been that healthy tension between the normativeness of revelation and its living acceptance through succeeding christian generations, each one understanding it within the cultural context of its own day.

But that is not precisely the question initially posed, or at least, the matter needs to be probed a bit deeper. Quite apart from the new insights of interpretation gained by examining a normative past revelation, is there any sense in which we can say that God continues to reveal himself in a new way without disturbing the normativeness of his historical revealings?

DISCLOSURE OF THE ULTIMATE

The Inexhaustibility of the Ultimate

To answer that question it is necessary to consider that revelation is an encounter with the ultimate. Ultimate implies, as we have seen, an inexhaustibility, an unreachability, a non-conceptualizability. Any encounter with the ultimate, which is the ground of all knowledge, must be expressed analogically, in symbolism, through a glass darkly, as St. Paul says. Even normative revelation of God's fullness is received by men through the medium of experience. God is so great that man can never completely grasp his fullness but must continue to deepen his knowledge of him.

It is also an encounter in the sense that it is a sharing between selves, the human self and the divine self. We have seen how another self can never be known all at once or immediately. One grasps the fact that one is dealing with a self, but one then has to examine various signs and gestures, and listen to the other self speak in order to get to know that self better. And there is always a sense in which there is more to the self than that self is able to explain or that can be grasped by another self. This is all the more true of God as a self, since in his greatness he is even further removed from the grasp of the men engaged in dialogue and encounter with him. Past revelation remains normative as a revelation of the fullness of God. But since that revelation is in our symbols and language it can never fully express the ultimate any more than a human self can fully express itself in its own conversation.

Like a Heuristic Field

This process can be compared to a heuristic field. In a heuristic field fullness of meaning is admitted, even if only dimly perceived. This awareness pulls one forward to deeper perception

266

and understanding, confident that what one is looking for will be found because it is already there.
A judge, for example, usually has no trouble interpreting and applying the law, but every once in a
while he runs into a case where the law is not lcear
and he must find the law even though he is not sure
where it is or just what it is. He presumes that
the law covers all contingencies; he also presumes
that a judge's function is to administer justice.
So he searches for the law in the interest of justice and in this excercise of judicial responsibility usually finds a meaning of the law which had
always been there but only dimly perceived up until
that point. This is not a mere reading of the law,
nor it is a mere interpretation of a text of the
law. It is a finding of the law.

Another example would be that of a scientist
who goes beyond the day-to-day applications of
science into the area of new discovery. Usually
this process begins when the scientist becomes
aware of an accumulation of anomalies with regard
to the laws or applications of regular science.
This faces the scientist with a problem. He begins
to search for a solution to that problem confident
that he will find it because he knows it is there
even though he does not at the moment know where
that is or just how he will go about successfully
finding it. He excercises his scientific responsibility in searching for an answer that he only dimly
perceives. But he recognizes it when he finds it.
In so doing he has gone beyond ordinary science
with its current solutions, he has gone beyond the
interpretation and further application of existing
scientific laws. He has gone to the world itself
and found an answer he did not fully perceive but
which he knew was there.

A third example is that of an artist. A
genuine artist who does not merely copy others or
slavishly imitate the externals of nature, is also
on a voyage of discovery. His heuristic field is a
sense, an intuition of the depths of meaning and

beauty which lie in reality. Such meaning need not
be mere superficial prettiness. It can be the
beauty of high tragedy such as Hamlet of the Pieta.
Michelangelo used to say that his chisel and hammer
were used by him to discover or uncover the form of
the statue that was hidden in the block of marble.
Even though the artist does not know just where to
look, or how to express it, he is driven by his
artistic intuition to somehow portray what he knows
is there but which he cannot as yet fully express.
It may take many sketches, many trials, many brushes
and many colors, but finally he will be able to step
back from the canvas and say that he has discovered
and captured what he was searching for. He is not
merely copying nature, nor merely interpreting
nature, he is in some sense, releasing what Hans
Hofmann used to call the "push-pull" of nature.

Revelation can be compared to such a heuristic
field. God calls man both in the past and in the
present. He revealed himself to man in the past
through great events in history and through the life
and person of Jesus Christ. That revelation has
become the framework of belief of the christian
community. By dwelling in that framework which
includes the normative revelation of the past, the
individual contemporary christian and the christian
community taken as a collectivity, can reach ever
deeper life and insights. For that framework of the
past can operate as a heuristic field in which it is
possible to make new discoveries that have been
perceived as already there, but only dimly. Once
again this is not a mere reading of what is set down,
nor is it mere interpretation, it is a new understanding of and from God. Paradoxically, then,
normativeness and newness are complementary rather
than contradictory.

Can This Be Called Grace?

This question might have been dealt with more
simply had the term God's grace been used to describe

this ongoing life and development of the individual
christian and of the community. But, for better or
for worse, the term grace has come to acquire two
static qualities of which it would need to be
purged before it could come to really stand for this
meaning of contemporary revelation. The first
staticity is an understanding of grace as an almost
physical inflow of divine help into the soul of the
christian. Obviously an exagerration that deviates
from the great classical understanding of grace, it
has had too pervasive an influence, especially in
spirituality, to be overlooked. The second staticic-
ity is an understanding of grace as an illumination
from God concerning an inert, passive collection of
divine truths called revelation. This goes back in
part to an understanding of revelation as a collection of propositions, firmly fixed, whose mysterious content could be clarified by invoking the
help of the God who gave them to us in the first
place.

If, however, we understand revelation as event
rather than proposition, and if we see it as encounter rather than mere ideas, and if we speak of the
relationship between God and man in personal rather
than merely physical terms, then the term grace
must acquire considerably different connotations
before it can be appropriately used in this context.

The Importance of Worship

Finally, and very briefly, worship is central
to this dynamic understanding of revelation. For
in worship man turns his whole mind and being to
God in the company of his fellow worshippers. As
they commemorate Christ's death and resurrection
and share in the eucharist, they approach that
core of deep silence where God speaks loudest
today.

DISCLOSURE OF THE ULTIMATE

The Christian Church and Other Communities

of Faith

There is another important aspect to the once
and for allness of christian revelation and that is
the question whether this means uniqueness in an
absolute sense. Though too vast and complex a
question to be treated adequately here, some very
brief indications of direction may be helpful.

We have seen God to be the ultimate, the ground
and source of all being, the supreme object of
worship. He cannot be such unless he is related to
the world as a whole, and therefore to all men. We
have also said that basic understandings of God's
nature have been given to us in special occasions
of christian religious history. What then about the
claims to religious knowledge and faith to be found
in either widespread and ancient religious traditions?
Are these "simply to be denied on the ground that the
disclosure of God through the special occasions of
the Judeao-Christian tradition is final and exhaustive and nothing else is required? This solution
has been advanced time and again in the source of
Western history; it is a solution, however that cannot be sustained." /43/

With the shrinking of the world in the jet age
and greater familiarity with other world religions,
their bizarreness and exotic aspect has diminished
considerably. It is now possible to approach them
in a calm and factual manner difficult for previous
generations separated by tremendous physical and
cultural obstacles.

One solution to this apparent impasse is through
an application of the principles of interpretation
that have been discussed so extensively. Even the
special occasions of disclosure by God we call Christian revelation have to be received in an essentially
dialogical situation and this reception means inter-

270

pretation. In order to understand what it is that
God is saying to us in his special disclosures, we
have to come to them and see them through our ordinary knowledge, as well as through "the general concept of God as it has been derived from the religious
dimension of experience which is universal. As we
progress in understanding the meaning of our historical tradition, we are led to introduce comparisons
with the other world religions and their ideas of
God." /44/

All this is totally removed from eclecticism
or a fuzzy kind of universal religion. It is not
falsely irenical but genuinely ecumenical in the
sense that it allows the christian community to
remain fully true to itself and to its revelation
all the while admitting the value of the religious
traditions of other communities of faith. The
paradoxical conceptual question involved is how is
it possible for the revelation of Jesus Christ to
remain absolute and unique for Christians without
diminishing the genuine absoluteness and value of
the belief of other world religious communities?
I think this can be shown along the lines indicated,
but to do it in detail is a task for another day.

Conclusion

Despite its length, this chapter has been no
more than the detailed explanation of three basic
definitions. The first defined experiential knowledge as encounter with a disclosing other through
indwelling in a framework and the integration of its
particulars into a coherent whole. This was specified by the second definition of religious experiential knowledge, namely, a n encounter through
indwelling and integration with an ultimate other
which discloses itself both as the limit of all
knowledge and of all life and thereby the holy object
of supreme worth to be worshipped and as the
revealer through history of its reality and nature.

Then, after an extensive examination of the first
two kinds of disclosure, both of which were seen as
aspects of the religious dimension of experience,
the third disclosure, that of positive, revealed
religion, was further specified as christian revelation. This was defined as the fulfillment of man's
quest for the ultimate through God's disclosure of
himself as love in events in history, in the life
and person of Christ and in the records, life and
worship of the church.

In the course of these discussions, the name
and role of the Christian God has been important.
The emphasis has been on encounter between God and
man. Experiential knowledge was emphasized over
rationalistic knowledge, directness over immediacy.
Yet these were mentioned only briefly. A nagging
problem remains. Given the fact of man's existential search for meaning and purpose in life and
given man's intellectual need for certainty and
clarity, wouldn't it be more useful and human, more
in conformity with the demands of scientific verification to try to prove the existence of God? In
the next chapter then, we shall examine the classic
debate on the proofs for and against the existence
og God and see what our own theory of religious
experiential knowledge adds to the discussion.

DISCLOSURE OF THE ULTIMATE AS LIMIT AND LOVE

NOTES

[1] John E. Smith, _Experience and God_ (New York: Oxford University Press, 1968), pp. 35-36.

[2] _____, _The Analogy of Experience_ (New York: Harper and Row, 1973), p. 40.

[3] John V. Apczynski, _Doers of the Word_, (Missoula, Montana: Scholars Press, 1977),pp. 53-54.

[4] Ibid., pp. 61-62.

[5] Ibid., pp. 141-142.

[6] Michael Polanyi, _Personal Knowledge_ (Chicago: Chicago University Press, 1962), p. 308.

[7] Apcztnski, op. cit., p. 143.

[8] Ibid., p. 162.

[9] Ibid., p. 163.

[10] Anne Carr, _The Theological Method of Karl Rahner_ (Missoula, Montana: Scholars Press, 1977), p. 46.

[11] Joseph Maréchal, _Le Point de Départ de la Métaphysique_ (Bruxelles: L'Edition Universelle; Paris: Desclee de Brouwer, 1944-1949) 2nd ed., 5 volumes.

[12] Carr, op. cit., p. 47.

[13] Maréchal, op. cit., vol. 5, p. 259.

[14] Carr, op. cit., p. 50.

[15] Ibid., p. 51.

[16] Smith, op. cit., p. 57.

[17] Ibid., p. 58.

[18] Ibid., p. 60.

[19] Ibid., p. 63.

[20] Michel Gervais, "Nature et Grâce Chez Saint Thomas d'Aquin," (I) _Laval Théologique et Philosophique_ (Vol. XXX, 3, October 1974),334. Own translation.

[21] _Summa Theologica_, Ia IIae, art. 2, q. 8, obj. 3. Can be found in any of numerous editions. The Fathers of the English Dominican Province have published a multi-volume translation of the _Summa_ (London: Burns, Oates and Washbourne Ltd., 1914, 1922)

[22] _The Trinity and Unicity of the Intellect_. Transl. by Sr. R. F. Brennan (St. Louis, B. Herder Book Company, 1946) Q.6, a. 4, 5a obj., p. 143.

[23] _Summa Theologica_ Ia IIae, art. 2, q. 8. resp. ad obj. 3.

[24] _Trinity and Unicity of the Intellect_, resp. as 5a obj., p. 197.

[25] _De Veritate_, p. 22, a.7.

[26] Gervais, op. cit., p. 344.

[27]Ibid., p. 335.

28 Summa Theologica Ia IIae, q. 5, a. 5, obj. & resp.

[29]De Virtute in Comm., q. i, a. 10, ad 2.

[30]Gervais, op. cit., p. 340.

[31]A few examples: "capax Dei", IIa, q. 4, ad 2: "capax adoptionis", :IIIa, q. 23, ad 3; "capax vitae aeternae", Ia q. 23, a. 1; "capax summi boni", : Ia, q. 93, a. 2, ad 3; "naturaliter anima est gratiae capax," Ia IIae, q. 113, a 10.

[32]For a detailed examination of the theory of pure nature from the point of view of the gratuity of the supernatural and its relation to the discussions of the Encyclical Humani Generis, see "Nature et Grâce chez Saint Thomas d'Aquin (II)," Laval Théologique et Philosophique (XXXI, Fev. 1975) 293-319. In this article Gervais, though critical of an unsophisticated version of the theory of pure nature suggests that many of the difficulties connected with the earlier controversy can be solved by using a more nuanced theory. He agrees with Karl Rahner that our being given a supernatural end is a gratiotous gift. It is necessary then to admit the possibility of human nature being without the gift and that the gift of the supernatural is gratuitous, thus necessarily implying a theory of pure nature. But, it is necessary to go beyond this stage of the argument and point out that this gratuity of the supernatural is not being postulated with regard to an hypothetical human nature but with regard to human nature as it actually exists. When dealing with human nature as it actually exists, we are not talking about the supernatural as a purely arbitrary superimposition.

Theoretically, that is almost identical with secularism. What is being affirmed in this modified version of the theory of pure nature is rather that though it would have been possible for man not to have had this ordination towards the vision of God, then this would have meant that man would not have been able to achieve his ultimate goal or that perfection capable of completely fulfilling the basic drive of his spiritual faculties. Thus instead of speaking of a humanity self-enclosed and self-sufficient, we are speaking of one with an opening towards the transcendent and which needs to reach it for its final fulfillment even though it cannot do so all by itself. Thus the supernaturality and the gratuity of the supernatural are preserved as well as man's native dignity.

[33] Smith, op. cit., p. 85.

[34] Epistle to the Philippians, 2:6-11.

[35] Matthew. 16: 16 foll.

[36] Luke, 22:70.

[37] Smith, op. cit., pp. 78-79.

[38] Ibid., p. 79.

[39] Ibid., p. 80

[40] Robert M. Friedman, "Merleau-Ponty's Theory of Subjectivity," Philosophy Today (XIX, n. 3/4, Fall, 1975), 235. Quotation from Merleau-Ponty, Signs, Transl. R. C. McCleary (Evanston: Northwestern University Press, 1964), p. 125.

[41] Apczynski, op. cit., p. 170

[42]Ibid., p. 173.

[43]Smith, op. cit., p. 74.

[44]Ibid., pp. 74-75.

DISCLOSURE OF THE ULTIMATE

CHAPTER SEVEN

THE EXISTENCE OF GOD

OR

THE REALITY OF GOD?

The attempt to prove the existence of God
is a response both to man's ongoing doubts about life
and his intellectual need for clarity and certainty.
It has a long and important history and is a vast
enterprise in itself. For our purpose here we will
confine ourselves to four major points. First,
there will be a historical survey of the classic
theistic arguments followed by the classical arguments against them. Second there will be a consideration of the question as to whether Roman Catholic
tradition, especially as exemplified by Vatican I,
allows any other option concerning the question of
God than St. Thomas' five ways. Third, based on an
affirmative response to the above question, three
possible theistic options will be examined: the first
is a reassertion of the classic proofs; the second is
a use of existential thought to approach the God
question; and the third is the use of process metaphysics as an instrument to pursue the problem.
Finally, our theory of experiential religious knowledge will be used to examine in specific detail the
classic arguments for the existence of God. It will

be there suggested that it is more appropriate to speak of God as a reality encountered than as a being intellectually proven.

The Ontological Argument: Pros and Cons

The ontological argument for the existence of God has had many exponents. It centers around the understanding of God as "the greatest perfection that one can perceive." The main supporters of the ontological argument are St. Anselm of Canterbury (1003-1109), St. Bonaventure (1121-1274), Rêné Descartes (1596-1650), Leibniz (1646-1716), and Hegel (1770-1831). Its major proponent today is Charles Hartshorne. Its two major opponents are St. Thomas Aquinas (1225-1274) and Immanuel Kant (1724-1804).

Anselm of Canterbury

Anselm argued that the existence of God is self-evident, which is why people believe in God even when they don't admit it to themselves. The self evidence arises from the fact that God is a being than which nothing greater can be conceived. This is a key passage from the Proslogion:

> It is one thing for an object to be in the understanding, and another thing to understand that it exists. When a painter considers beforehand what he is going to paint, he has it in his understanding, but he does not suppose that what he has not yet painted already exists. But when he has painted it, he both has it in his understanding and understands that what he has now produced exists. Even the fool then must be convinced that a being than which none greater can be thought exists at least in his understanding, since when he hears this he understands it, and what-

ever is understood is in the understanding.
But clearly that than which a greater cannot
be thought cannot exist in the understanding
alone. For if it is actually in the
understanding alone, it cannot be thought
of as existing also in reality, and this
is greater. /1/

This argument was opposed in Anselm's own time
by a monk named Gaunilo. He wrote a reply to the
Proslogion entitled A Book on Behalf of the Fool. /2/
Gaunilo admits that Anselm was correct in saying that
the human mind must necessarily think about God, but
contrary to Anselm's claim, he said that this does
not mean that we must conclude that God exists as
an actual fact. He used an example as an analogy.
He said that it is possible to conceive of a wonderful island, a perfect paradise, the most perfect
that could exist, but this would not mean that that
island actually exists.

Anselm answered Gaunilo by saying that both his
example of an island and his reasoning concerning
it were correct, but that the analogy he made to
God does not hold. This is because in the case of
the island it is possible to conceive its non-exis-
tence as well as its existence, whereas in God's
case it is not possible to conceive his non-exist-
ence. Since in the case of God we are thinking of
that which is most perfect, the greatest of all
degrees of being, it is possible to conclude that
God necessarily exists.

Thomas Aquinas

Two centuries later, Thomas Aquinas dealt with
the ontological argument by rejecting it in accord
with the Aristotelian tradition to which he was so
deeply commited. Aquinas preferred the cosmological
argument which starts from created things in the
world about us and argues to their origin or goal.

In the <u>Summa Theologica</u> he first repeats the ontological argument by way of an objection (Obj. 2)
then refutes it in favor of the cosmological
approach:

> Obj: As soon as the signification
> of the term God is understood, it is at
> once seen that God exists. For by this
> name is signified that thing than which
> nothing greater can be conceived. But
> that which exists actually and mentally
> is greater than that which exists only
> mentally. Therefore, since as soon as
> the name God is understood it exists
> mentally, it also follows that it
> exists actually. Therefore, the propos-
> ition that God exists is self-evident.

> Resp:I say that this proposition,
> God exists, of itself is self-evident
> for the predicate is the same as the '
> subject, because God is his own exist-
> ence as will be hereafter shown. Now
> because we do not know the essence of
> God, the proposition <u>is not self-evi-
> dent to us</u>, but needs to be demonstrated
> by things that are more known to us,
> though less known in their nature--
> namely by his effects. /3/

Aquinas then went on of course to develop his
cosmological argument according to the five ways,
but more of that later.

Rene Descartes

Because of Aquinas's opposition to the ontological argument and his tremendous influence on
succeeding theological generations, it largely drop-
ped out of sight until given new life in the seventeenth century by the French philosopher Rene
Descartes. It is his formulation of the ontological

argument in his <u>Meditations</u> /4/ that has provided
the basis for most modern forms of the discussion.
But from this and other of his writings, it is not
clear as to whether Descartes was directly influenced
or not by Anselm.

Just as the cultural climate some five hundred
years later differed considerably from that of Anselm's day, so the method of argumentation used by
Descartes in his version of the ontological argument
differed a good deal from Anselm's. Descartes was
a philosopher-mathematician and he argued here by
means of scientifico-mathematical examples. He begins
by restating Gaunilo's objection then goes on to
answer it:

> But though, in truth I cannot conceive
> God unless as existing, any more than I can
> a mountain without a valley, yet just as it
> does not follow that there is any mountain
> in the world merely because I conceive a
> mountain with a valley, so likewise, though
> I conceive God as existing, it does not
> seem to follow on that account that God
> exists; for my thought imposes no necessity
> on things; and as I may imagine a winged
> horse, though there be none such, so I
> could perhaps attribute existence to God,
> though no God existed. But the cases
> are not analogous and a fallacy lurks
> under the semblance of this objection; for
> because I cannot conceive a mountain
> without a valley in existence, but simply
> that the mountain or valley, whether they
> do nor do not exist, are inseparable from
> each other, whereas, on the other hand,
> because I cannot conceive God unless as
> existing, it follows that existence is
> inseparable from him, and therefore that
> he really exists; not that this is brought
> about by my thought, or that it imposes
> any necessity which lies in the thing
> itself, that is, the necessity of the

existence of God, determines me to think
in this way: for it is not in my power
to conceive a God without existence, that
is, a being supremely perfect, and yet
devoid of an absolute perfection, as I
am free to imagine a horse with or without
wings. /6/

As proof he offers the example of the imaginary
triangle. It is possible to imagine a triangle as
existing only in the mind, he says. But there is a
curious thing about this imaginary triangle. While
certain elements depend upon its being imagined,
there are other aspects which do not. Thus the fact
that the sum of a trinagle's three angles equals two
right angles does not depend in the imagination.
There is an analogy between this necessary aspect of
a triangle and the existence of God. For just as
the very idea of a triangle implies that the sum of
its angles equals 180 degrees, so the very idea of
existence is implied in the idea of an infinitely
perfect being. It is just as impossible to deny one
as the other. Though clothed in more modern, scientific terms, this is essentially the Anselmian
argument.

Immanuel Kant

Kant took the ontological argument very seriously and addressed himself directly to Descartes'
formulation of it:

> Thus the fact that every geometrical
> proposition, as for instance, that a
> triangle has three angles, is absolutely
> necessary, has been taken as justifying us
> in speaking of an object which lies
> entirely outside the sphere of our under-
> standing as if we understood perfectly
> what it is that we intend to convey by
> the concept of that object....

THE EXISTENCE OF GOD OR THE REALITY OF GOD?

So great indeed is the deluding influence exercised by this logical necessity, that, by the simple device of forming an a priori concept of a thing in such a manner as to include existence within the scope of its meaning, we have supposed ourselves to have justified the conclusion that because existence necessarily belongs to the object of this concept-- always under the condition that we posit things as given (existing)--we are also of necessity, in accordance with the law of identity, required to posit the existence of its object and that this being is therefore itself absolutely necessary....

My answer is as follows. There is already a contradiction in introducing the concept of existence--no matter under what title it may be disguised-- into the concept of a thing which we profess to be thinking solely in reference to its possibility. /6/

For Kant the concept of highest possible perfection did not include necessary existence. Nor did this mean that it lacked anything as a concept. Concepts cannot be improved by adding reality to them. Thus if one has a concept of a thousand dollars, this concept is not increased when a real dollar bill is added to it. A real dollar cannot be added to an imaginary thousand dollars any more than an imaginary thousand can be added to the real dollar in my pocket. Kant thus opposed both Anselm and Descartes by denying that the concept of perfection includes necessary existence.

The Cosmological Arguments: Pros and Cons

285

DISCLOSURE OF THE ULTIMATE

Plato

The cosmological argument for the existence of God is the most ancient. When Plato discussed it in Book Ten of The Laws, /7/ he was undoubtedly already echoing an earlier tradition. Discussing motion, he said that there are two aspects to it: motion which has the power to move something else and motion which has the power to move itself. Of the two the second is obviously the primary power of motion, for production is prior to reception. Thus as the beginning of any chain of causes there must be an uncaused cause. Since for Plato, only a soul has the power of being able to move itself then the uncaused cause with the power to move itself and the world must be a living soul, one necessarily different from the human soul:

> If, my friend, we say that the whole path and movement of heaven, and of all that is therein, is by nature akin to the movement and calculation of minds, and proceeds by kindred laws, then, as is plain, we must say that the best soul takes care of the world and guides it along the good path. /8/

Aristotle

Continuing this Platonic tradition, Aristotle argued in his Metaphysics that you cannot have change without an unchanging source of change:

> But if there is nothing eternal, then there can be no becoming; for there must be something which undergoes the process of becoming, that is, that from which things come to be; and the last member of that series must be unregenerated; for the series must start with something, since nothing can come from

nothing. /9/

Thomas Aquinas

The classic development of the cosmological argument falls to St. Thomas Aquinas. This is to be found principally in his <u>Summa Theologica</u>, Part I, Question II, "The Existence of God." This question is divided into three articles, of which the third article is the most important, cosmologically speaking. All of these passages should be read in their fullness to appreciate Aquinas' reasoning in all its complexity and compression. That compression especially characterizes the third article, which contains the famous five ways of proving the existence of God. The first way is the argument from motion, the second the argument from effecient causality; the fourth way is the argument from degrees of being and the fifth from order in the world. The third, however, is the argument from possibility and necessity, or from the "contingency" of the world:

> We find in nature things that are possible to be and not to be, since they are found to be generated and to be corrupted, and consequently it is possible for them to be and not to be. But it is impossible for these always to exist, for that which can not-be at some time is not Therefore, if everything can not be, then at some time is not. Therefore, if every- thing can not be, then at one time there was nothing in existence, because that which does not exist begins to exist only through something already existing. Therefore, if at one time nothing was in existence, it would have been impossible for anything to have begun to exist and thus even now nothing would be in existence--which is absurd. Therefore

287

not all beings are merely possible, but
there must exist something the existence
of which is necessary. But every necessary
thing either has its necessity caused by
another, or not. Now it is impossible to
go on to infinity in necessary things
which have their necessity caused by
another, as has already been proved in
regard to efficient causes. Therefore
we cannot but admit the existence of
some being having of itself its own
necessity, and not receiving from
another, but rather causing in others
their necessity. This all men speak
of as God.

David Hume

David Hume (1711-1776) was one of the main
opponents of the cosmological proof of the existence of God. Though in his <u>Dialogues Concerning
Natural Religion</u> he is mainly concerned with the
argument from design, his discussions in part IX
of that work are more directly pertinent to the
cosmological argument. /10/

Hume began by having Demea explain the traditional cosmological argument at considerable length.
Demea does this in terms very close to the passage
from Aquinas just quoted. Cleanthes then replies
that he must point out the weaknesses of this metaphysical reasoning because it is ill-founded. In
this connection, it is interesting to note that
Hume made a point in this same section that is
frequently overlooked. He said that these arguments are "of so little consequence to the cause
of true piety and religion, that I shall myself
venture to show the fallacy of it." /11/ And at
the end of the passage he says again, "Other people,
even of good sense and the best inclined to religion
feel always some deficiency in such arguments,
though they are not perhaps able to explain dis-

tinctly where it lies. A certain proof, that men ever did, and ever will derive their religion from other sources than from this species of reasoning." /12/ This is an important point to which we shall return later in our evaluation.

Hume's basic objection was to the demonstrative proof of an existential propostion, namely that something "exists":

> I shall begin by observing that there is an evident absurdity in pretending to demonstrate a matter of fact, or to prove it by any arguments a priori. Nothing is demonstrable unless the contrary implies a contradiction. Whatever we conceive as existent, we can also conceive as non-existent. There is no being, therefore, whose non existence implies a contradiction. Consequently there is no being whose existence is demonstrable. I propose this argument as entirely decisive and am willing to rest the whole controversy upon it. /13/

To this Hume added two arguments. First that if the arguments for a necessary being were acceptable, then it would be possible to argue that the material universe could be this necessary being and that the arguments against its being so apply equally well against the deity. Second his important argument about the nature of causality where he claimed that the uniting of parts into a causal whole is formed merely by an "arbitrary act of the mind and has no influence on the nature of things." /14/

Immanuel Kant

In his Critique of Pure Reason there is a section devoted to the Existence of God. One of the divisions of this section is entitled "Of the Impossibility of a Cosmological Proof of the Existence of God," and is followed by another section entitled "Detection and Explanation of the Dialectical Illusion in all Transcendental Arguments for the Existence of a Necessary Being." In order to understand the full weight of the Kantian objection, it is necessary to place it in the context of the Kantian system as a whole. Suffice it to say that he does not admit the necessary existence of an individual thing:

> It is a very remarkable thing that, supposing that something exists, I cannot escape the inference that something exists necessarily. Upon this perfectly natural (though not on that account reasonable) inference the cosmological argument rests. But whatever concept I form of a thing, I find that I cannot conceive the existence of the thing as absolutely necessary and that nothing hinders me (whatever the thing or being may be) from conceiving its non-existence. I may thus be forced to admit that all existing things have a necessary basis while I cannot conceive any single or individual thing as necessary. In other words, I can never complete the regress through the conditions of existence without conceding the existence of a necessary being; yet on the other hand I cannot make a <u>beginning</u> from this being. /15/

According to Kant, then, the principle that every event must have a cause applies, as far as we can tell, only to the world of sense experience, whereas the cosmological argument carries us beyond the empirical limits of such sense experience. Such an extension, according to Kant, is unwarranted and unjustified, for there is no basis for presupposing that principles used to analyze our experience can be applied to that which lies beyond it.

290

Furthermore, there is no justification for assuming that there must necessarily be a first cause when we can never be sure that we have arrived at the end of a series of causes. Attempts, therefore, to reason beyond that of which we can be certain by our rational faculties is illegitimate and fruitless. As these arguments show, there is a clear connection between the theories of both Hume and Kant and their foundational theories of knowledge.

The Teleological Argument

or Argument from Design: Pros and Cons

Thomas Aquinas

The design argument for the existence of God, namely that the reality of a design or order in the world necessarily implies the existence of a designed or orderer, was also stated by St. Thomas Aquinas in the section previously quoted. It constitutes his fifth way:

> The fifth way is taken from the governance of the world. We see that things which lack knowledge, such as natural bodies, act for an end, and this is evident from their acting always, or nearly always, in the same way so as to obtain the best result. Hence it is plain that they achieve their end, not fortuitously, but designedly. Now whatever lacks knowledge cannot move towards an end, unless it be directed by some being with knowledge and intelligence; as the arrow is directed by the archer. Therefore some intelligent being exists by whom all natural things are directed to their end; and this being

we call God. /16/

William Paley

Several centuries later, William Paley (1743-1805) developed the argument for design in a form influenced by the growing scientific and technological advances of his day. His two major works, in which the argument from design plays an important part, are his <u>Evidences of Christianity</u> /17/ and his <u>Natural Theology: or Evidences of the Existence and Attributes of the Deity Collected from the Appearances of Nature</u>. /18/

His arguments are highly detailed and specific. This section on the watch and watchmaker are typical of his method:

> In crossing a heath, suppose I pitched my foot against a <u>stone</u>, and were asked how the stone came to be there. I might possibly answer, that, for anything I knew to the contrary, it had lain there forever; nor would it perhaps be very easy to show the absurdity of this answer. But suppose I found a watch upon the ground. And it should be inquired how the watch happened to be in that place. I should hardly think of the answer which I had before given...For this reason and for no other, voz., that, when we come to inspect the watch, we perceive (what we could not discover in the stone) that its several parts are framed and put together for a purpose....This mechanism being observed ....the inference we think is inevitable, that the watch must have had a maker; that there must have existed, at some time, and at some place or other, an artificer or artificers who formed it

THE EXISTENCE OF GOD OR THE REALITY OF GOD?

for the purpose which we find it actually
to answer; who comprehended its construction, and designed its use. /19/

David Hume

Some twenty-three years before Paley's first
publication, David Hume's _Dialogues Concerning
Natural Religion_ were published. posthumously,
three years after his death. Though the work
contained strong criticism of the argument from
design, there are no indications that Paley was
aware of it.

Since the argument from design for the existence of God is the most complex and detailed so far,
Hume's arguments against it are also the most complex. He said first that the argument must be judged
not as to whether it will be convincing to someone
already predisposed to believe in God, but rather
whether it will be such to one not so predisposed.
Second, even when one admits the necessity of a
watchmaker for Paley's watch, it is illegitimate
to apply the need for a watch designer to the universe as a whole. There is no appropriate comparison
between as individual object such as a watch and the
totality of the universe. What applies to one does
not necessarily have to apply to the other.

Hume found some difficulties within the argument itself. For though the design of the watch
implies intelligence, what about the laws of nature
that are found in natural and unmanufactured objects
such as stone? He suggested that there are some
forms of order which, as far as we can tell, are not
the result of intelligence.

A response which has been made to Hume is though
there are many things in nature for which we cannot
find a human or natural agency, this does not mean
that they just happened. But the difficulty with
this reply is that as science advances the areas

293

of such unaccountability continually shrink. One of
the reasons for the impact of the theory of evolution
in the nineteenth century was the way it struck down
so many examples of what had been thought to be clear
eaxmples of orderly design in nature.

Hume continued by saying that even if the argument shifts from apparently exceptional cases in
nature to the fundamental laws of nature, this does
not change matters. For, according to Hume, no
argument can be based on the fundamental laws of
nature since we have to consider tham as ultimate
facts or ultimate givens.

Finally, Hume suggests that if an analogy can
be drawn between a watch and a watchmaker on the one
hand and God and the universe on the other, then
there are alternative analogies which need to be considered. The world can be conceived, for example,
as an animal analogy, understanding it as alive in
the same way. Such a living world would be animated
by God who not only gives it life but identifies
with it. And thus we arrive at pantheism. Another
analogy is to conceive the world as generated. as a
number of primitive religions have done. Even the
watch-watchmaker analogy contains a number of hidden
questions that have not always been clearly faced.
Thus how do we know whether or not the world is the
result of a whole series of earlier, discarded
failures? How do we know whether there may not have
been many makers cooperating together in order to
fashion so complex a reality as the universe? How
can a good watchmaker have made such an imperfect
and painful world? The analogy itself poses rather
than answers to these and other questions, according
Hume.

Immanuel Kant

Kant objected to the teleological argument on the
grounds that it does not prove the kind of God that

it seems intended to prove. The argument deals
with a designer of the universe, but it does not
handle the question of where the designer got the
materials which he used in building the universe
he designed. Thus the teleological argument needs
the support of the cosmological argument and can
be said to be a version of it. But, added Kant,
no matter how these arguments are combined, they
do not provide us with a demonstration of the
existence of the God portrayed in the Bible.

Despite these differences, Kant saw the teleological argument as "the oldest, the clearest and
the most accordant with the common reason of mankind." /20/ Though, as Kant argued, it will not
prove the existence of God or compel the assent
of anyone, it remains a powerful argument perhaps
best understood in relation to its underlying
religious experience as will be shown later.

The Moral Argument: Pros and Cons

Immanuel Kant

Having rejected the ontological, cosmological
and teleological arguments for the existence of
God on the grounds that theoretical reasons cannot
go beyond the boundaries of human experience and
therefore cannot establish without doubt the existence of a transcendent God, Kant went on to argue
that what theoretical reason cannot do, practical
reason can. Thus he claimed that practical or
moral reason necessarily presupposes the existence
of a transcendent God. God thus becomes a postulate
of critical reason. /21/

Whatever theoretical reason may do or fail
to do in these other arguments, practical reason
has to presuppose certain metaphysical facts in its
very operation. Among such metaphysical facts are

freedom, immortality and the existence of God.

Kant's chain of reasoning here began with the premise that the only thing in the world that is unqualifiedly good is a good will. Such a good will, however, is not necessarily the highest goog (summum bonum) in the world. The summum bonum is by definition the best possible state of things and the best possible state of things would necessarily have to include more than moral goodness. In order for the summum bonum to be achieved, moral goodness would have to be crowned with happiness.

Morality's claim upon us then was seen by Kant as postulating the divine existence. For morality to make sense, the achievement of the summum bonum must not only be possible but necessary. And if it is necessary then it is also necessary that there be some being capable of bringing about the summum bonum. Since human beings are not capable of adding happiness to virtue, then there must be a rational end moral being who can bring about such a harmony of goodness and happiness. And finally, since such a proportioning of goodness and happiness cannot take place in this life, human immortality is a further necessary condition.

Kant's argument has been criticized at the key point of the possibility of the summum bonum. He said that in order fpr the summum bonum to be possible, God must exist. But "possible" is ambiguous and open to interpretation. It could mean only logically or theoretically possible. If so, the existence of a divine being is not necessarily postulated. If man be said to be under an obligation to do all that he can to achieve the summum bonum, how can he be said to be also obliged to proportion happiness to such achievement. This is beyond his powers. Thus the factuality of happiness is not proven, according to Kant's critics, nor is the existence of an agent such as God deemed necessary to confer it.

THE EXISTENCE OF GOD OR THE REALITY OF GOD?

The Argument From Religious Experience

As noted earlier in this work, it is necessary to distinguish religious experience as an inferential argument for the existence of God from the religious dimension of experience. If taken inferentially, this argument from religious experience is a variation of the cosmological argument and what was said above about the cosmological argument applies here.

Some Conclusions with Regard

to the Classic Arguments

Concerning the Existence of God

In his book <u>Religion and Trationality</u>, Terence Penelhum neatly summarizes the status of these arguments concerning the existence of God in the eyes of most modern thinkers:

> Each of the three traditional proofs
> ascribed a different sort of irrationality
> to atheism. The ontological proof repres-
> ents atheism as self-contradictory and
> theism as logically necessary. This breaks
> down because of a mistake about the concept
> of existence. The cosmological proof
> represents atheism as commited to a meta-
> physically intolerable incompleteness in
> the explanation of the existence and
> nature of finite beings and theism as the
> only framework that will allow our world
> to be finally and fully intelligible.
> This proof breaks down because the intel-
> ligibility it insists upon is either the
> same as that of the ontological proof
> or is explanatorily barren. And it results
> in a concept of the deity that entails
> an increasingly intolerable series of

297

logical absurdities construing conceptual
relationships in our talk of God as
necessary relationships in the divine
nature. The argument from design represents atheism as defying the scientifically tested canons of evidence and
probability and theism as the only soundly
based explanatory hypothesis to account
for some salient features of our observed
environment. This breaks down because
such a general hypothesis is not necessary
at all and does not in any case have to
take such an orthodox form. /22/

In a section of his Principles of Christian
Theology entitled "Philosophical Criticism of
Natural Theology," John Macquarrie makes much the
same kinds of criticism of the traditional proofs
of the existence of God as does Penelhum. /23/ He
then goes on to say that of course there have been
any number of attempts to reformulate these arguments
to try to take into account the criticisms leveled
against them. He adds, however, that even those who
make such modifications and modernizations do not
usually claim that their arguments have the cogency
of proof and that whatever conclusions they come to
do not do justice to the fullness of religious faith.
Macquarrie then adds that some value remains in the
arguments if one sees them as closely related to the
religious experience of mankind. Thus he sees the
ontological argument as showing that man has a
native taste for the infinite; the cosmological
argument as articulating an awareness of the mystery
of life and existence, and the teleological argument
as pointing out the amazing complexity of our lives
and of the universe.

Penelhum puts the matter another way. He says
that though the attempt involved in the traditional
arguments to prove the existence of God must be
considered a failure, these arguments could hardly
have become so widespread and persisted so long in
the face of so much counterargumentation, if there

were nothing more than empty sophistries. They "do not completely distort the beliefs they are supposed to support, and so they manage to draw their plausibility from them. Instead of the philosopher lending intellectual respectability to the simple faith, it is the other way around." /24/

These remarks of Macquarrie and Penelhum lead us into an examination of the experiential approach to the reality of God. But before developing this in detail, a number of the other options need to be taken up, both non-theistic and theistic. While the non-theistic ones will be considered only briefly, three major modern theistic options will be gone into at greater length. The question of the relationship of Roman Catholic to any other theistic option than the five ways will be studies as a prelude.

The Non-Theistic Options

What then are the options before us? First of all, of course, there are the non-theistic options. It is possible to accept the conclusion that since the classic proofs for the existence of God do not work, then there is no God and religion must be explained by some other hypothesis. This is the source of the reductionism of some in the social sciences who consider religion to have strictly human origins and objects. When faced with the question as to how religion could have exercised such a powerful and continuing influence upon mankind, such reductionists reply that religion was supported because it in turn supported political tyranny. Or if this was seen as too crude an explanation, others suggested that religion indeed had some truth in it, but that it needed scientific interpretation to discover what that really was. Thus religion was seen as a phase of the history of science or as a phase of the development of human morality, a projection of human nature, the opium of the people, an expression of the Oedipus complex, or a morality of wthical individualism.

Another non-theistic response is materialism where only matter and hard fact are accepted as real. In its more sophisticated forms, it can be called scientific reductionisn or scientistic imperialism, both quite different from and inimical to genuine science. One of the more modern forms of such materialism is atheistic existentialism which sees mankind and the world as absurd and existence as despair. As Camus once remarked, the only real choice then seems to be suicide. In such a situation, all that man can do is acknowledge defeat and muster as much dignity as he can while the proud ship of the universe sinks slowly into the sea of nothingness.

Another alternative is agnosticism or "not sureness." Religion and God are not denied outright but neither are they affirmed, leaving life strangely unfocussed.

The Theistic Options

Does a failure of the classic theistic proofs lead only to such non-theistic conclusions? Not at all, says John Hick:

> A philosopher unacquainted with modern developments in theology might well assume that theologians would, ex officio, be supporters of the theistic proofs and would regard as a fatal blow this conclusion that there can neither be a strict demonstration of God's existence nor a valid probability argument for it. In fact, however, such an assumption would be true only of certain theological schools. It is true of the more traditional Roman Catholic theology, of sections of conservative Protestantism, and of most of those Protestant apologists who continue to work within the tradition of nineteenth century

300

idealism. It has never been true, on the
other hand, of Jewish religious thought; and
it is not true of that central stream of
contemporary Protestant theology which has
been influenced by the "neoorthodox"
movement, the revival of Reformation studies
and the "existentialism" of Kierkegaard and
his successors; or of the most significant
contemporary Roman Catholic thinkers. /25/

Roman Catholics and the Classic Proofs

Before proceeding any further, then, it is necessary to pause and consider a question of considerable
importance to Roman Catholics: is anything more than
a reassertion or modernization of the classic theistic
proofs a realistic option for them given the long
Catholic tradition of the reasonableness of the preambles of faith and the definition of Vatican I in
the matter? "The same Holy Mother Church holds and
teaches that God, the beginning and end of all things,
may be certainly known by the natural light of human
reason, by means of created things, 'for the invisible
things of him from the creation of the world are clearly seen, being understood by the things that are made.'
(Romans 1:20)" (26)

This seems so definite and clear that many Roman
Catholic writers simply reassert the traditional
proofs and accuse atheists of either ill-will or
ignorance.

Even those Catholics who have some strong criticism to make about the classic theistic proofs often
then go on to try to adapt them to the modern mind
in what are ultimately accidental ways. Writing on
the Thomistic proofs, F. Van Steenberghen says, "none
of the *quinque viae* constitutes, as it stands, a
complete and satisfactory proof of the existence of
God. The first and second need to be prolonged, the
third and the fifth need to be corrected and completed
and the fourth is unusable." /27/ But no dramati-

cally new directions emerge from this. A number of
other Catholic members of what might be called the
neo-Thomistic school have tried to modernize the
classic proofs. There is a long and honorable
tradition here that includes Gilson, Maritain and
even, to a certain degree, Karl Rahner and Bernard
Lonergan. This is certainly one of the directions
in which it is possible to go, but to appreciate it
adequately would require a separate study with a
somewhat different focus.

We are going to opt for another philosophical
system than that which sustains the classic theistic
proofs and to argue theistically with it in a way
that still remains faithful to the Catholic tradition summed up in the Vatican I text cited above.

Thomas Aquinas

In order to do this, let us begin by taking
a closer look at St. Thomas Aquinas and his cultural
milieu. It seems fair to say that St. Thomas' cultural context differs widely not only from our own
but even from that of his Enlightenment critics.
It is not appropriate either for them or for us to
assume that his presuppositions are the same as
ours and proceed to argue positively or negatively
from there. Thus there is little to indicate that
St. Thomas' purpose in developing the quinque viae
was to set out arguments to convince an unbeliever
that he should accept the Christian God or even a
Christianity of which he may never have heard.
The very geo-political situation of Aquinas' day
makes such a cultural supposition difficult. It
would be more accurate to speak of Thomas' ways
as demonstrations rather than as proofs. He was
writing within a cultural context that was Christian. A case could be made that he was more interested in confirming the faith of a Christian than
in creating it is a supposed believer. Furthermore,
the very word reason as used here by Aquinas does
not have that logical simplicity that it acquired

in more modern times. The simple identification of
reason with formal logic and scientific abstraction
that characterized Western society from the Renais-
sance-Enlightenment on cannot be simply equated with
Thomas' understanding of reason, despite its strong
Aristotelian character. His understanding of it is
both richer and subtler. Finally, taking the text
of the Summa Theologica as a whole, St. Thomas was
dealing with here with what was essentially a technical problem in medieval scholasticism: If the
existence of God is an element of faith, then how
is it possible, it was asked, to have genuine "knowledge" of it. (Knowledge and faith as understood in
the medieval context differ sufficiently to warrant
raising this question). Thomas' answer is that the
existence of God can remain an element of faith
because the "knowledge" involved deals with the
preambles of faith and that the connection that must
then be made between the being whose existence is
concluded to and the God of faith can be made by
the will which brings the mind to acknowledge God.
This final point opens up the meaning of "will" in
Thomas. Perhaps his use of will in this context,
if analyzed more deeply, would show it to be considerably closer to the solution we are about to propose
than is generally thought.

Vatican I

To properly understand the definition on faith
and reason of Vatican Council I it is helpful to
take a look at a series of Roman Catholic pronounce-
ments in this area throughout the nineteenth century.
The Vatican I statement can then be seen as both a
part and a culmination of a long series of such
statements. As a matter of fact, the series can be
extended, partially as a gloss upon Vatican I, all
the way through to Vatican Council II in the 1960's.
/28/

Though many of these documents are harshly
polemical in tone, if one examines them closely one

can discover a long, drawn-out attempt to hit the proper balance between reason and faith in christian life at a time when both of these were under considerable attack from a variety of sources. Though an individual document may react strongly to one kind of attack and defend the prerogatives of faith, say, against an overstrong emphasis on rationalism, the documents as a whole try to strike a proper balance and relationship between the two. They rule out excesses on both sides. Thus fideism (or fundamentalism) is rejected as too narrow and the need for human reason is asserted. In turn, the rationalist claim that reason left to itself could come up with all the truths and realities of christianity is rejected as too strong and the need for revelation is man's limited and sinful condition is reasserted. Vatican I's declaration then has to be seen on a double historical level, the immediate theoretical circumstances in which it was held and in which it was attempting to work, and the general, lengthy history of attempts to deal with these questions through the middle and latter part of the nineteenth century.

Such a historical background is important, because it helps us to be able to say that, properly understood, Vatican I's definition of the relation of faith and reason does not require Roman Catholics to consider the classic theistic proofs of the quinque viae as the only way to arrive at a positive answer to the question of the reality of God.

Karl Rahner

Karl Rahner, in a discussion of the relationship between philosophy and theology, deals directly with this issue from Vatican I. He says despite the criticism which has been directed against the Council as being too reactionary and too tied in with the reassertion of nineteenth century church viewpoints and prerogatives, and despite the fact that the intellectual framework of the Fathers of

the Council looked backwards rather than forwards,
Vatican I can be called a great and exciting council
precisely because of the definition in question.

He says that one must put aside for the moment
the exact meanings of the terms used, namely "reason," "proof" and "knowledge," and look behind the
definition to see what it was really trying to say.
This is how Rahner understands the essence of the
definition:

> The heart and centre of it is this:
> man cannot escape from having to do with
> God, and even at a stage prior to any
> christian revelation conceived of in
> explicit or institutional terms. This
> is inescapable and is something he
> encounters before any particular pro-
> phets or pastors have reached him....
> What is astonishing about the First
> Vatican Council, in other words, is the
> fact that it recognizes something that
> takes place in man which is significant
> for his salvation (if we want to put
> it in theological terms) and yet which
> is, independently of Christianity or
> the Church, present inescapably and
> always....What is exciting in this
> conciliar declaration is the assertion
> that there is a factor of decisive
> importance for human existence apart
> from faith in revelation at the biblical
> and ecclesiastical level, a factor which
> is of radical significance for Christian
> faith despite the fact that it is said
> to have its basis within itself....
> But what is utterly astonishing is that
> the faith of the official Church, of its
> own volition, ascribes so fundamental
> a significance to a factor which lies
> outside the Church's own conscious
> faith in revelation. /29/

What is equally exciting and significant about this interpretation of Vatican I's declaration on human reason and the knowledge of God is that it is almost identical with the understanding of the two-pronged religious dimension of experience that we have examined at such length in this work, most recently in the preceding chapter.

Vatican II

Since we are dealing at the moment with concillar documents, however, we cannot conclude the discussion without examining what Vatican II had to say about faith and reason in its Dogmatic Constitution on Divine Revelation. /30/ In it are two brief, pertinent passages: "God, who through the Word creates all things (John 1:3) and keeps them in existence, gives men an enduring witness to himself in created realities (Romans 1:19-20).... This Sacred Synod affirms 'God, the beginning and end of all things, can be known with certainty from created reality by the light of human reason (Romans 1:20), but the Synod teaches that it is through his revelation that those religious truths which are by their nature accessible to human reason can be known by all men with ease, with solid certitude, and with no trace of error, even in the present state of the human race." /31/

Vatican II, in this most controversial and revised of all its central documents, clearly reaffirms the basic position of Vatican I that in man's religious activity there is a human stage prior to the revelational that is essential to it and which is illuminated by it. As Frederick C. Grant, an official Protestant observer at the Council, writes in a commentary on the Declaration "The article rules out the erroneous idea that God is the great unknown, not only to all men in general but even to Christians, for it safeguards the sound principle that God has revealed Himself to all men, in nature, in history, and may be known by the light of human reason.

306

THE EXISTENCE OF GOD OR THE REALITY OF GOD?

This has always been one of the most stable and dependable principles in Catholic theology, and its modern repudiation in some areas of Protestantism has been a major tragedy." /32/

Karl Rahner draws two important practical conclusions from all this. The first is that God's intervention in human history and experience takes place continuously and in forms, shapes and even expressions new or unfamiliar to us. It is far more important and productive to search out and examine them despite the dangers and complexities involved than to merely lament the evils of materialism and atheism. The second is that this complex human dimension so important to religious integrity cannot be simplistically analyzed and explained by one conceptual approach. Almost of necessity it requires pluralistic philosophical examination. Rahner himself uses the unusual term "gnoseological pluralism." The fact that prior to any question of truth properly so called we have to recognize a pluralism of philosophies too great for us to master or control, compels us today to recognize a pluralism of theologies prior to the question of theological truth, without prejudice to a general orientation of all such theologies towards the original message of faith and the single teaching authority of the Church. /33/

Three Theistic Options

If all this is true then, it is not necessary to simply reassert the basic forms of the quinque viae approach to the proof of the existence of God in order to remain faithful to Vatican I and II or to the basic thrust of a sound christian faith. There are other options, other approaches and these ought to be judged on their own merits.

Before coming to the option which we will advocate, in the light of the theories developed and positions taken so far in this book, we will

307

examine briefly two other options that have much to commend them.

The Existentialist Option

In the classic medieval theistic arguments, God is seen as the creator and sovereign ruler of the universe and the one supremely necessary being. Modern existentialists thought theistic rather than atheistic in bent, however, sees God as the transformer of personal human existence. The focus shifts from the cosmos or the logical mind to the full human self. Rudolph Bultmann, the most influential modern theistic existentialist, says that we should consider God as acting not so much in the objective sphere of nature as in man's existential self-understanding. Presupposed here is a basic conflict between the world of nature and the world of value or the human. Essential to this dichotomizing view is an understanding of nature as a rigidly determined and closed mechanical order which is neater to Newton than it is to Einstein. It is this conflict between the physical and the human that leads Bultmann to his program of demythologization of the Bible. He says that the Bible falsely represents God when it accepts the mythical language of space-time in which to describe God and his actions. The real action of God, which is existential and directed towards the human self needs to be disengaged from this mythological framework and liberated into a genuine I-thou relationship, (in terms of Martin Buber), if we are to really understand what the Bible is revealing to us and we are to enter into a genuinely religious and worthwhile relationship with God.

It is unfair to Bultmann to see his demythologization program in merely negative terms, however. His intentions are positive, to reinterpret man's whole existence, his fears, his hopes, his decisions, his understanding of life and death so that God's trus meaning and action can be seen. Bultmann and

other Christian existentialists are thus performing
a very important and valuable service with their
emphasis upon what could be called the religious, the
human, the personal dimension of Christianity and
of belief in God.

At the same time, without pursuing further what
is obviously a complex and important area, there are
two major difficulties with the theistic existentialist option. First, Bultmann seems to be moving
towards a dehistoricized faith in which Christ
becomes not an independent reality but a parable of
the possibilities of human existence. Second, God's
activity in nature, while perhaps overemphasized
in the medieval arguments, is underemphasized in
Bultmann when he says that God cannot violate the
integrity of a closed mechanical system and therefore
must confine himself to the human self. Any reference to cosmological activity must be considered to
be mythological. At issue is both Bultmann's view
of nature as a closed mechanical system and his
program for radical demythologization. For it is
clear that he is retreating from the external world
of cause and effect to the inner world of personal
experience. His view of nature as an inviolable
and mechanically determined causal system...is closer
to nineteenth century than to contemporary science.
One interpretation of all this is to say that Kant's
division between nature and spirit has become so
accepted that God is banished from the world in
order to leave it to science while faith continues
to have its safe and independent sanctuary within
the human person. Epistemologically speaking, as has
been pointed out earlier in this work, such a dichotomy is not necessary. The division between the
world and the self, between the personal and the
impersonal is not an unbridgeable one. As a matter
of fact, there is a dynamic and living relationship
between the two. There is not only no contradiction
but something ultimately more satisfying in seeing
God as genuinely active both in the world of nature
and in personal existence.

DISCLOSURE OF THE ULTIMATE

Recent existentialist thought has acknowledged a number of these difficulties and modified and further refined a number of existentialist positions with regard to God. It may very well be that further close dialogue will indicate that there are now much closer affinities between such a renewed christian existentialism and the program of experiential religious knowledge developed here than would at first seem to be the case.

A Second Theistic Option

The Anglo-American system called Process Philosophy is another theistic option. In medieval thought God is understood as creator and ruler of the world and the greatest that can be conceived; in Christian existentialism, God is thought of as the transformer of personal existence; whereas in process philosophy, God is understood as the one who influences the processes of the world. Thus process is closer to the medievalist position in that it sees God as involved in the physical world and not confined to the realm of the personal. Unlike the classical theistic understanding of God, however, process philosophy attaches certain qualifications to the divine qualities such as omnipotence immutability, impassivity, absolute simplicity, timelessness, etc. Also, insofar as it attaches more importance to the "human" qualities of God and his immanence in the world and in the human person, it comes closer to christian existentialism than to medieval theism.

Alfred North Whitehead is the main figure in process philosophy. "Whitehead views every new occurrence as a present response (self-cause) to past events (efficient cause) in terms of potentialities grasped (final cause). Each event is represented as a moment of experience under the guidance of its 'subjective aim' every entity has a 'mental' pole, though the contribution of the latter may be vanishingly small." /34/ In all this, God is seen

310

as the primordial ground of order. "He embodies
within himself the order of possibilities, the
potential forms of relationship that are not
chaotic but orderly even before they are actualized.
This aspect is an answer to the question: why does
the world have the particular type of order it has
...rather than some other type?" /35/

God, however, is also seen as the ground of
novelty in an attempt to answer the further question:
why do certain new things come into existence instead
of merely repeating what already exists? God is seen
as representing new possibilities to the world and
giving it alternatives that are genuinely open. The
self creation of individual entities is left to their
freedom within a directional structure. The final-
izing tendency at work here is a subtle one. By
valuing certain potentialities more than others, God
determines the world without coercing it. He draws
it on by the lure of greater perfection and the vision of the good, both of which open up new possibilities for nature and for man.

God is also seen to be influenced by the world.
This is process philosophy's strongest departure
from the classical view of God's nature. God influences the world as described above, but at the same
time, the world is understood as influencing God.
This takes place in what Whitehead calls the "consequent nature" of God. "The central categories of
process philosophy (temporality, interaction, mutual
relatedness) apply to God; he is understood to
be temporal in the sense that his experience changes,
for he both receives from the world and contributes
to it. /36/ As Whitehead himself puts it,

> For the kingdom of heaven is with
> us today. The action of the fourth phase
> is the love of God for the world. It is
> the particular providence for particular
> occasions. What is done in the world is
> transformed into a reality in heaven, and

311

the reality in heaven passes back into
the world. By reason of this reciprocal
relation, the love in the world passes
into the love of heaven, and floods back
again into the world. In this sense, God
is the great companion--the fellow
sufferer who understands. /37/

One of the difficulties usually brought up in
relation to process thought's approach to God is the
loss there of God's

> traditional characteristics of immut-
> ability, impassivity, absolute simplicity,
> timelessness and the like...(But) These
> characteristics...are traditional only
> because the ancient theoretical schemes
> available for the interpretation of the
> Christian model demanded them; they are
> not especially required by the imaginative
> picture of God found in Christian
> Scripture. It may indeed be argued
> that the substitution of the mutable,
> essentially-related God-concept of
> Whitehead in place of the icy absolutes
> of Plato and Aristotle represents the
> discovery of a theoretical structure
> for theology far more congenial in
> formal structure to the God of the
> biblical model than was the traditional
> theory. /38/

Two other difficulties with process thought are
more substantial. First, there is the extreme
complexity of the metaphysical system itself. As
any bewildered first reader of Whitehead's fundamental work Process and Reality knows, /39/ the
beauty of the system's conclusions is not matched
by the simplicity of its structure or the clarity
of its language. Subsequent process thinkers such
as John Cobb /40// have simplified and synthesized
these principles to some degree, but process remains

a formidable philosophical bite to chew, particularly if taken as a preamble to a deeper conceptual
understanding of God. The second difficulty is
more theological.

> It is hard to know just how well
> Whiteheadian metaphysics can explicate
> Christian insistence on the uniqueness
> of Jesus and his significance for men.
> As a theoretical matrix for a general
> theistic religion of creativity the
> Whiteheadian scheme will serve to
> whatever extent it can meet the demands
> of critical reason and be shown to be
> consistent, coherent and adequate. But
> the Christian model, while dominated by
> God, has historically included more
> specific elements as essential to its
> image. How will the so-called "scandal
> of particurity" be represented by the
> very general Whiteheadian concepts
> available? /41/

Though a number of Whiteheadian theologians
recognize this problem and are studying it seriously
/42/ this second question remains a nagging one.

If difficulties ruled out philosophical systems,
however, there would be very few around and process
thought is proving to be of considerable importance
on the current philosophical and theological scene.
Charles Hartshorne, for example, has written prodig-
iously in this area, developing what has turned out
to be a distinctively personal contribution and has
alsmost singlehandedly revitalized interest in the
ontological proof. Many theologians, including many
Roman Catholics, are much interested in process
thought and are beginning to develop a corpus of
works that are among the most dynamic and productive
on the current scene. Finally, much of process
thinking about God is compatible with the more experiential approach of this work. Whitehead himself
is proof of this as he "turns from God as the

'primordial' ground of order to God's 'consequent' nature interacting with the world, he makes more frequent references to religious as against purely philosophical considerations." /43/

The Third Option

This brings us to the third option, the one that we have been exploring throughout this work. If in the first option God could be described as One who transforms personal existence and if in the second option he could be described as One who draws out and influences the processes of the world, then in this third option he could be described as the One who is encountered in religious experience both communal and individual, both human and revealed. The reality of God is thus affirmed without the existentialistic separation from the cosmos or process thought's awkwardness with the historical, the christological and the self.

Background: Two Traditions of Thought

Before developing this third option in more detail it may be helpful to recall some of the general background involved. The third option clearly favors one of the two great traditions of Western Christian thought, namely the Platonic-Augustinian over the Aristotelian-Thomistic. Although this was discussed earlier in chapter five, the following looks as some fresh angles.

In comparing the two traditions, it is important to point out immediately that no attempt is being made to say that one is wrong and the other right. That would be chauvinistic in the extreme. What is involved is saying that one system of thought is better suited to one kind of intellectual discourse than the other and that instead of being contraries the two systems should be understood

314

as complementary. They do not clash unless they trespass into the area of each other's special competence. Thus the Aristotelian-Thomistic (AT) tradition is particularly strong with regard to the areas of science and technology and the propositional abstraction associated with these, whereas the Platonic-Augustinian tradition (PA) is particularly strong in the areas of morality, art, politics and religion.

Looking at their relationship historically, it is clear that after some centuries of domination of Western Christianity, the PA tradition was gradually displaced as the prime Christian philosophical-theological system by the AT tradition beginning in the early Middle Ages. Most historians of thought agree that the older tradition found itself incapable of dealing, without considerable revision, with the unfolding developments of the slowly dawning age of science. The AT tradition proved itself a better tool for handling these advances and it gradually became the dominant system even it was itself reacted against in later centuries. The case can be made, historically, that the pendulum has not swung the other way, and that the contributions at of the AT system to the modern scientific-technological world have been made and that the problem not is that we are faced with the failures of its attempted extension into other areas as the human, the personal, and the experiential. Any number of indications, as has been observed earlier, show the need for a return to the more experiential aspect of life and the need to resist imperialistic claims on all knowledge by any one system of thought no matter how great.

The processes of the two traditions differ considerably. AT moves by inference, starting with facts or realities supposedly open to all and moving on to something that lies beyond. The PA tradition does not move away from its starting point so much as moves within it. It reflects upon or interprets the experiences of the self in order to discover intelligible patterns that make sense of the whole of experience. In Polanyian terms, we discover that we know more than we can tell. The AT tradition's experiential base is the normal, the standard, the universal. The PA's the individual self living within its cultural framework. The AT's intelligibility is achieved through logical implications between propositions resulting in compelling proof. The PA's intelligibility is achieved through an examination of the internal meanings and interconnections of experience as well as through the relations of these to the whole pattern of the self and its cultural framework. The AT's tradition's purpose is to convince the neutral or hostile person of something by force of logic. Since the PA's position is to support and clarify the experience of the enquirer, it sees nothing invalid or irrational for the starting point to be found in the conclusion. If such clarification of experience serves as a helpful example to someone else, that is an added advantage, but it is secondary to the movement involved.

Finally, it can be argued that the God arrived at through these two systems has differing characteristics. To take one central difference, it can be claimed that the God of the PA tradition is more easily compatible with the God of Christianity than the God of the AT tradition. It has always been a source of considerable difficulty for the AT tradition to explain how its uncaused cause, its prime mover, its final cause is simply another way of speaking of the God of the Bible. Of course there was no great difficulty in simply stating this equivalence, as Thomas himself does, in those ages when there was no particular conceptual doubt of the existence of the Christian God. But stating such equivalence and demonstrating it are two different things. The God of the PA tradition, the ultimate of life and thought, a God whose love is experienced in the community of faith and in the individual believer, is much easier to see as God of Christ-

ianity. It is interesting that some of the strongest
critics of the traditional AT proofs of the existence
of God, such as Hume and Kant, go out of their way to
indicate that even if one were to concede much of
the theistic arguments, it is difficult to see how
the God they concluded to is to be related to the
God of Christian faith. It was this very difficulty
that impelled Kant, for one, to develop at such
length his moral arguments.

Background: Two Epistemologies

The contrast involved, however, goes beyond that
between the two great traditions, Thomistic and Augustinian. Despite their differences, both traditions,
even the Thomistic in its high period, shared an
unarticulated realistic theory of knowledge that included the reality of the faith experience as legitimately foundational. As time went on, however, the
internal logic of the Aristotelian-Thomistic tradition
showed greater and greater strains due to the tension
between the empirical advances of the new science and
the inner world of faith and value. This led ultimately to Descartes' dichotomy between mind and substance, which led to the further dichotomy between
fact and value. Out of both these dichotomies grew
the classic challenges to the classic proofs of God
made by the Empiricists and Kant.

What is involved here, once again, is a conflict
between the epistemological presuppositions of classical empiricism and the position developed earlier
in this work. Thus whereas the classical empiricists
claim that experience or knowledge is a veil standing
between the person who experiences and the so-called
external world; that experience and sensation are
co-extensive and that the experiencer is primarily
a theoretical knower of data, we have claimed, to
the contrary, that experience is an objective disclosure of what is there to be encountered; that it is
a meaningful result of a multidimensional encounter
between a concrete person and whatever there is to

be encountered, and that finally, such experience
includes a number of dimensions of human life such
as the moral, esthetic, scientific and religious.

Basic Principle: The Nature of Religious Faith

One final major contrast between the two great
traditions of thought discussed above, is the relation of their methodologies to the nature of religious faith and its experience of God. The AT tradition builds by inference, proceeding from the
world of the generally know, to a compelling
conclusion with regard to the heretofore unknown.
While it doesn't equivalate understanding with
faith, it does say that it understands the preambles
of faith and therefore believes. Intelligo
preambulas fidel et credo. Understanding here is
taken in the inferential sense described. Whatever
its merit, such a process goes counter to the way
that religious experience works in fact. In
practice people do not arrive at genuine religious
faith through an inferential process. They encounter God in themselves and in their religious tradition. As was said earlier, such encounters with
God in one's religious tradition are none the less
real and personal for happening within an inherited
framework of experiences and ideas. Our analysis
of the human way of knowing showed that such suppo-
sitional frameworks are endemic to the way the
human mind works, even in its scientific aspects.
We live in a body of subsidiary awareness that do
not come to focal awareness except on particular
occasions and for particular needs. The religious
view of the world is an interpretation of the same
world that we live in, but with a particular vision,
namely the encounter there of God. These encounters
are broadly historical, as in our acceptance of God
and commemoration of the Exodus and the Eucharist
and intensely personal and individual as in the case
of saints and mystics. The process of PA thought,
thus, with its stress on the intelligibility of

religious experience, "Nisis credideritis non
intelligitis," seems closest to the nature of religious faith.

The Theistic Arguments as Expression

of Religious Faith

The case can therefore be made that the traditional arguments for the existence of God, the
ontological argument of Anselm and the five ways of
St. Thomas, were developed in a period of strong
reli_ious and Christian faith, when there was little
real doubt about the existence of the Christian God,
in order to clarify the nature of the God in whom
they already believed. In intent, the arguments were
meant to confirm rather than convince only the
already convinced are short of the mark because that
is what they were intended to do and what they in
fact do. This is obviously a different approach to
the theistic proofs than many, especially Roman
Catholics, are accustomed to, so it may be helpful
to reexamine these traditional proofs briefly to
see whether such a claim can be supported.

The Ontological Argument

The major difficulty with the ontological argument, of course, has always been that to claim that
something exists demands more than the assertion of
logical consistency. In our general experience,
existing beings are known through encounter. We
don't reason to a stone wall, we point to it. We
don't reason to the existence of family and friends,
we point to them. We can reflect abstractly upon
such pointing, of course, but this is not the same
thing as arguing to the fact of existence through
logical necessity.

So why not admit that the ontological argument
is based on just such an encounter with God and is,

as a matter of fact, pointing at him rather than asserting his existence through logical necessity? It certainly seems to make much more sense historically and psychologically:

> Anselm inherited the record of the
> continuing experience of God contained
> in the biblical tradition. He understood
> the God of Christianity as the God of
> Majesty, of awe-inspiring sublimity,
> as a God of perfect love and truth who
> alone is worthy of an absolute loyalty
> and devotion. Anselm incorporated this
> conception into his own experience,
> relived and repossessed it in meditation
> and reflection; his task was to find a
> conceptual formula of a philosophical
> sort that would express the God of an
> absolute religious devotion. The
> formula "than that which nothing greater
> can be conceived," is the result of
> Anselm's search. /44/

The argument for an experiential base for the proofs of God, including the ontological is supported both by Henri DeLubac and Karl Rahner. DeLubac says that the criticisms directed against the proofs are inspired by a too narrow conception of the human intelligence and focused too much upon their conceptual apparatus, looking upon "their 'logical forms' in a superficial way, without regard to the spirit that informs them...For the artifice developed by the learned proof...is simply the elaboration and rational organization of a permanently subsisting proof which is natural, spontaneous and in many cases unformulated." /45/ Karl Rahner says, "There is and can be only one proof, in the whole questionable nature of man seen as a totality which man is aware of in the concreteness of his existence." /46/

THE EXISTENCE OF GOD OR THE REALITY OF GOD?

The Cosmological Argument

The basic question involved in the cosmological argument is of course why does anything exist when it might not? The answer that since what in fact exists but might not does not have the reason for its existence within itself then there must be at least one existent capable of giving existence to itself and thence to others, is an answer which depends on the use and validity of the principle of sufficient reason. But what if the principle of sufficient reason is not accepted? Wouldn't the cosmological argument then fail? And it has been challenged.

And yet in our experience the principle of sufficient reason does give intelligibility to reality.

> This point may be expressed in another and quite surprising way by saying that such complete intelligibility is what we would expect reality to exhibit if God were real. The principle itself, namely, that there is an ultimate intelligibility both for the features exhibited in the world and for the existence of the world itself, is a way of expressing what it would be for God to be real. /47/

Doesn't it make sense to see the cosmological argument as primarily seeking the intelligibility of religious experience rather than arguing inferentially? This is not to deny that there is a logical transition involved which goes beyond the limits of direct experience, but this transition remains logically related to that experience as a starting point. So we are back where we were with the ontological argument. We have as a matter of fact started with the religious experience of God, or, more explicitly, with the experience of our own insufficiency as finite beings both as persons and as part of a limited cosmos face to face with an

321

ultimate who has also spoken to us about himself and about us. The cosmological arguments then, and these include teleological, make more sense as attempts to spell out the functions of the universe of God as they are revealed by that cosmos and supported by his revelation. Such an attempt assumes that God has a certain nature and a certain role in the cosmos that can be found and analyzed and made more intelligible. Since God's nature is complex, his role in the cosmos is complex, with a variety of different functions. One of the points of the cosmological arguments, in their diversity, is to separate out these functions and by focussing the mind upon them, make them stand out in such a way as to make these functions of God more intelligible.

So God is assumed in the cosmological argument as in the ontological, and this is seen as no more valid and irrational in one than in the other.

Is Such a Circular Process Rational?

But is such a circular process really rational? The problem is posed succintly and well by John Hick.

> Historically, then, the philosophical proofs have normally entered in to support and confirm but not to create belief. Accordingly, the proper philosophical approach would seem to be a problem of the actual foundations and structure of a living and operative belief rather than of theoretical and non-operative arguments subsequently formulated for holding these beliefs. The question is not whether it is possible to prove, starting from zero, that God exists: the question is whether the religious man, given the distinctively religious form of human existence in which he participates, is properly entitled as a rational person to believe what he does believe? /48/

THE EXISTENCE OF GOD OR THE REALITY OF GOD?

There are two ways of answering that question
positively, the first, Hick's own, is through a
process of analyzing the nature of rationality
itself and the relationship between the evidence
involved and the belief. The second is through an
explanation of the epistemology involved in the
theory of religious experiential knowledge such as
has been presented in this work.

Rational Belief in God

What then is meant by a rational belief? It
is important to distinguish clearly between a rational belief and a rational believer. One is a proposition, the other a person. Persons are rational,
propositions are either true or false. Putting
aside the question of analytical propositions, the
rationality of a person has to be judged in each case.
For rationality depends on the relationship between
the proposition believed and the data upon which it
is based. It is possible for a belief to be rational for one person based on the evidence which he has,
and irrational for another person because of a lack
of such evidence or the presence of contrary evidence.
These general principles apply to the question of
belief in God.

> What is at issue is not whether it
> is rational for someone else, who does not
> participate in the distinctively religious
> mode of experience to believe in God on
> the basis of the religious man's reports...
> .It is not the non-religious man's theo-
> retical use of someone else's reported
> religious experience that is to be
> considered, but the religious man's own
> practical use of it. The question is
> whether he is acting to live on the
> basis of it. /49/

Hick argues for the rationality of religious

DISCLOSURE OF THE ULTIMATE

belief in God by developing at some length an
analogy between belief in the existence of the
external world and belief in the reality of God. If
nothing else, such an argument shows the importance
of epistemological considerations in this matter.
He says that the vast majority of men claim to be
conscious of the physical environment of the world
around them, seeing it as independent of themselves
and an arena in which they can and must act. Most
men accept the external world as true, its indepen-
dence from them as real and their actions within it
as genuine and necessary. They do so even though
when pressed for a theoretical justification of such
assumptions, when asked to "prove" them, they cannot
do so, (Even Descartes' major effort to do so
ultimately fails.) yet they accept it and live as if
it were true. Daily experience confirms rather than
derogates such an understanding. If they try to
live otherwise than if there really were an external
world, they are judged by other people to be abnormal
or "insane".

Just as the external world has a giveness to it,
so the realities of religious experience have a
giveness to them, especially as these are experienced
by the great religious figures of history. The world
is a given, and a profound interpretation of its meaning and purpose is experienced as equally given. In
the case of both givennesses, men act upon them and
judge their validity in part by successful actions.
Despite occasional lapses and human failures, the
general and religious history of mankind shows that
actions of men based on religious experience have
been widely considered to be realistic and successful

All this is not to say that there are no differences between the experience of the external world
and religious experience. The first is had by all,
for example, whereas the second is not. But once
the religious experience has been freely chosen, as
it has been so consistently down through the millenia
of mankind's the same qualities of givenness and

actability can be observed.

Delusion and Falsity

Could it be, however, that such religious experience and especially that more intense kind found in
the great religious leaders are simply delusional?
"Since those who enjoy a compelling religious experience form such a small minority of mankind, ought
we not to suspect that they are suffering from a
delusion comparable with that of the paranoiac who
hears threatening voices from the walls and the
alcoholic who sees green snakes?" /50/ Delusion
is possible, but it cannot be assumed; it has to be
shown, like anything else, to be really there. And
the evidence is much to the contrary. The obviously
high character and keen intelligence of the great
religious leaders down through history lend little
credence to the delusional charge and they were
certainly not perceived as such by their followers
in their own day. If we examine their lives we
find that they were not disoriented, that they were
able to live warmly and productively in society, that
they gave wholeheartedly and unselfishly of themselves
and were supported and honored for such. The life,
person and message of Jesus Christ has been scrutin-
ized and imitated by millions and millions of people
down through the centuries and their lived reaction
to a charge of paranoical delusion would be strongly
negative.

Suppose, however, putting delusion aside, the
data upon which the religious person bases his beliefs
in all good faith as it were, are in point of fact,
false? At one time men thought that the sun revolved
around the world, and it was rational to believe that
this was the case because man's data gathering apparatus was not sufficient to refute the data of the
naked eye. Once the Copernian system was shown to
be correct, however, it was no longer rational to
believe in the Ptolemaic. Suppose then that the
data upon which the religious person bases his faith

is equally false. Suppose that new and forthcoming
discoveries in the depths of the psyche, from outer
space or in psychical research were to show that
these data are false, then the religious man's
beliefs would be equally false and it would be
irrational to hold them. Is such falsehood possible?
Yes it is. Just as it is possible that there is no
external world out there. But the possibility
diminishes in proportion to the kind of data involved
It is at a maximum with regard to data with a theoretical element to it, such a high-level scientific
hypotheses, but it is at a minimum level with regard to data arising from perceptual beliefs, among
which is included the experience of the external
world. Religious experience is not some hypothetical
scientific theory referring to an inferred deity;
it is an experienced encounter of a personal kind,
a perceptual belief:

> If this is so, it is appropriate
> that the religious man's belief in the
> reality of God should be no more pro-
> visional than his belief in the reality
> of the physical world. The situation is
> in each case that, given the experience
> which he has and which is part of him he
> cannot help accepting as "there" such
> aspects of his environment as he exper-
> iences. He cannot help believing either
> in the reality of the material world
> which he is conscious of inhabiting,
> or of the personal divine presence which
> is overwhelmingly evident to him and to
> which his mode of living is a free
> response. And I have been suggesting
> that it is _as_ reasonable for him to hold
> and to act upon the one belief as the
> other. /51/

Epistemological Foundations

Hick's argument from the analogy between our

perception of the external world and religious experience is compelling and convincing as long as the epistemological theory of critical realism that underlies it holds up. But such critical realism has been strongly challenged and it has been one of the main efforts of this work to respond to that challenge with a theory of experiential knowledge and experiential religious knowledge which has been called intersective realism. We have done so because its centrality to so many important arguments, the epistemological dimension is too frequently assumed rather than explained.

The theory of intersective realism, as developed at length earlier, supports the analogy Hick draws between experience of the external world and religious experience. It goes beyond it and claims that there is a sense in which all knowledge, including the creatively scientific, arises out of personal commitment, is oriented towards discovery and is heuristic in nature. Without developing this position once again, it is legitimate to conclude that there is nothing irrational or invalid about a belief in the reality of God which attempts to bring to a focal awareness subsidiary experiences of God. It assumes that all human reasoning is based on experience, that this involves the circularity of reflection upon that experience, and that therefore human reasoning about God is neither irrational or invalid if it proceeds in the same way with the experience of God, understanding that God as the Ultimate can be perceived only through symbol and analogy. Instead of being constantly on the defensive against the charge of not being able to prove the existence of God, the believing person can legitimately ask the other person to show how the acceptance of the experience of the reality of God is any more irrational than the acceptance of the reality of the external world. Instead of trying to convince unbelievers with inferential argument, would it not be more practical and effective to simply ask others who have not experienced God to try to share with the believer, as best they both can, the religious experience of believing individuals, including that of the great leaders and that of the religious community of faith with its special experiences and revelatory dimensions? Pointing seems somehow more appropriate than abstraction. In the ultimate analysis, for those who do not believe, no proof is possible, for those who do believe, no proof is necessary.

In the next and final chapter we will take up one remaining major question, namely, what good is all this God-talk if the name of God and religious language itself are purely and simply meaningless?

THE EXISTENCE OF GOD OR THE REALITY OF GOD?

NOTES

[1] *A Scholastic Miscellany: Anselm to Ockham.*
Ed. and Trans. by E. R. Fairweather (Philadelphia:
The Westminster Press, 1956) Vol. X *Library of
Christian Classics*, p. 73. John Hick ed. *The
Existence of God* (N. Y.:Macmillan, 1964) notes on
page 30, "Anselm uses four different but synonymous
formulations: aliquid quo nihil maius cogitari
potest, aliquid quo nihil maius cogitari possit,
aliquid quo maius cogitari non valet, and aliquid
quo maius cogitari nequit."

[2] "Gaunilo: A Book on Behalf of the Fool: Anselm:
A Reply." Transl. A. C. McGill in John Hick, *Classical and Contemporary Readings in the Philosophy
of Religion*, 2nd Ed. (Englewood Cliffs, N. J.:
Prentice-Hall, 1970/64), pp. 28-37.

[3] *Summa Theologica*, Part I, Q. II, Art. 1.

[4] Réné Descartes, *The Meditations and Selections
from the Principles*. Transl. by John Veitch (La
Salle, Illinois: Open Court Publishing Company, 1966)

[5] Ibid., Med. V, pp. 78-79.

[6] Immanuel Kant, *Critique of Pure Reason*. Transl.
Norman Kemp Smith (London: Macmillan and Company,
1933), pp. 501-504.

[7] *The Dialogues of Plato*. Trans. by B. Jowett
(Oxford: The Clarendon Press, 4th ed. 1953) Vol. IV,
pp. 463-69; Book X, 894A- 899C.

[8] Ibid., p. 467.

[9]Aristotle, Metaphysics. Transl. by Richard Hope (Ann Arbor: The University of Michigan Press, 1960), Eeta 4 (999b), p. 51.

[10]Richard Wollheim, ed. Hume on Religion (Cleveland: World Publishing Company: Meridian Books, 1963)

[11]Ibid., p. 162.

[12]Ibid., p. 165.

[13]Ibid., pp. 162-163.

[14]Ibid., p. 164.

[15]Ninian Smart, ed. Historical Selections in the History of Religion (N. Y.: Harper and Row, 1962), pp. 261-262. Critique of Pure Reason: Transcendental Dialectic, BookII, ch. iii.

[16]Summa Theologica, Part. I Q. II, Art. III.

[17] William Paley, A View of the Evidences of Christianity: In Three Parts (London: J. Faulder, 1814), Vols. I and II.

[18]William Paley, Natural Theology or Evidences of the Existence and Attributes of the Deity Collected from the Appearances of Nature (London: J. Faulder, 1813).

[19]Ibid., pp. 1-3.

[20]Immanuel Kant, Critique of Pure Reason, p. 520

330

[21] Immanuel Kant, Critique of Practical Reason. Transl. Lewis White Beck (N. Y.: Liberal Arts Press, 1956) Book II, Chapter II, Sec. V, pp. 128-136.

[22] Terence Penelhum, Religion and Rationality: An Introduction to the Philosophy of Religion (N. Y.: Random House, 1971), p. 85-86.

[23] John Macquarrie, Principles of Christian Theology (N. Y.: Scribner's Sons, 1977/66), pp. 46-49.

[24] Penelhum, op. cit., p. 84.

[25] John Hick, Arguments for the Existence of God (N. Y.: The Seabury Press, 1971), p. 101.

[26] The Teaching of the Catholic Church as Contained in Her Documents. Ed. Neuner, Roos, Rahner. Transl. G. Stevens (Staten Island, N. Y.: Alba House, 1967), pp. 31-32.

[27] F. Van Steenberghen, Revue Philosophique de Louvain (XIV, 1947) 168.

[28] Teaching of Catholic Church: The following texts are included in this collection: The Articles Subscribed by Bautain (1840); Pius IX's Address: Singulari Quadam (1854); Articles Subscribed by Bonnetty (1855); Ontologist Errors Condemned by Pius IX (1861); Letter of Pius IX to the Archbishop of Munich Freising against the Rationalism of Frohschammer (1862); The Syllabus of Errors (3-9) of Pius IX (1864); Vatican I (1870); Articles of Rosmini Condemned by Leo XIII (1887); Form of Oath against Modernism prescribed by Pius X (1910); Encyclical Letter: Humani Generis of Pius XII (1950); Encyclical Letter Sempiternus Rex of Pius XII (1951) and Vatican II (1960-64)

[29] Karl Rahner, _Theological Investigations: Vol. XIII: Theology, Anthropology, Christology_. Transl. D. Bourke (N. Y.: Saebury Press, 1975), pp. 67-68.

[30] _The Documents of Vatican II_. Ed. W. Abbott (N. Y.: America Press and Guild Press, 1966), pp. 111-128.

[31] Ibid., I:3 , p. 112; p. 114.

[32] Ibid., p. 129.

[33] Rahner, op. cit., p. 72.

[34] Ian G. Barbour, _Issues in Science and Religion_ (N. Y.: Harper, 1966), p. 434.

[35] Ibid., p. 440.

[36] Ibid., p. 446.

[37] Alfred North Whitehead, _Science and the Modern World_ (N. Y.: Macmillan, 1925), p. 275.

[38] Frederick Ferré, _Basic Modern Philosophy of Religion_ (N. Y.: Scribner's Sons, 1967), p. 434.

[39] Alfred North Whitehead, _Process and Reality: An Essay in Cosmology_ (N. Y.: Macmillan, 1960/57)

[40] John Cobb Jr., _A Christian Natural Theology based on the Thought of Alfred North Whitehead_ (London: Lutterworth Press, 1966): _God and The World_ (Philadelphia: Westminster Press, 1969)

THE EXISTENCE OF GOD OR THE REALITY OF GOD?

[41]Ferré, op. cit., p. 435.

[42]Two recent and important examples of process christologies are John B. Cobb,Jr., *Christ in a Pluralistic Age* (Philadelphia: Westminster Press, 1975) and David Griffin, *A Process Christology* (Philadelphia Westminster Press, 1973)

[43]Ferré, op. cit., p. 445.

[44]John E. Smith, *Experience and God* (N. Y.: Oxford University Press, 1968), p. 123.

[45]Henri DeLubac, *The Discovery of God.* Transl. A. Dru (N. Y.: P. J. Kenedy, 1960), pp. 83-88.

[46]Karl Rahner, *Theological Investigations, IX, Writings of 1967-68, I* (N. Y.: Herder and Herder, 1972), p. 140.

[47]Smith, op. cit., p. 139.

[48]John Hick, op. cit., p. 108.

[49]Ibid., p. 109

[50]Ibid., p. 114.

[51]Ibid., p. 116.

DISCLOSURE OF THE ULTIMATE

CHAPTER EIGHT

THE DISCLOSIVE NATURE

OF RELIGIOUS LANGUAGE

AND THEOLOGICAL MODELS

The previous chapter discussed the existence and reality of God. But one final question remains: what if the very word God and other elements of religious language are meaningless? Such a question is a new one. Up until around World War I, it was a general philosophical and cultural assumption that the truth or falsity of a proposition was something that could be determined by means of a careful examination. Around that time, however, there developed, beginning in what is called the Vienna Circle, a new school of thought which held that meaning comes before truth. According to the logical positivists, if a proposition is meaningless, then it is useless to pursue the question of its truth or falsehood. By meaningful they of course mean cognitively meaningful not psychologically. If the proposition is verifiable in human experience, if it "makes a difference to someone", then it is meaningful. Otherwise it is not.

This has been a largely Anglo-American philosophical development and those Christians, including Roman Catholics, whose philosophical and theological

335

ideas are strongly influenced by Continental European thought in its Barthian, Neo-Thomistic and Existentialistic forms, have tended either to be unaware of the developments of logical analysis or uninterested.

Yet as an attempt to deal creatively with the question of truth in the thoroughly pragmatic and scientific culture that exists in the United States, logical or linguistic analysis deserves to be taken more seriously by Anglo-American theologians and especially by Roman Catholics than it has been. The assumption, furthermore, that logical analysis is exhausted by and identified with logical positivism's assertion of the meaninglessness of religious language cannot be supported by the facts. There are both early and later schools of linguistic analysis and differing shades of thought at both times. Some of the more recent schools not only take a position in support of the meaningfulness of religious language but provide valuable new conceptual tools which are highly stimulating for a genuinely contemporary theology. For these reasons, this chapter will begin with a study of logical positivism and its evolution as seen in Ayer, Wisdom, Flew, Hare, Mitchell and Hick. It will then examine two non-cognitive theories of religious language in Randall and Braithwaite and finally, go on to an exposition of the positive modular theory of religious language found in Ramsey and Barbour. This last will be shown to be in essential agreement with the theories of religious experience and intersective realism developed in this book.

Historical Background

British analytic philosophy along with its American counterpart begins with David Hume. Hume tempered his skeptical empirical analysis with moral conviction based on common sense. But as time went on, later empiricists were more rigorous in drawing skeptical conclusions from Hume's premises. As a

counterreaction to this deepening religious and
moral skepticism of the empiricists, a number of
idealistic philosophers appeared in the latter part
of the nineteenth century. As a movement it was
called absolute idealism and for several decades
it dominated British-American philosophy.

The two main figures of absolute idealism were
T. H. Green and F. H. Bradley. Green held that in
order to understand the world it is necessary to
recognize a universal self whose consciousness is
what provides the relationship between our sensations and whose will in all its goodness is experienced in our moral decisions. Bradley held that
it is false to say that all objects are constituted
by clusters of their qualities because relations
are internal and not external. In order, then, to
explain the reality of anything, it is necessary
to go beyond the individual fact or object to a
universal reality where contradictory and completely
factual universality.

Analytic philosophers began as disciples of
such absolute idealism and eventually rose in opposition to it. Bertrand Russell, for example, was
originally a disciple of Bradley:

> The development of this form of
> philosophical analysis leads from Russell's
> espousal of an alternative metaphysic of
> "logical atomism" to Ludwig Wittgenstein's
> rigorous development of this, which led
> ironically to the denial of the possibliity
> of metaphysics. It then moves through
> the logical positi.ists' analysis of
> scientific knowledge--which, assuming
> the elimination of metaphysics, is
> alleged to provide us with our only
> "positive knowledge of the world--
> and the analysis of moral and religious
> discourse in the light of positivist
> assumptions...Out of this development..
> .emerged a specific cluster of criticisms

DISCLOSURE OF THE ULTIMATE

and appraisals of religious and theological discourse. /1/

Ayer and the Analysis of Scientific Language

Rather than attempt a kind of history of the
logical positivist movement, something long and
involved, one principal figure in it will be
examined in some detail. Alfred Ayer is a good
example, because in the course of his life he embodied the developments and changes that took
place in the movement as a whole, going from strict
positives to a much more open-ended position.

Ayer had been one of Rudolf Carnap's disciples
at the University of Vienna and upon returning home
to England he published in 1936 his influential
Language, Truth and Logic which popularized the
logical positivism of the so-called Vienna Circle.
/2/ In this early work, Ayer says that the philosopher must not be asked to develop speculative
truths in the way scientists do, for a philosopher's
task is much more simple, that of analyzing language.
By language he does not mean the language of ordinary
life but the language of science. The philosopher's
function is to analyze these scientific propositions
and exhibit their logical relationships by defining
the symbols they contain. In doing so, the philosopher is not setting himself up as judge over the
scientific theories themselves. These are matters
of fact with which the philosopher does not deal.
But what he does do is help the scientist to define
and clarify the concepts which are being used in
scientific theories. Such definition and clarification can be of considerable assistance to scientists
because it coordinates their work and frees them
from ony metaphysical burden which they may be carrying, allowing them to work even more productively.
Science and philosophy, then, for Ayer are closely
interconnected: science is blind without philosophy
and philosophy is empty without science. They are

both about the same task, with science handling the
speculative aspect and philosophy the logical.

Philosophical propositions, according to Ayer,
are linguistic and deal with the use of words.
Lexicography of course also analyzes the use of
words, and in so doing is empirical, but philosophy
is more concerned with verbal definitions than with
matters of fact.

All propositions are either analytic or empirical. Analytic means that the proposition's validity
is dependent only on the definition of its symbols.
An example of an analytic proposition would be: all
pediatricians are child-doctors. As long as the
definitions of the symbols are known, the truth of
the proposition is known. Such analytic propositions
though they are a priori and independent of experience, are not meaningless; they can teach us something new by pointing to a linguistic usage that
might otherwise be missed.

An empirical proposition is one whose validity
is determined by experience. By determination is
meant verifiability. Though some empirical propositions are strongly verifiable, such as for example,
"I don't feel well," most can only show their probability. Even when an empirical proposition is not
verified as a matter of fact, it should remain
theoretically capable of being so.

All this leads Ayer to say that metaphysical
propositions are meaningless since they assert something about reality which cannot be verified by
sense experience. Since they are unverifiable in
principle, they are meaningless. "God Exists" is
just such kind of unverifiable proposition and that
is why it must be judged to be meaningless.

What about the verification principle itself?
Can it be verified? According to Ayers there is
no difficulty because it is not an empirical proposition but an analytic one. So, in the first

339

edition of Language, Truth and Logic, he defines
it as firm and unarbitrary. By the time he issued
the second edition, he had modified his stand and
conceded that there was an arbitrariness to the
verification principle which allowed different
persons to adopt different criteria of meaning.
Though such an understanding of the verification
principle would seem to leave room for a metaphysical criterion of meaning, Ayer still refused to
accept any other criterion for verifiability than
sense experience.

In his more recent works, however, he does
admit that questions of analysis cannot be distinguished quite so neatly from questions of fact and
that philosophy does involve some such questions of
empirical fact. He thus largely abandons logical
positivism and stands as a symbol of a general
trend in the modern Anglo-American philosophical
scene.

Wittgenstein and the Analysis of Ordinary Language

Though obviously an oversimplification, the
gradual move away from strict logical positivism
can be described as a move away from the analysis
of scientific language exclusively to the analysis
of ordinary language as well.

Another person who exemplifies in himself this
kind of change is Ludwig Wittgenstein. Though at
one time in his Tractatus Logico-Philosophicus /3/
he had been one of the most uncompromising of the
logical positivists and in many ways the foundation
store of the movement, he later became in his
Philosophical Investigations /4/ one of the most
outspoken critics of positivistic assumptions The
literary character of these two works alone is
indicative of this change. The first is highly
organized and contains a meticulously developed
philosophical system. The second seems to have no
organization at all and gives the impression of

being musings-out-loud captured on paper. This contrast reflects the contrast between their respective
philosophical viewpoints.

The early Wittgenstein, as was seen in chapter
four, had been impatient with the vagueness of ordinary language in order to overcome it. Later on he
saw that this was an enterprise foredoomed to failure.
Though it is true that scientific language has great
clarity about it, it is a mistake to identify it
and its clarity with human language as a whole. Such
an overidentification of scientific language with
human language arose from two basic misconceptions.
"The assumption that the basic or normative, if not
the sole, function of language is to state facts:
and the assumption that sentences which state facts
'picture' the facts which they state." /5/

If the function of language then are broader
than scientific clarity, how are they discovered?
By empirical examination answered Wittgenstein.
Such a study will disclose that language, besides
asserting facts, tells stories, expresses wishes,
greets persons, makes business deals and so on. Any
analysis of language which is going to be sound and
accurate must include all these functions. The
varoius functions of language can be compared to the
tools in a tool box. It makes as much sense to say
that language has only one function as to say that
all the tools in a tool box do exactly the same
thing. Just as it is necessary to ask what specific
tools do, so it is necessary to look at the specific
roles of language. In both cases, differences are
as important as similarities. These differences
were called "language games" by Wittgenstein. Each
major area of human life has its own "language game"
with its own goals and rules and these need to be
respected. The use of the word game in this context,
however, should not be taken as belittling linguistic analysis or that the rules being discussed are
mere matters of convention. Wittgenstein himself
tried to specify matters futher by describing

341

language games as "forms of life", though in his
writings this last term remains somewhat ambiguous.
By it he meant that language games "are the living
expressions of the knowledge, convictions, hopes,
fears and visions of human beings involved in the
business of life. Languages derive their importance from the 'forms of life' they articulate." /6/

Verification-Falsification: A Tale of Several Tales

Another direction taken by logical analysis was
from questions of meaningfulness and verifiability
to those of falsifiability. A good example of this
development is the debate carried on by a group of
British philosophers using a string of parables to
make their respective points.

John Wisdom

It begins with John Wisdom's now famous parable of the gardener:

Two people return to their long-
neglected garden and find among the weeds
a few of the old plants surprisingly
vigorous. One says to the other "It must
be that a gardener has been coming and
doing something about these plants."
Upon inquiry they find that no neighbor
has ever seen anyone at work in their
garden. The first man says to the other
"he must have worked while people slept."
The other says, "No, someone would have
heard him and besides, anybody who cared
about the plants would have kept down
these weeds." The first man says, "Look
at the way these are arranged. There is
purpose and a feeling for beauty here.
I believe that someone comes, someone
invisible to mortal eyes. I believe
that the more carefully we look the more

342

we shall find confirmation of this."
They examine the garden ever so carefully
and sometimes they come on new things
suggesting that a gardener comes and
sometimes they come on new things
suggesting the contrary and even that a
malicious person has been at work.
Besides examining the garden carefully
they also study what happens to gardens
left without attention. Each learns all
the other learns about this and about
the garden. Consequently, when after all
this, one says "I still believe a gardener
comes" while the other says
"I don't" their different words now
reflect no difference as to what they
have found in the garden, no difference
as to what they would find in the
garden if they looked further and no
difference about how fast untended
gardens fall into disorder. At this
stage, in this context, the gardener
hypothesis has ceased to be experimental,
the difference between the one who
accepts and one who rejects is not now
a matter of the one expecting something
the other does not expect. What is the
di-ference between them? The one says,
"A gardener comes unseen and unheard.
He is manifested only in his works with
which we are allfamiliar," the other says
"There is no gardener" and with this
difference in what they say about the
gardener goes a difference in how they feel
towards the garden, in spite of the fact
that neither expects anything of it
which the other does not expect. /7/

What is implied in this parable is that there
is no disagreement between theist and atheist about
the facts that they experience. The disagreement
lies in the way they react to these same facts.
These reactions are not contradictory as much as

they are simply different. Each one is expressing
his feelings about what he has seen. Since they are
expressing their personal reactions to these facts,
it is not possible to qualify one as wrong and the
other right, but as purely and simply different.
To express one's feeling is not to make any claims
about reality. All we can say about them is that
they are more or less satisfying to the individual
who feels and expresses them. In short, neither
the theist or the atheist position is, according
to this parable, verifiable in principle.

Anthony Flew

More recently, the discussion has shifted from
this idea of verifiability to that of falsifiability.
This asks whether there is anything that could conceivably happen that would definitely show theism
to be false. Is theism compatible with whatever
we may experience? Anthony Flew presents this
question in terms of the conflict between the
Christian understanding of God as loving and evil
in the world, or a variation of the classic problem
of evil. /8/

Anthony Flew comments on Wisdom's parable by
examining its nature as an assertion. "The gardener
exists" is taken as equivalent to such phrases as
"God exists," or "God created the world." He says
that at first sight all these expressions look
like assertions. But an assertion implicitly contains a denial of the opposite. If we are not sure
that something is an assertion then we "attempt to
find what we would regard as counting against or
being incompatible with its truth. For if the
utterance is indeed an assertion, it will necessarily be equivalent to a denial of the negation of
that assertion." /9/ However if that supposed
assertion doesn't deny anything, then it really
cannot be an assertion. This is what the skeptic
means in Wisdom's parable when he says, "Just how
does what you call an invisible, intangible,

344

eternally elusive gardener differ from an imaginary gardener or even from no gardener at all?" /10/

Flew adds that religious people give the impression that there is no conceivable event or series of events that would justify conceding that there really is no God and that he really does love us. But when faced with the problem of evil and suffering in the world, religious people reply that God's love is genuine if mysterious. And, Flew continues, "what is the assurance of God's (appropriately qualified) love worth....What would have to occur or to have occurred to constitute a disproof of the love of, or of the existence og God?" /11/

Richard Hare

Hare takes up Flew's challenge by saying that he will attempt to deal with religion in general rather than Christianity in particular "because you cannot understand what Christianity is, until you have understood what religion is." /12/

He answers Flew by telling another parable:

> I must begin by confessing that, on the ground marked out by Flew, he seems to me to be completely victorious. I therefore shift my ground by relating another parable.

> A certain lunatic is convinced that all dons want to murder him. His friends introduce him to all the mildest and most respectable dons that they can find, and after each of them has retired, they say, "You see, he doesn't really want to murder you; he spoke to you in the most cordial manner; surely you are convinced now?" But the lunatic replies "Yes, but that was only his diabolical cunning; he's really plotting against me the

whole time, like the rest of them;
know it I tell you." However many
kindly dons are produced, the reaction
is still the same. /13/

Hare then points out that the lunatic will
accept no test as contrary to this theory. If so,
then according to Flew, he is asserting nothing.
Does this mean that there is no difference between
what the lunatic thinks about dons and what the
rest of us think? There is, says Hare, or he would
not be called a lunatic.

"Let us call that in which we differ from this
lunatic, our respective _bliks_. He has the insane
blik about dons, we have the sane one....it is very
important to have the right _blik_." /14/ Why is it
important to have the right _blik_? Because our
human existence depends on it. It is possible to
have a _blik_ which distrusts the qualities of steel,
so that we will not go into a building with steel
girders, ride in an elevator or drive a car. It
will not be removed merely by tests showing the
tensile strength of steel. The steel _blik_ is compatible with any number of such tests. "It seems,
indeed to be impossible even to formulate as an
assertion the normal _blik_ about the world which
makes me put my confidence in the future reliability
of steel joints,...and in the general non-homicidal
tendency of dons." /15/

Here claims that Flew's mistake is to consider
the kind of talk in the parable as some kind of
explanation in the scientific sense whereas it is
nothing of the kind. A _blik_ is something by which
we decide what is and what is not an explanation.

Finally, Hare points out an important difference between Flew's interpretation of Wisdom's
parable and his own:

The explorers do not _mind_ about
their garden; they discuss it with

interest, but not with concern. But
my lunatic, poor fellow, minds about
dons, and I mind about the steering
of my car; it often has people in
it that I care for. It is because I
mind very much about what goes on in
the garden in which I find myself,
that I am unable to share the explorer's
detachment. /16/

Basil Mitchell

Mitchell answers Flew by saying that the
Christian theologian does not deny the fact of pain
and evil in the world. Nor does he discount it as
counting against the love of God, thereby constituting what is called the problem of evil. Despite
this difficulty, he says, his basic faith in God
continues; he does not allow the difficulty to
count decisively against his trust in God. Why?
Because he is not a detached observer but a believer:

> Perhaps this can be brought out by
> yet another parable.
>
> In time of war in an occupied country,
> a member of the resistance meets one
> night a stranger who deeply impresses
> him. They spend that night together
> in conversation. The Stranger tells
> the partisan that he himself is on the
> side of the resistance--indeed that he
> is in command of it, and urges the
> partisan to have faith in him no matter
> what happens. The partisan is utterly
> convinced at that meeting of the
> Stranger's sincerity and constancy
> and undertakes to trust him.
>
> They never meet in conditions of
> intimacy again. But sometimes the Stranger

347

is seen helping members of the
resistance, and the partisan is
grateful and says to his friends, "He
is on our side."

Sometimes he is seen in the uniform
of the police handing over patriots to the
occupying power. On these occasions his
friends murmur against him; but the
partisan still says, "He is on our side."
He still believes that, in spite of
appearances, the Stranger did not deceive
him. Sometimes he asks the Stranger for
help and receives it. He is then thankful.
Sometimes he asks and does not receive it.
Then he says, "The Stranger knows best."
Sometimes his friends, in exasperation,
say, "Well, what would he have to do for
you to admit that you were wrong and that
he is not on our side?" But the partisan
refuses to answer. He will not consent
to put the Stranger to the test. And
sometimes his friends complain, "Well, if
that's what you mean by his being on our
side, the sooner he goes over to the other
side the better."

The partisan of the parable does not
allow anything to count decisively against
the proposition "The Stranger is on our
side." This is because he has committed
himself to trust the Stranger. But he of
course recognizes that the Stranger's
ambiguous behaviour does count against
what he believes about him. It is precisely
this situation which constitutes the
trial of his faith. /17/

What then if the partisan asks for help from
the stranger and doesn't get it? If he says that
the stranger really is on the right side but has
reasons for not helping, is this a reasonable thing
to say? Yes, under two conditions: first, the

initial trust in the goodness of the stranger must
have itself been strong, and, second, the partisan
has to feel genuine conflict within himself in trying
to sort all this out.

Mitchell adds that this is where his own parable
differs from Hare's. The partisan does admit that
some things cann add up against his belief in the
stranger. The don-hating lunatic does not. Nothing
can go against his _blik_ because nothing goes against
bliks. In the lunatic's case, with no reason for his
blik, there is no assertion; in the partisan's case,
there is a reason for his having originally committed
himself to the stranger, so there is an assertion.
So Mitchell is agreeing with Flew that theological
statements must really be assertions. The partisan's
assertion makes sense of his behavior. Theological
assertions make sense of Christians' behavior without being conclusively falsifiable. They are thus
significant articles of faith.

John Hick

John Hick disagrees with Hare's _blik_ solution
to the parable, on the grounds that despite the
fact that he insists on the necessity of finding
the right _bliks_, _bliks_ themselves are considered to
be unverifiable and unfalsifiable. He agrees however with Mitchell's stress on the similarity
between religious beliefs and ordinary, factual
beliefs. He then proposes to continue along this
line by developing a parable of his own concerning
what he calls eschatological verification:

Two men are travelling together along
a road. One of them believes that it leads
to the Celestial City, the other that it
leads nowhere; but since this is the only
road there is, both must travel it.
Neither has been this way before; therefore,
neither is able to say what they will find
around each corner. During their journey

349

they meet with moments of refreshment
and delight, and with moments of
hardship and danger. All the time one
of them thinks of his journey as a
pilgrimage to the Celestial City.
He interprets the pleasant parts as
encouragements and the obstacles as
trials of his purpose and lessons in
endurance, prepared by the king of that
city and designed to make of him a
worthy citizen of the place when at
last he arrives. The other, however,
believes none of this, and sees their
journey as an unavoidable and aimless
ramble. Since he has no choice in the
matter, he enjoys the good and endures
the bad. For him there is no Celestial
City to be reached, no all-encompassing
purpose ordaining their journey; there
is only the road itself and the luck of
the road in good weather and in bad.

During the course of the journey,
the issue between them in not an experimental one. They do not entertain
different expectations about the coming
details of the road, but only about its
destination. Yet, when they turn the
last corner, it will be apparent that
one of them has been right all the time
and the other wrong. Thus, although
the issue between them has not been
experimental, it has nevertheless been
a real issue. They have not merely felt
differently about the road, for one was
fheling appropriately and the other
inappropriately in relation to the
actual state of affairs. Their opposed
interpretations of the situation have
constituted genuinely rival assertions,
whose assertion-status has the peculiar
characteristic of being guaranteed

350

retrospectively by a future crux.

This parable, like all parables, has
narrow limitations. It is designed to make
only one point: that Judaic-Christian theism
postulates an ultimate unambiguous existence
in patria, as well as our present ambiguous
existence in via. /18/

So much then for the meaninglessness-verifia-
bility debate concerning religious language. Another
important approach is the one which denies the cognivity of religious language because it does not
measure up to scientific standards of cognitivity.

Non-Cognitive Theories of Religious Language

John Herman Randall, Jr.

To pursue this we now turn from British philosophers to an important American philosophical
figure of the first part of the twentieth century,
John Herman Randall, Jr. His numerous and influential writings are both an expression of a broad
cultural climate concerning the relationship between
religion and science in America during this period,
and an important contribution to its development
and refinement.

Relationship of Science and Religion

Randall is very much aware of the fact that if
philosophy is to be taken seriously and is to make an
important cultural contribution then it must itself
seriously take into account both the arts and religion. If metaphysics deals with the existence of man
then it must include consideration of all important
areas of man's existence.

The problem that tops the list, of course, in
any contemporary discussion of religion, according
to Randall, is the relationship between science

351

and religion.   But, he says, the days of intense
confrontation between them that characterized the
nineteenth century are over in these more enlightened
times, for one of the results of these discussions
was a clearer understanding of just what religion is
and what role it plays in men's lives.

These older discussions presupposed a "traditional" understanding of religion where religious
knowledge and belief were considered to be paramount
concerns of religion. Im more recent times, however,
a "scientific" understanding of religion has been
developed where the moral, esthetic and social functions of religion in life are emphasized.

> Yet Randall is profoundly reluctant
> to call the "teachings" of any art or
> religion "true" or to suggest that either
> may result in genuine knowledge. His
> reluctance is apparently due in part at
> least to the fact that "the arts,"
> including religion, do not significantly
> employ "signs" of anything else. Their
> resemblance to language signs lies not
> in their agressive function; it lies in
> the "impressive function."...Or in terms
> Randall has perhaps used most consistently,
> the artist and the prophet and the saint
> teach how, and not that. "The painter
> shows us how to see the visible world
> better--how to see the grass. Even so,
> the prophet and the saint show us how to
> see the Divine better--how to see God." /19/

Since science obviously deals with the "that"
of things and is expressive of them rather than
impressive, that is, it deals with things and not
with the impressions that these make on human beings
then there is really no conflict between the two.
They dwell in separate spheres, one dealing with
reality the other dealing with vision and impressions and there is no need to see them as being in

conflict with each other:

> Knowing how, according to Randall, is
> fundamentally different from knowing that;
> and it is the function of science to teach
> that certain things are so. Thus he
> concludes that the arts and religions
> should be said to belong to the class of
> "non-cognitive symbols" which "do not have
> as their function to participate in
> activities that eventuate in knowledge and
> truth." ...For Randall, the method of
> physics is obviously the paradigm of
> cognitive activity or of knowledge and
> understanding. /20/

The Cognivity of Religious Symbols

Are there any circumstances or conditions in
which Randall would consider religious symbols to be
cognitive? Yes, and here he approaches the grounds
of the debates of logical analysis discussed earlier.
They could be considered cognitive if they were propositions capable of verification. Insofar as they
would be subject to such verification, they would be
said to be true. In order for a religion to be considered as making truth claims, it would have to make
verifiable assertions about the existence of God,
the demands of moral action and the ultimate destiny
of man. Since he considers such assertions to be,
as a matter of fact, unverifiable, then they cannot
be described as cognitive. They must be seen as
impressive symbols which deal with man's most important concerns.

There are, according to Randall, only three possibilities with regard to the cognitivity of religious
assertions:

1. A "special and privileged religious knowledge."

2. A "consistently rational philosophical theology," which would show that "religious 'truth' must agree with man's best knowledge of the world."

3. Acceptance "that there is no theoretical 'truth' at all in religion." /21/

According to the first view, the truth revealed in Christianity is unlike any other kind of truth in the world because it deals with a supernatural realm inaccessible to man's reason. This contrast was described in medieval times as one between faith and reason; in Kant's time, as one between fact and value and, more recently, as one between objectified, impersonal knowledge and existential, participatory knowledge.

According to the second view, reinterpretation of the doctrine of revelation brings about its identification with "an acceptable philosophic scheme of understanding." This is ultimately based on the principle that for a religious belief to be accepted as true it must be found to be in agreement with the best knowledge about reality that can be gained from non-religious sources. /22/

Finally, according to the third view, religion does not produce knowledge on its own. Since religion is a practical matter, involving feeling and doing rather than thinking or explaining, it has no cognitive value.

Since Randall obviously holds the third view, yet at the same time is not unaware of certain difficulties inherent in that position, he develops his sustaining arguments at considerable length.

Religion as a Body of Symbols

Making a great deal of the relationship between

354

the religious and the esthetic, Randall explores
the idea that religion is a body of symbols and
myths.

> What is important to recognize is
> that religious symbols belong with social
> and artistic symbols, in the group of
> symbols that are both <u>nonrepresentative</u>
> and <u>noncognitive</u>. Such noncognitive symbols
> can be said to symbolize not some external
> thing that can be indicated apart from
> their operation, but rather what they
> themselves <u>do</u>, their peculiar function. /23/

Such symbols have four functions. First of all,
they "provoke in men an emotional response, and
stimulate appropriate human activities." /24/
They deal more with the will and the imagination
than the intellect. As motives, they lead to action
and in this they differ from signs which merely lead
to other things.

Second, "they provoke in a group of men, the
community for whom they serve as symbols, a common
or shared response." /25/ Even when focussed mainly
in an individual, such a response is derived from
communitarian orientations. Such a symbol is shared
generally, though it can of course receive different
interpretations.

Third, "noncognitive symbols are able to communicate qualitative or 'shared' experience, experience that is difficult to put into precise words
or statements and may well be ineffable." /26/
This is seen most clearly in art. Art affects men
in a number of powerful ways, but it is difficult
to say with any degree of precision what this 'means.'
Such symbols, once again, should be clearly distinguished from mere representative signs, with no
power of their own.

In addition to these three characteristics,
religious symbols have a fourth one, namely, that

"they can be said to 'disclose' or 'reveal' something about the world in which they function...If
we ask what it is that such symbols do reveal or
disclose about the world, it is clear that it is
not what we should call in the ordinary sense
'knowledge,' in the sense already defined." /27/

Critique of Randall

John Hick, in his analysis and critique of
Randall takes a strongly negative position.

> Randall's position represents a
> radical departure from the traditional
> assumptions of Western religion. For in
> speaking of "finding the Divine" and of
> being shown "visions of God," Randall
> does not mean to imply that God or the
> Divine exists as a reality independently
> of the human mind,...The Divine, as
> defined by Randall, is the temporary
> mental construction or projection of a
> recently emerged animal inhabiting one
> of the satellites of a minor star.
> God is not, according to this view,
> the creator and the ultimate ruler
> of the universe; he is a fleeting ripple
> of imagination in a timy corner of
> space-time. /28/

Other critics are more qualified in their
assessment, even though they disagree with Randall's
theory of the noncognitivity of religion. This is
summed up by John Smith's remark that "Randall's
approach to the issue and its resolution is subtle
in the extreme....Randall's own position is itself
dialectical and not without internal tension that
brings it perilously close to inconsistency." /29/

The disagreement of these critics with Randall'
position is very much the one that has been taken
consistently in the course of this book, namely a
refusal to accept as dogma the theory that only

scientific knowledge is real human knowledge. "The failure in Randall's account, however, is not his claim that religion does not provide the same sort of knowledge as science, but his claim that there is a clear and immense difference between the cognitive status and function of religions and the sciences, so that the results of the religions are never appropriately called 'knowledge'." /30/

This is a refusal to accept the assumption that for religion to be cognitively significant, religion must develop propositions about such things as God's existence, ways of worship and of acting. To proceed on the basis of this assuption about the exclusive claim of science to 'knowledge', is to seriously misunderstand other dimensions in human life, and to overestimate the nature of scientific process and knowledge.

Though religion can and should be studied externally using the methodology of the social sciences, this is neither primary nor exhaustive. If overemphasized it can fail to deal with the essential, namely, religion's self-interpretation. While religion may not now be seen as primarily containing knowledge which gives a theoretical explanation of the world, this does not mean that it has no knowledge at all. It has its own kind of knowledge, which is genuinely cognitive and which is summed up best by its theologians.

Also, to overstress the monopolistic cognitivity of the sciences is to overestimate their objectivity. "As Randall himself has made us abundantly aware, all sciences, especially cultural sciences, reflect the commonsensical and philosophical assumptions of a period, which means that these sciences are not purely descriptive but are controlled by some conception of the nature of religion not uniquely derived from free inquiry." /31/

If religion is understood as an experience integrating actuality and possibility then the truth of religion does not depend as claimed upon "a special and privileged" form of religious knowledge or on a "consistently rational philosophical theology," but simply on the fact, that "the religious aspects of experience are as dependable and as inescapable, as cogent and dependable, if we do not demand too much of them, as the sensory and logical features of experience." /32/

Religion and God

John Hick points out that one of the effects of taking religion to be noncognitive is that religion eventually becomes more important than God. In earlier times it was God's existence and nature that were analyzed and debated. Today, as Randall indicates, it is the nature, function and usefulness of religion that are analyzed and examined. The existence of religion is obvious to all, the existence of God is not. The usefulness of religion in helping human beings adjust to their environment can be clearly observed, the role of God cannot. The net result of all this is a paradoxical one: instead of religion being understood as the way men respond to God, God is understood as a subdivision of the science of religion. "Faith" thus becomes an end itself; whether it has a real object is irrelevant.

This view of religion represents a logical development within an increasingly technological society, of what has been variously called scientism, positivism, and naturalism. This development is based on the assumption, engendered by the tremendous, dramatic, and still accelerating growth of scientific knowledge and achievement that the truth concerning any aspect or alleged aspect, of reality, is to be found by the application of the methods

of scientific investigation to the
relevant phenomena. God is not a
phenomenon available for scientific
study, but Religion is. /33/

Braithwaite

Moral Assertions

Another theory which sees religious language
as noncognitive is that of Richard Braithwaite. He
compares religious assertion to moral assertion. He
rejects theory of moral action for what he calls a
conative one, namely, "the primary use of a moral
assertion (is) that of expressing the intention of
the asserter to act in a particular sort of way
specified in the assertion." /34/ Thus he would
understand a utilitarian to be declaring that to the
best of his ability he intends to act in accordance
with the policy of utilitarianism. Though there are
difficulties and vaguenesses here, all that we have
to do, according to Braithwaite, is to recognize
that when a man asserts that he ought to do something, his assertion is simply making it known that
he intends to do that something.

The advantage of this account of
moral assertions has over all others,
emotive non-propositional ones as well as
cognitive propositional ones, is that it
alone enables a satisfactory answer to be
given to the question: What is the reason
for my doing what I think I ought to do?
The answer it gives is that, since my
thinking that I ought to do the action is
my intention to do it if possible, the
reason why I do the action is simply that
I intend to do it, if possible. /35/

DISCLOSURE OF THE ULTIMATE

Religious Assertions

Braithwaite then applies this theory of moral
assertions to religious ones. Here too he rejects
the theory of religion as merely subjective emotion-
ality in favor of conativity. "The view I put forward for your consideration is that the intention
of a Christian to follow a Christian way of life is
not only the criterion for the sincerity of his
belief in the assertions of Christianity; it is the
criterion for the meaningfulness of his assertions."
/36/ By saying this, Braithwaite is reversing the
usual order of understanding of religious belief and
morality. Instead of seeing religious beliefs as
the source of the believer's actions, he sees the
intention of the believer to act in a certain way
as constituting religious conviction.

In replying to the objection that the intention
to carry out a policy necessarily implies that what
that policy is has to be known ahead of time, he
says that this is irrelevant to an empiricist enquirer. All an empiricist has to do is to consider
the system as a whole and see the activity taking
place. And in analyzing that activity there is no
need to go any further than saying that in passing
from an intention of doing an action to doing it, a
religious action has taken place. Religious assertions are discovered by examining the principles
of conduct which the believer understands the assertions to involve.

He adds that these moral assertions have to be
taken as parts of a whole system, that they are frequently given by means of concrete examples, and
that the conduct involved is not merely external or
social but can be internal, and, in the case of
Christianity "agapeistic."

Though these qualification may be sufficient
to allow us to distinguish between a moral assertion

and a religious one, they are not much help when it comes to discriminate among the religious assertions put forward by different religions. How can we tell the difference?

> The really important difference, I think, is to be found in the fact that the intentions to pursue the behavior policies, which may be the same for different religions, are associated with thinking of different stories (or sets of stories). By a story I shall here mean a proposition or set of propositions which are straightforwardly empirical propositions capable of empirical test and which are thought of by the religious man in connection with his resolution to follow the way of life advocated by his religion. /37/

The difference then between a moral assertion and a religious one is that the religious assertion will have a propositional element whereas the moral one will not.

There will of course be any number of different interpretations of these stories, just as there are any number of differing Christian theological theories, but all of these will remain interpretations of empirical propositions.

The Truth of Religious Assertions

What about the truth of these stories? According to Braithwaite it is not necessary "for the asserter of a religious assertion to believe in the truth of the story involved in the assertions: What is necessary is that that the story should be entertained in thought, i.e. that the statement of the story should be understood as having a meaning." /38/ He does not insist on the word story of course. Other equally acceptable terms to him as allegory, parable, tale and myth. Story he feels is the most neutral in that it doesn't contain any implication as to whether anyone believes it or not.

If such stories are not necessarily believed as true, then what function can they really play in religious faith?

My answer is that the relation is a psychological and causal one. It is an empirical psychological fact that many people find it easier to resolve upon and to carry through a course of action which is contrary to their natural inclinations if this policy is associated in their minds with certain stories. /39/

As an example, he gives the powerful psychological and religious impact in England of a story which is fictitious, namely Bunyan's Pilgrim's Progress.

Braithwaite himself sums up his position concerning the noncognitivity of religious knowledge this way:

A religious assertion, for me, is the assertion of an intention to carry out a certain behavior policy subsumable under a sufficiently general principle to be a moral one, together with the implicit or explicit statement, but not the assertion of certain stories. Neither the assertion of the intention nor the reference to the stories includes belief in its ordinary senses. /40/

Critique of Braithwaite

Any critique of Braithwaite's theory would have to begin with his ethical theory which claims that a moral assertion is the expression of an intention

to act in accordance with that assertion. without
going into an extended discussion of ethics, it can
be said that there is a certain inconsistency in
this argument, since according to it, it is impossible to intend to act wrongly. As St. Paul test-
ifies and everyday experience confirms, people do
sometimes purposely intend to act wrongly.

Second, Braithwaite's description of Christian
stories is very unsophisticated. It lumps all elements of the Bible together, making no attempt to
distinguish what so many biblical scholars have
taken great pains to distinguish, namely the different literary forms that one finds in the Bible.
Because one can find imaginary stories in the Bible,
this does not mean that the whole thing is a work of
fiction. Furthermore, such a view leaves out of
account entirely statements in the Bible which are
clearly propositional and not in story form as all
such as "God is love."

Third, his view that beliefs about God and such
stories are needed for psychological reinforcement,
leaves out the question of any underlying rationality
is acting in one way and then another.

Another possible view of the matter
is that the ethical significance of these
beliefs consists in the way they render a
certain way of life both attractive and
rational. This view would seem to be
consistent with the character of Jesus'
ethical teaching. He did not demand that
people live in a way that runs counter to
their deepest desires and that would thus
require some extraordinary inducement.
Rather, he professed to reveal to them the
true nature of the world in which they live. /41/

Finally, Braithwaite's epistemology is based on
the essential incompatibility between fact and value.
Fact is the domain of science and value that of reli-

gion and the two go their separate ways. If then, as Braithwaite says, the only true knowledge is scientific and fact related, then his system is an ingenious and plausible one that appeals to the empirically and pragmatic minded especially. But if this dualism is simply not so, if scientific knowledge is not the only kind of genuinely human knowledge, if other dimensions of men's life, including the artistic, the moral and the religious, are genuinely cognitive, as we have affirmed several times already, though in a way different from science. Braithwaite's proposal is seriously underminded. All this underscores once again the importance of epistemological foundations for all these questions.

Modular Theories of Religious Language

Though the discussion so far might give the impression that the contemporary schools of linguistic and logical analysis are somehow intrinsically inimical to the understanding of religion and of God that has been developed in these pages, such is not the case. On the contrary, what we have discussed so far is only some of the schoolofanalytic thought. There are other schools, and other thinkers, whose positions are not only more favorable to religious thought, but which also strongly support the views adopted here. The following section will treat of two such important figures, Ian T. Ramsey and Ian G. Barbour.

Ian T. Ramsey

Ramsey himself takes a positive view towards the relationship between religion and linguistic analysis. At the very beginning of his Riddell Memorial Lectures he says that though there is a serious complaint against such philosophy as soul destroying verbalism and though others consider theology itself to be empty, vacuous chatter, neither position is adequate:

RELIGIOUS LANGUAGE AND THEOLOGICAL MODELS

What I hope to show in these
lectures is that the way of philosophizing
which is the subject of the first complaint,
far from being soul-destroying, can do
much to help us soften the second complaint,
for it can help theology to put its house
into some kind of logical order so that
the better find our way about Christian
discourse. /42/

The theoretical way to go about doing this was
developed at considerable length in his earlier
Whidden Lectures. There he makes a comparison
between the nature and use of models in science and
in theology. He claims that despite other differences, the various modern intellectual disciplines
have more in common than is frequently realized.
"It is by the use of models that each discipline
provides its understanding of a mystery which confronts them all, and indeed its own contribution to
the fellowship of faith and learning which should
characterize a university." /43/

Picture Models

In attempting to clarify the meaning of the term
"model" he begins with Kelvin's understanding of
scientific models as mechanical. Kelvin saw such
a relationship between a scientific model and the
understanding of scientific theories that he went
so far as to say that if it is not possible to make
a mechanical model of some theory then it is not understandable. Such mechanical models have also been
called copies, pictures and "scale" models. /44/
In more ordinary lnaguage this is the meaning of
model in such terms as model railroad, model air-
planes, model buildings, etc.

Such mechanical or picture models have many
advantages. They allow "the scientist and the theologian respectively, to be articualte...(and) being
replicas, they reproduced identically important and

relevant properties which also belonged to the object modelled." /45/ They are so useful, specific and manageable that it is easy to see how the conclusion could be drawn that they picture how things really are.

If picture models were replicas of reality, however, it would be difficult to explain and deal with the diversity of models, many of which supposedly "picture" the same reality. Light, for example, is modelled at one and the same time as a continuous wave motion and as discontinuous discrete particles. How do we know which is the accurate "picture"? Even theology has this kind of modular diversification, with God at times pictured as loving and at times as judging.

Why then has there been such an emphasis upon picture models? Because, says Ramsey, there was concern for enunciating the clear, direct account of things as they are:

> Let us take as an alternative to
> the concept of a picturing model, a
> concept of a model...which stands some-
> where between a picture and a formula,
> which deals in hints rather than identities,
> what Black calls an "analogue model,"
> and what I shall presently call a
> disclosure model. /46/

In such a model there must be a structural similarity between the model and the phenomena it helps us to understand without at the same time merely reproducing or picturing it. It could be called similarity-with-a-difference. And it is precisely this point that is the source of new insight.

RELIGIOUS LANGUAGE AND THEOLOGICAL MODELS

Similarities

between Scientific and Theological Models

Ramsey then develops three areas of similarity between scientific and theological models: first, scientific models allow presently uninterpreted phenomena to be clarified by a theory or mathematical treatment. The same thing is true in theology. "Models can be seen as builders of discourse, as giving rise to large-scale interpretations of phenomena that so far lack a theological mapping." /47/ As an example he gives St. Peter's speeches in Acts, where Jesus is referred to under a variety of titles which are then summed up under the heading of Messiah.

Second, when the theories of science become too complex, particularly when mathematics is used, then a model may help to signify things by focussing on fundamental notions which are echoed in the disclosure from which it arises. In theology also there are models which allow some kind of sense and simplicity to emerge out of complex and confusing discourse. As examples he gives the models of grace and atonement.

Third, in science, models are used to stand for a topic or point which otherwise eludes us. Thus when an object is too small or too big or too far away to be observed, there is a need for a model. So too in theology, though the way that God eludes our grasp differs sginificantly from the way atomic nuclei do, nevertheless models concerning God do become necessary and helpful. "Speaking broadly then, in these three ways models enable us to become theologically articulate as they enable us to be scientifically articulate." /48/

Finally, there are two conditions that need to be met if theological models are to be genuinely articulate. The first is that there must be a real relationship between the model and the phenomena which is the source of the insight or disclosure. There must be something in the world which matches man's experience of say a loving father, a judge or a king. The second condition, the more important one, sharply distinguishes the scientific model from the theological one. A scientific model stands or falls on its verifiability. A theological model does not:

> It is rather judged by its stability over the widest possible range of phenomena, by its ability to incorporate the most diverse phenomena not inconsistently....The theological model works more like the fitting of a boot or a shoe than like the "yes" or "no" of a roll call.... Here is what I might call the method of empirical fit. /49/

Models in Psychology and the Social Sciences

Ramsey then turns to the use of models in psychology and the social sciences. He argues for the usefulness of models in psychology and sociology. He says that psychology benefits from the use of behavioristic and even mathematical models. Thus modern experimental psychology can pursue much of the same directions as natural science and this is helpful as far as at goes. The important point is that behavioristic models cannot be understood as picture models. Those parts of the human person that are observable can be splendidly portrayed by models, but unfortunately they are not the whole person. There are other aspects of the human person that are not so observable. There is the question, for example, of the role of observation itself in any attempt to model. Helpful as they are, such behavioristic models are only partially accurate.

Supplementing these psychologically oriented
models with sociological ones, though it adds some
helpful clarifications, does not solve the basic
problems. For neither are picture models, they are
disclosure models:

> So my main point has been whether
> the models are scientific or social, they
> are born in insight, which in this case
> reveals for each of us his own subjectivity
> ....Let none of us repeat in our own time
> the naive futilities which physics has so
> notably outgrown. Let us all be content
> with the exploration of a mystery, with
> constructing maps, scientific or social,
> which are never final, though it is no
> less our professional duty, whatever our
> disciplines to construct the best map
> we can. /50/

Metaphors and Models

Ramsey then goes on to show that there is a close
connection between metaphors and models unlike that
between similes and models. Similes he understands
to be very much the same kind of thing as picturing
models. They describe some important feature of what
they represent: the room is as hot as an over, for
example. But this can hardly be developed much further. No one would conclude that the room could
therefore bake a cake. A metaphor, on the other hand,
is closer to what has been called a disclosure model.
A good metaphor provides us with many possibilities
of articulation. To speak of Martin Luther King,
for example, as a beacon of hope to his people, leads
to any number of developments and articulations.

Because of this richness, metaphors and models
are not mere verbal or literary ornamentations. They
are not ways of speech reserved only for an earlier,
non-scientific stage of man's developemnt. They are

used rather, when the ordinary powers of speech fail us, when we are unable to articulate our insights in any other way than through their rich and mysterious language. That is why they are not capable of being simply translated into barren, ordinary prose. Something irreplaceable and intangible is lost by any such attempts. Witness what Shakespeare looks like in those student summary books sold for help in examinations. If all that is wanted is the bare plot, fine, but the magic, the mystery, the beauty and the music have been lost, and these are not merely subjective emotionalisms:

Now how does the secret and mystery arise out of such a co-operation and connexion between contexts? My answer is that it does so when and because the point of connexion expressed in the metaphor itself generates a disclosure ....Generalizing, we may say that metaphorical expressions occur when two situations strike us in such a way as to reveal what eludes them but is no mere combination of them both. Metaphors and models, both enabling us to be articulate about an insight, are thus the basic currency for mystery, and we can spend our lives elucidating ever more faithfully the mystery in which metaphors and models are born /51/

With regard to the scientific disciplines, though they may have neglected the role of models in their processes, and may sometimes have overlooked and even denied the insights derived from them, the damage has been minimized by their ties with observable facts.

The same is not true of theological models, however, Theology must acknowledge the mystery which is at its heart. "For theology...is founded in occasions of insight and disclosure, when, to put

370

it at its most general, the universe declares itself
in a particular way around some group of events
which thus take on cosmic significance." /52 Dealing with such a process of cosmic disclosure involves the use of many phrases and combinations of phrases which create a diversity of models. Rather than
this being a "death by a thousand qualifications,"
/53/ it is life "by a thousand enrichments." /54/

Ramsey then suggests that what he calls theological qualifiers play an important role in this
process. A qualifier is a word or phrase which by
its diversity and richness indicates the route from
model of mystery. Sometimes, one word metaphors or
models are satisfactory, such as Father, for God,
but qualifiers such as "loving" or "eternal" provide
new models which show that the mystery involved
eludes them all.

Disclosure Models

One final point. Where Ramsey speaks of disclosure models, what does he mean is being disclosed?
First, it is clear that he is operating with a realistic epistemology for he gives "cognitive signifi-
canse...to insight and imagination:"

> The very aptness of the word I
> use--disclosure--is that the objective
> reference is safeguarded, for the
> object declares its objectivity by
> actively confronting us....Models, like
> metaphors, enable us, as I have said, to
> be articulate, and both are born in
> insight. But it is an insight which,
> viewed as a disclosure, reminds us that
> in such insight the universe is reveal-
> ing itself to us. /55/

At the conclusion of his Christian Discourses,
he returns to the same theme. He says that the
disclosure involved here is a disclosure of

objectivity. But this objectivity is not that of
dream images, nor the objectivity of the natural
sciences, nor that of the social sciences. "It is
the objectivity of what declares itself to us--
challenges un in a way that persons may do. It is
in this sense that God declares his objectivity."/56/

Once again epistemological concerns come to the
fore. The system of metaphors and models developed
by Ramsey depends upon a realistic epistemology.
Ramsey candidly acknowledges this. But unfortunately,
he does not develop these realistic foundations very
much at all. He asserts realistic disclosure but
does not demonstrate it. To this extent, his theory
is weakened. If however, it is allied with and
supported by a developed theory of knowledge, such
an intersective realism, it becomes much more fully
operative and offers many helpful methods and insights.

Ian G. Barbour

Ian Barbour is a former scientist, now theologian, who is impressively at home in both worlds.
His Issues in Science and Religion /57/ is a model
of interdisciplinary dialogue, marked by clarity
of thought and incisiveness of language. More recently, he has published Myths Models and Paradigms,
which develops a valuable set of conceptual tools for
dealing with religion and religious language. /58/

Barbour's general theme is that science is not
as objective and religion is not as subjective as is
often supposed. In support of this, he examines
three themes which are influential in the scientific
community and which can serve as a means of strength-
ening productive dialogue between scientists and
Christian thinkers. The first theme is that of the
diverse functions of language as was seen earlier
with regard to the later Wittgenstein. It is now
fairly widely acknowledged that each field, whether

that of science, philosophy, literature or religion, has a logic and a language appropriate to what it is and what it is trying to do. The second theme is the use of theoretical models in both science and religion, where there are both similarities and differences. A theoretical model is an imaginative mental construct developed to explain certain observed phenomena. The third theme is the use of paradigm in both science and religion. Paradigms here means standard examples of investigation which embody a certain set of assumptions and which ultimately become a research tradition until replaced by another set of assumptions. It also means shared exemplars. Finally, all this is based on a position of epistemological realism which Barbour calls critical realism. According to this view, models in science and religion are neither literalistic nor instrumentalistic but "partial ways of imagining what is not observable." /59/

The following is a summary of Barbour's overall position:religious language contains symbols and myths many of which are metaphors based on analogies with man's experience and which can be expressed in models. These theoretical models in religion, like those in science are neither literally true, nor useful fictions but lead to conceptually formulated religious beliefs.

Myth

According to Barbour then, a myth is a complex narrative embodying religious symbols and images telling a story taken to manifest some aspect of the cosmic order. In eastern religions, myth is tied more closely to phenomena in nature than in Western religions where it is tied in with historical events.

A myth should not be confused with a fairy tale. A fairy tale is simply a story for entertainment and delight, whereas a myth has a number of important effects in the personal and corporate life of man.

DISCLOSURE OF THE ULTIMATE

Among these, five are particularly significant:

1. "Myths offer ways of ordering experience.
   Myths provide a world view, a vision of
   the basic structure of reality." /60/

Most myths deal with the formative period of creation
and contemporary time is compared and contrasted
with this primordial time as a means of giving it
greater sense and orientation.

2. "Myths inform man about himself. He takes
   his self-identity in part from the past
   events which he believes to have made him
   what he is." /61/

It is the key events of their history that makes a
people a people and these need to be remembered and
evoked. Thus a myth that is alive brings about
personal commitment rather than mere contemplation,
an action that brings men into adjustment with a
group and an ordained order.

3. "Myths express a saving power in human
   life." /62/

In the cosmic order there is first an ideal state
which is the origin of life. Then there is the
actual condition of man clearly separated from that
ideal by ignorance, sin and suffering. Finally,
there is a saving power that can overcome these
difficulties and reestablish the reign of the ideal
state.

4. "Myths provide patterns for human action.
   They hold up not an abstract ideal but a
   prototype for man's imitation." /63/

This is the vivid, narrative, biographical aspect
of myth, which provides examples of significant
activities exemplary for guiding men to concrete
action.

5. "Myths are enacted in rituals. Myths are
   expressed, not only in symbolic words, but
   also in symbolic acts--dance, gesture, drama

and formalized cultic acts or rites." /64/ The ritual is often justified by the myth while the ritual gives vitality to the myth and helps to pass it on from group to group and generation to generation. In some way, past events and primordial time are made present and influential.

Allegory and parable are forms of myth. Allegory is a narrative in which there is one-to-one correspondence between the details of the event narrated and the hidden message of the story. A parable, on the other hand, is a narrative form of myth which by analogy makes a comparison and calls for a decision on the part of the hearer.

Besides the five functions mentioned above, myth has some noncognitive ones as well. Thus "in the face of the insecurities of illness, natural disaster and death, myths and rituals contribute to the reduction of anxiety." /65/ Against a variety of threats to human life, they are a mechanism of defense. Psychoanalytic thought sees them as symbolic expression of unconscious wishes.

Another function of this kind is the social. Myths are seen as integrating society, binding people together, giving them communal identity and harmony, thus sanctioning and supporting the existing social order. Claude Levi-Strauss tries to show that the recurring structural patterns within myth help individuals and societies to cope with conflicts.

The Cognitivity of Myths

Does all this, and especially these last functions of myth shows that myths are not genuinely cognitive? That is what a number of interpreters say. Thus the instrumentalists claim that it is wrong to speak of myths as being true or false, all that can be said of them is that they are useful fictions. Part of the reason for this position is the fact that the same mythology can contain without apparent difficulty differing and even opposing accounts of important events such as creation. But religious people do not strip myths of cognitive function. Their belief systems cannot be dismissed quite as easily and lightly as the instrumentalists do. Even though a myth and its ritual are closer to daily living and acting than to speculation, this does not mean that there is no truth-claim whatsoever involved. And differing accounts are simply imaginative attempts to express complex realities.

Nineteenth century anthropologists also held that myths were noncognitive. They understood myths to be primitive attempts to explain natural phenomena In other words, that they were an earlier, more literary and imaginative form of science, superseded, of course, as science advanced and became more theoretical. Modern anthropologists who understand better both primitive man's not so primitive mental capacities and the complex nature of modern science itself have quietly deemphasized the description of myth as early science.

A third group which emphasizes the noncognitive character of myth includes many psychologists who see myths as truthful symbols only of man's inner life. Myths for them "would be valid insofar as they expressed man's feelings, hopes and fears, or his experience of guilt, reconciliation and liberation from anxiety." /66/ Karl Jung goes further and says that these projections of inner psychic dramas are products of what he calls the collective unconscious embodied in archetypal figures, common to both ancient and modern man, which express nothing more than man's inner life. There are others, however, who, while they admit this creative relationship between man's inner life and symbols and myth, refuse to accept any need for thus concluding to their total subjectivity.

Symbol, Metaphor and Myth

There is disagreement, then, between those who see religious language, including myth and symbol, as cognitive and those who do not. In order to support their cognitivity, Barbour suggests that one must begin with a realistic theory of knowledge out of which flows an understanding of symbol which supports metaphor, which grows out of analogy, which in turn develops into myth and which finally flows into religious language.

A symbol is anything presented to us as standing for something else. More specifically, there are conventional symbols and intrinsic symbols. A conventional symbol is better called a sign because it has no internal connection with what it represents. Though a red light is an indicator that a vehicle should stop, its redness has no intrinsic connection with halting physical motion. An intrinsic symbol, on the other hand, does have such an internal connection with what it represents. Water has long been seen as a symbol for life and it is obvious that water is intrinsically connected with life.

Such intrinsicity is the key to cognitivity. This brings us to metaphor, for a genuinely intrinsic symbol is basically a metaphor. It is the incorporation of such metaphors into myths that gives them their cognitive value. What then is a metaphor? A metaphor proposes analogies between the normal context of a word and a new and often unexpected context. This juxtaposition of two frames of reference, especially when it is fresh and new, produce a novel insight. Ramsey said much the same earlier. While a metaphor does not claim to be literally true, it does claim to be more than a useful fiction or a mere sign precisely because there are significant analogies existing between the things compared.

It is important to distinguish metaphors from

similes, because similes do not have this intrinsicity and inner creativity arising from analogy. A simile may be translated into soberer, more literalistic statements without much loss, but this is not the case with metaphors. While it may be true that there is some latitude for the translation of a metaphor into ordinary language, and while it may also be true that old and tired metaphors (green with nevy lend themselves to this kind of translation, a true metaphor is open-ended and contains more than it can tell. The extravagant language of a love letter would never be considered to contain the fullness of the lovers' feelings. The same with a rich metaphor. If it is translated too literally, its rich potentialities will be prematurely frozen and impoverished A metaphor then needs to be taken on its own terms and not as merely an imaginative statement of something more literal.

At the same time, it must be affirmed that metaphors, like myth, also have functions which are noncognitive. Metaphors also express emotion and valuational overtones. These noncognitive functions do not cancel out the cognitive. They stand in a state of tension one with the other.

According to Barbour, then, religious language contains myth which contains symbol, which contains metaphor, which contains analogy. The word contained however, may be understood too mechanically. It might be better to say that analogy is essential to myth and myth is essential to religious language, In any case, it is important that the notion of analogy be clarified.

Analogy and Religious Language

Analogy is a familiar term, especially to Roman Catholics, perhaps too much so, since it is often used uncritically. Analogy is generally defined as the resemblance of similarity without identity

of properties or relations. But this does not mean
that there is only one kind of analogy. On the contrary, there are various kinds, each based on the
metaphysical and epistemological systems which support it. Many Roman Catholics are unaware, for
example, of the dependence of the traditional
analogies concerning the existence of God on classical metaphysics. The first of the two classical
forms, the "analogy of proportionality", says only
that the goodness of God is related to the divine
nature in the way that human goodness of related
to man's nature. "But unless we have some prior
knowledge of God's nature, or assume an ontology of
'levels of being' with some continuity between the
levels, the 'proportionality' tells us nothing about
God," /67/ and ends up close to agnosticism.

The second classical form, the "analogy of
attribution," says that a characteristic can be
predicated formally of God but only derivatively of
created beings. "But the argument rests on the
assumption that causes resemble their effects and
that God is the cause of the world. The conclusion
then asserts only what was already in the premise:
the creator is good in whatever way necessary to
produce goodness in his creatures," /68/ and ends
up close to anthropomorphism.

Analogies based on human experience, however,
avoid many of these difficulties while remaining
genuinely cognitive. As John Smith says:

> The proposal to employ experience
> as the basis for analogy in the religious
> sphere has two aspects: on the one hand,
> it means the appeal to specific experiences
> as a way of understanding religious
> concepts. On the other hand, it means
> an ontological claim concerning the status
> and function of experience as such, namely
> that it is capable of serving as a medium
> of interpretation between the finite

world and its ultimate ground. /69/

Analogy and Models

The major thrust of Barbour's study, however, is to develop the analogical nature of models, so the question of analogy is better pursued in that context. Analogy is common to symbols, metaphors and models. In the case of symbols and metaphors, there is only brief and limited insight, whereas models can be developed systematically. Both in science and in religion they provide the opportunity for conceptual clarification. In religion they provide, in addition, the opportunity for the expressio of attitudes.

A model represents the enduring structural components which myths dramatize in narrative form. So one model may be common to many myths. Compared to myth, a model is relatively static and lacks a myth' imaginative richness and dramatic power. A model arises from reflection on the living myths transmitt by religious communities.

Models in Science

Barbour develops at considerable length a comparison between the use of models in science and in religion. For present purposes only certain key elements in that extended discussion will be selecte First, Barbour does what Ramsey did, he distinguishe among scientific models. He sees four kinds of scie tific models: experimental, which can be can be actually conducted in the laboratory; logical, or a set of entities which satisfy the axioms of a formal deductive system; mathematical, or symbolic representaions of quantitative variables in physical systems and last, but most important, theoretical models. These he understands as "imaginative mental construc invented to account for observed phenomena. Such a

380

model is usually an imagined mechanism or process, which is postulated by analogy with familiar mechanisms or processes and used to construct a theory to correlate a set of observables." /70/ The billiard ball model of a gas is an example of this kind of theoretical model. Such theoretical models, then, have three main features: they are analogical, they contribute to the extension of theories and they are intelligible as a unit. These features alone do not guarantee the validity of the model. There must also be careful testing of a model's deductions, and such testing can lead to either a discarding or a modification of the original model.

There was a time when such models were considered to be real pictures of the world as it is. Though such naive realism was almost universally accepted up until the present century, it has now been largely abandoned. A more contemporary theory is to see them as summaries of data or formulas for summarizing experience. They are thus called theoretical only because they are a convenient way of classifying such observational data. This more positivistic approach itself has also been largely abandoned since it was discovered that it limits the extensibility of a theory to new situations when such extensibility was one of the main reasons for devising the theory in the first place.

Another explanation is more instrumentalistic. While agreeing with the positivists that such theoretical models are not representative of the world, instrumentalists claim that they do determine truth or falsehood either. They are seen as merely useful devices for correlating observations and making predictions. In other words, useful fictions.

Then there is the more realistic understanding of the critical models, that of Barbour's critical realism and this book's intersective realism. This kind of realism agrees with the naive realists in seeing models as representative of the world, but disagrees with the positivists that they must therefore be confined to the correlation of data in the mind of the viewer. Also contrary to the instrumentalists, it sees theoretical models as both true and useful since the world and nature are understood to be active as well as passive. They are not merely to be recorded. They themselves are disclosive. "Science is discovery and exploration as well as construction and invention." /71/ The role of the imagination is acknowledged as important in the formation of theoretical models since they are understood to be only partly representative of reality. Room is left for refinement and improvement by the imagination. This protects both the power of man's mind and the power of patterns in nature. "The scientist today usually takes his models seriously but not literally." /72/

Models in Religion

Barbour sees the use of theoretical models to be as widespread and necessary in religion as in science. These religious models are seen to have four functions. "1.the interpretation of experience; 2. the expression pf attitudes; 3. the evocation of disclosures, and 4. the construction of metaphysical systems....The first two...will be taken a primary for religious models." /73/

Besides these cognitive functions, religious models also express emotions and attitudes, since religion, as a way of life, is more practical than theoretical. These two sets of functions, one cognitive and one noncognitive are complementary rather than contradictory.

When it comes to comparing scientific theoretical models with religious ones, Barbour sees both similarities and differences.

382

First, the similarities: "1. they are analogical in origin, extensible to new situations and comprehensible as units; 2. they have a similar status. Neither is a picture of reality, yet neither should be treated as useful fiction....3. the use of scientific models to order observations has some parallels in the use of religious models to order the experience if individuals and communities..." /74/

The differences are: "1. religious models serve noncognitive functions which have no parallel in science; 2. religious models elicit more total personal involvement than scientific models; 3. religious models appear to be more influential than the formal beliefs and doctrines derived from them, whereas scientific models are subservient to theories." /75/

Paradigms

The latter half of Barbour's book is concerned with the analysis of paradigms in science and in religion. Following the lead of Thomas Kuhn and others discussed earlier in chapter four, he shows that the assumptions concerning scientific method that underlie much of the positivistic criticism of religious language simply are not accurate, since science itself does not provide a totally neutral, objective ground of observation as once was thought in more naive days:

> I have suggested, however, that science is not as objective, nor religion as subjective, as the view dominant among philosophers of religion has held. Man the knower plays a crucial role throughout science. Scientific models are products of creative analogical imagination. Data are theory-laden; comprehensive theories are resistant to falsification; and there are no rules for paradigm choice. To be sure, each of these subjective features

> is more prominent in religion; there
> is a greater diversity of models,
> greater influence of interpretation
> on data, greater tenacity in commit-
> ment to paradigms, and greater ambiguity
> in paradigm choice. But in each of
> these features I see a difference of
> degree between science and religion
> rather than as absolute contrast. /76/

All this brings him to the conclusion that to
demand as Flew did in the sections quoted earlier
in this chapter and which formed the basis on an
ongoing debate, that falsifying conditions for religious belief need to be specified, is an unreasonable
demand because it cannot be done and is not being
done even in science. If comprehensive scientific
theories cannot meet this demand, then how can it be
demanded of religion? Instead of there being only
falsifiable and non-falsifiable statements, there
are degrees of resistance to falsification.

> Though no decisive falsification
> is possible in religion, I have argued
> that the cumulative weight of evidence
> does count for or against religious
> beliefs. Religious beliefs, like
> scientific ones, are not falsified
> by data, but are replaced by promising
> alternatives. Commitment to a paradigm
> allows its potentialities to be system-
> atically explored, but it does not exclude
> reflective evaluation. /77/

What are some of the criteria for such evaluation
of a religious paradigm? They are partly similar
to those in science: simplicity, involving both internal consistency and systematic interrelatedness,
and supporting evidence from religious and moral
experience and key historical events. Another
criterion is extensibility of application (fit or
fruitfulness) and finally, comprehensiveness, or the

384

coherent ordering of different types of experience
within a systematic metaphysics. Of course, the
choice between paradigms by means of these criteria
is more problematical in religion than in science,
but they are operative nevertheless.

What exactly does Barbour mean then by paradigm?
He follows Kuhn's lead here. In his original work,
the Structure of Scientific Revolution,/78/ Kuhn had
proposed a wide variety of definitions and explanations of the term paradigm. In response to criticism of this vagueness, he clarified his meaning.
/79/ He points out that in their primary meaning
paradigms are shared crucial examples or exemplars.
Thus science is learned more by problem solving
through the help of concrete examples than by explicit theoretical rules. Another way of putting
this is to say that a scientific paradigm is "a
research tradition transmitted by key historical
examples or exemplars." /80/ Applying this to
religion then, a religious paradigm would be a religious tradition transmitted by key historical
examples or exemplars. In the case of Christianity,
the prime exemplar is of course Christ, but to him
can be added the great men and women of Christian
history or the Saints. Crucial historical events
are obviously connected with historical exemplars.
All of which brings us back to the centrality of
revelation through interpretation of the action
of God in key events and persons in history. It
also brings us back to Polanyi's framework. This
understanding of paradigm is broader than that of
model:

> Metaphors may momentarily encourage
> us to see patterns which we may not have
> noticed...but models systematically
> suggest distinctive ways of looking at
> things. In using religious models we
> find new patterns in the world around
> us and in our lives....A given community
> can use a variety of models in such

interpretation, but its paradigm tradition sets limits on the range of acceptable models and gives emphasis to those experiences whose interpretation it considers most significant. /81/

A paradigm, then, is like a heuristic framework which an individual inherits and works within as part of a community, whether it be a scientific or a religious one.

Theological Method

Based firmly on epistemological realism of a critical kind, these analyses of myth, symbol, metaphor, analogy, theoretical models and paradigms provide a firm set of conceptual tools for theological work. With them it is possible to explore purposefully such disciplines as the p_nomenology of religion, the psychology or religion, the philosophy of religion and various facets of the great world religions. Most importantly, they sustain and direct the theological conceptualization of Christianity in a way suitable to the cultural climate of our time and to the nature of Christianity itself. One current example of the successful use of such a method is Avery Dulles' book Models of the Church. /82/

Conclusion

We have pursued the present task from the religious dimension of experience, through a basic epistemological position to a full-fledged theological method, and it is now time to bring it to a halt. Though we do not expect that everyone will agree with them, we have proposed some clear cut definitions for the principal terms and areas of fundamental theology in the hope that such attempted clarity will help to advance further discussion. Thus we understand fundamental theology to be the serious reflection of the christians of each age upon the how and why of their living faith.

We distinguished religious experience from the religious dimension of experience, both centered on the ultimate dimension of human existence, but the first more emotional and the second more cognitional. We attempted to define experiential knowledge as an encounter with a disclosing other through indwelling in a framework and the integration of its particulars into a coherent whole. Building upon this, then we defined religious experiential knowledge as an encounter through indwelling and integration with an ultimate other which discloses itself both as the limit of all knowledge and of all life and thereby as the holy object of supreme worth to be worshipped and as the revealer through history of its reality and nature. Since this definition is a generic one, applicable to world religions in general, the revelational aspect in the last part was further specified in christian terms thus: christian revelation is the fulfillment of man's quest for the ultimate through God's disclosure of himself as love, in events of history, in the life and person of Jesus Christ and in the reocrds, life and worship of the Church. Using these ideas, then, we went on to examine the differences between the existence of God and the reality of God.

Finally, in the chapter just concluded, we examined a number of these same themes from the point of view of the challenge they have received from the claim of some linguistic and logical analysts that religious language is meaningless. An attempt was made to show how certain presuppositions concerning scientific method which underlie much of this approach are unsound, out-of-date or at the very least, improperly applied. While normal differences remain, the similarities between scientific method and religious method were shown to be greater than many have thought. And all this was seen as providing a body of conceptual tools for the theological task.

DISCLOSURE OF THE ULTIMATE

So this study ends where it began, with the conviction that the continuing discussion of fundamental theology by christian theologians is a task that can be carried on in a spirit that combines genuine inquiry with firm commitment.

RELIGIOUS LANGUAGE AND THEOLOGICAL MODELS

NOTES

[1] James Alfred Martin, Jr., _The New Dialogue Between Philosophy and Theology_ (New York: The Seabury Press, 1966), p. 40.

[2] Alfred J. Ayer, _Language, Truth and Logic_ (London: V. Gollancz Ltd., 1936).

[3] Ludwig Wittgenstein, _Tractatus Logico-Philosophicus_ (New York: Harcourt Brace and Company, 1955)

[4] Ludwig Wittgenstein, _Philosophical Investigations_ Transl. by G. Anscombe of 3rd Edition (New York: Macmillan, 1973)

[5] Martin, op. cit., p. 106.

[6] Ibid., p. 110.

[7] John Wisdom, "Gods," first published in _Proceedings of the Aristotelian Society_ (London, 1944-45), reprinted in John Hick, ed., _Classical and Contemporary Readings in the Philosophy of Religion_ (Englewood Cliffs, N. J.: Prentice Hall, 2nd ed., 1970), p. 434.

[8] Anthony Flew, _New Essays in Philosophical Theology_ (London: SCM Press, 1955)

[9] John Hick, op. cit., pp. 465-466.

[10] Ibid., p. 466.

[11] Ibid., p. 466.

[12]Ibid., p. 466.

[13]Ibid., p. 467.

[14]Ibid., p. 467.

[15]Ibid., p. 468.

[16]Ibid., p. 469.

[17]Ibid., pp. 469-470.

[18]John Hick, _Philosophy of Religion_ (Englewood Cliffs, N. J.: Prentice Hall, 2nd ed., 1973), pp. 91-92.

[19]Willard E. Arnett, "Are the Arts and Religion Cognitive?" in John P. Anton, ed., _Naturalism and Historical Understanding: Essays on the Philosophy of John Herman Randall, Jr._ (Albany: State University of New York Press, 1967), p. 234.

[20]Ibid., pp. 234-235.

[21]Ibid., p. 237.

[22]John E. Smith, _Experience and God_ (N. Y.: Oxford University Press, 1968)pp. 255-256.

[23]John Herman Randall, Jr., _The Role of Knowledg in Western Religion_ (Boston: Beacon Press, 1958) p. 114.

[24]J. H. Randall, Jr., "A Form of Religious Natur alism," in John Hick, ed., _Classical and Contemporary Readings_, p. 415.

[25] Ibid., p. 415.

[26] Ibid., p. 315.

[27] Ibid., pp. 415-416.

[28] John Hick, Philosophy of Religion, op. cit., p. 77.

[29] John E. Smith, "Randall's Interpretation of the Role of Religion in Religion," in Anton, ed., Naturalism and Historical Understanding, p. 255

[30] Arnett, op. cit., in Anton, ed. Naturalism and Historical Understanding, p. 238

[31] John E, Smith, "Randall's Interpretation of the Role of Knowledge in Religion," in Anton, ed., op. cit., p. 254.

[32] Arnett, op. cit., in Anton, ed. Naturalism and Historical Understanding, p. 241.

[33] John Hick, Philosophy of Religion, p. 79

[34] John Hick, Classical and Contemporary Readings, p. 394.

[35] Ibid., pp. 395-396.

[36] Ibid., p. 396.

[37] Ibid., p. 400.

[38] Ibid., p. 402.

[39] Ibid., p. 402

[40] Ibid., pp. 403-404.

[41] Hick, Philosophy of Religion, p. 82

[42] Ian T. Ramsay, Christian Discourse: Some Logical Explorations (London: Oxford University Press 1965), p. 1.

[43] Ian T. Ramsay, Models and Mystery (London: Oxford University Press, 1964), p.1.

[44] Max Black, Models and Metaphors: Studies in Language and Philosophy (Ithaca: Cornell University Press, 1962), p. 221.

[45] Ramsay, Models and Mystery, p. 5

[46] Ibid., p. 9; Black, op. cit., p. 227.

[47] Ibid., p. 14.

[48] Ibid., p. 15.

[49] Ibid., pp. 16-17

[50] Ibid., pp. 45-46.

[51] Ibid., pp. 51, 53.

[52] Ibid., p. 58

[53] A.G.N.Flew, op. cit., p. 97.

[54]Ramsay, op. cit., p. 60.

[55]Ibid., pp. 57, 58, 71.

[56]Ramsay, _Christian Discourse_, p. 88.

[57]Ian Barbour, _Issues in Science and Religion_ (New York: Harper and Row, 1966)

[58]Ian G. Barbour, _Myths, Models and Paradigms_ (New York: Harper and Row, 1974)

[59]Ibid., p. 48

[60]Ibid., p. 20.

[61]Ibid., p. 20.

[62]Ibid., p. 20.

[63]Ibid., p. 21.

[64]Ibid., p. 21.

[65]Ibid., p. 23.

[66]Ibid., p. 25.

[67]Ibid., p. 19.

[68]Ibid., p. 19.

[69]John E. Smith, _The Analogy of Experience_ (New York: Harper and Row, 1973), p. 52.

[70] Barbour, op. cit., p. 30.

[71] Ibid., p. 37.

[72] Ibid., p. 38.

[73] Ibid., p. 68.

[74] Ibid., p. 69.

[75] Ibid., p. 69.

[76] Ibid., p. 171.

[77] Ibid., p. 192.

[78] Thomas S. Kuhn, The Structure of Scientific Revolutions (Chicago: University of Chicago Press, 2ne ed., 1970)

[79] T. Kuhn, "Second Thoughts on Paradigms," (including critiques and replies), in Frederick Suppe ed., The Structure of Scientific Theories (Urbana: University of Illinois Press, 2nd ed., 1977), pp. 459 517.

[80] Barbour, op. cit., p. 133.

[81] Ibid., p. 149.

[92] Avery Dulles, S.J., Models of the Church (Garden City, N. Y.: Doubleday and Company, 1974)

Analogy : 35, (57), 232, 249, 252, 255, 266, 294, 324, 326, 327,
378 —